AGE OF ICONS

Exploring Philanthrocapitalism in the Contemporary World

Celebrities are increasingly front and centre in public debates on everything from solving world poverty to halting genocide, confronting obesity, and finding spiritual contentment. Bono, Bill Gates, Al Gore, Bob Geldof, Oprah, Madonna, and Angelina Jolie are just some of the entertainers, politicians, pundits, elite business people, and policymakers whose highly visible political activism has become an integral part of their public personas.

These pop icons tend to be celebrated as "philanthrocapitalists" with a unique ability to remedy the world's problems. However, as *Age of Icons* demonstrates, the solutions these icons promote for addressing global injustice, when examined critically, can be seen to work through the very same institutions that create these problems in the first place.

This volume assesses the growing role of popular icons in the construction of a culture that appears to incorporate a critical attitude towards the capitalist experience while, in fact, legitimizing the neoliberal character of the modern world. It will be an eye-opening read for anyone interested in the juncture between current events and celebrity culture.

GAVIN FRIDELL is Canada Research Chair in International Development Studies and an associate professor at Saint Mary's University. He is also the author of *Fair Trade Coffee: The Prospects and Pitfalls of Market-Driven Social Justice*.

MARTIJN KONINGS is a senior lecturer and Australian Research Council DECRA Fellow in the Department of Political Economy at the University of Sydney.

D1381684

Age of Icons

Exploring Philanthrocapitalism in the Contemporary World

EDITED BY GAVIN FRIDELL AND
MARTIJN KONINGS

UNIVERSITY OF TORONTO PRESS
Toronto Buffalo London

ISBN 978-1-4426-4349-9 (cloth)
ISBN 978-1-4426-1203-7 (paper)

Library and Archives Canada Cataloguing in Publication

Age of icons : exploring philanthrocapitalism in the contemporary world /
edited by Gavin Fridell and Martijn Konings.

Includes bibliographical references.
ISBN 978-1-4426-4349-9 (bound). – ISBN 978-1-4426-1203-7 (pbk.)

1. Social change. 2. Celebrities. 3. Celebrities – Political activity.
4. Philanthropists. 5. Capitalism. 6. Neoliberalism. I. Fridell,
Gavin, author, writer of introduction, editor of compilation
II. Konings, Martijn, 1975– writer of introduction,
editor of compilation

HM836.A34 2013   361.7   C2013-904616-X

University of Toronto Press acknowledges the financial assistance
to its publishing program of the Canada Council for the Arts
and the Ontario Arts Council.

Canada Council   Conseil des Arts
for the Arts   du Canada

ONTARIO ARTS COUNCIL
CONSEIL DES ARTS DE L'ONTARIO
50 YEARS OF ONTARIO GOVERNMENT SUPPORT OF THE ARTS
50 ANS DE SOUTIEN DU GOUVERNEMENT DE L'ONTARIO AUX ARTS

University of Toronto Press acknowledges the financial support of the
Government of Canada through the Canada Book Fund
for its publishing activities.

Contents

Contents

Acknowledgments

The editors would like to thank the Canada Research Chair program, the Social Sciences and Humanities Research Council of Canada, Saint Mary's University, Trent University, and the University of Sydney for the support that made this book possible, as well as two anonymous reviewers, Daniel Quinlan at University of Toronto Press, and John Carlaw. Special thanks are owed above all to Bhavani, Kate, Sasha, and Sebastian.

AGE OF ICONS

Exploring Philanthrocapitalism in the
Contemporary World

Introduction
Neoliberal Capitalism as the Age of Icons

GAVIN FRIDELL AND MARTIJN KONINGS

This book is about the age of icons, an era in which "big names" have become connected to "big issues" to a previously unprecedented degree. Bono and Geldof and African poverty, Gates and the global AIDS epidemic, George Clooney and the crisis in Darfur, Madonna and child poverty in Malawi – it has become nearly impossible to think of one without the other. Rich and powerful individuals – Leonardo DiCaprio, Angelina Jolie, George Soros, Oprah Winfrey – have become connected to any number of humanitarian issues, often serving as "Goodwill Ambassadors" or honorary advisors for the UN or other international or non-governmental organizations. These icons are mostly Western personalities, having built their reputations in collaboration with Western media and business interests; regardless of how far these personalities travel, their audience, and the source of their wealth and power, is predominantly Western. Abroad, they tend to represent the ideals and fantasies of Western capitalism (chief among them consumerism and individualism), while at the same time representing back to Western audiences a particular picture of life elsewhere. And yet, at the same time, with rapid technological change in global communications, these icons have an increasingly global reach beyond their traditional support bases. Superstar icon Oprah Winfrey's famous talk show, *The Oprah Winfrey Show*, despite garnering its largest audience from within the United States, is now syndicated in 150 countries – three quarters of all of the countries in the world – from Afghanistan and Australia, to India, Uzbekistan, and Zimbabwe (*The Times of India* 2012; *The Grio* 2009; *Oprah Winfrey Show* 2012).

Within the West, and increasingly on a global scale, powerful icons play an ever-larger role in structuring the nature of debate in the contemporary public sphere (Richey and Ponte 2011; Bishop and Green 2009; Brockington 2009; Cooper 2007). For this reason, we argue that they are more than idols, celebrities, or pop-stars, and are best understood as "icons," embodiments of the tremendous potential and promise held out by Western capitalism. Whereas the conventional understanding of "idols" is premised on the assumption that they derive their celebrity status from a cult of personality, predicated on issues of consumption and style, eliciting often blind admiration from fickle fans, the major iconic figures of our day reach deeper, evoking intensely held loyalties and emotional connections, urging people to act, and advocating specific programs of social and political change at a macro level (ending global poverty or climate change) or a micro level (getting rich quick, learning to love oneself) to a historically unprecedented degree (Goodman and Barnes 2011; Littler 2008).

In the age of icons, major iconic figures play an ever-increasing role in political life. In emotionally charged and contradictory ways, contemporary icons convey boundless faith in a better world under construction while simultaneously embracing the status quo, lashing out at the ills of global capitalism, while at the same time representing and defending its triumphant possibilities and inevitable forward march. Today's icons offer the promise of limitless change without changing the limits of existing society, which is central to their popularity as well as to their defining contradiction: Western icons conduct widely celebrated *superhuman* feats with only *modest, pragmatic* outcomes.

A recent case of icon-in-action demonstrates the issues surrounding this trend. On 12 January 2010, a devastating earthquake registering 7.0 on the Richter scale hit the island nation of Haiti. Following a long and tumultuous history – first as a slave colony for the French; then, after independence, facing imperialist aggression and intense civil strife; and finally subjected to a series of Western-backed dictators and coups – the country was in no shape to deal with the effects of such a massive quake (Schwartz 2010; Engler and Fenton 2005; Dicum and Luttinger 1999, 30; Knight 1990, 193–221). Buildings collapsed, social and economic infrastructure crumbled, and disease spread. In the end, almost 230,000 people lost their lives and over 2 million were left homeless. Thirteen thousand U.S. troops were dispatched to the country, and aid agencies, national governments, and international institutions initiated a major emergency relief effort.[1] It was not just the conventional aid institutions that offered assistance, however. John Travolta, star of such movies as *Saturday Night Fever*, *Grease*, and *Pulp Fiction*, also heard the call for help and leapt into action.

Operating from his multimillion-dollar Florida mansion, equipped with its own private runway, Travolta selected one of his five airplanes (a customized Boeing 707), loaded the plane with food and medical supplies, and set off for Haiti (Carroll 2010; *CBS News World* 2010; *London Evening Standard* 2007). He brought along not only his wife and medical doctors but also Scientology ministers, trained in an alleged healing technique said to use the "power of touch … to reconnect nervous systems shaken by trauma" (*Daily Mail* 2010c). Bypassing a huge backlog of hundreds of planes waiting to land at the Port-au-Prince airport, Travolta's plane touched down to immense fanfare and media coverage. Travolta spent the night in Haiti, acting, by his own account, as "commander" of his relief mission, "guarding" the supplies during the night and even giving a free tour of his luxury plane to a wounded 7-year-old boy, orphaned when his parents were killed in the earthquake (*Daily Mail* 2010b). Walking the red carpet in New York a few days later, the actor reflected on the moral aspects of his adventure: "We were there right away, with this airplane, because you know we have the ability and the means to do this so I think you have responsibility on some level to do that" (*Daily Mail* 2010a).

In a world where overt cruelty seems to be increasingly within the bounds of public discourse in North America – true to form, multimillionaire conservative pundit Rush Limbaugh actually called on Americans to *not* give money to support Haitian relief! (Hinckley 2010) – Travolta's actions stand out for their kindness and generosity. Yet they did not go without criticism. Aid organizations, frustrated over the long waiting list for their relief planes bringing urgent supplies, expressed dismay over the fact that Travolta's plane managed to get permission to land. Critics also questioned his decision to use the resources at his disposal to fly in Scientology healers. An anonymous doctor at a hospital in Haiti was quoted as cynically commenting, "I didn't know touching could heal gangrene" (Carroll 2010; *CBS News World* 2010; MacKey 2010).

While such concerns were drowned out in the overall media spectacle, it is not inappropriate to ask if Travolta's actions were the most efficient manner of doing what needed to be done and to wonder what the "opportunity costs" were of flying in Scientology healers. What could experts in emergency relief have accomplished with the same resources? What if Travolta had just signed a cheque and donated money to an organization with experience in aid relief and resigned himself to following the news on television, foregoing the excitement of a self-directed rescue mission? Of course, Travolta no doubt saw his own role not merely as a provider of resources but equally as someone who was able to draw media attention to the crisis. But one might ask if it did not do more to precisely divert the media focus away from the reality of death, disease, and destruction, replacing shocking images of desperation and need with upbeat ones of celebrity, charity, and generosity (Richey and Ponte 2011; Brockington 2009; Cameron and Haanstra 2008; Littler 2008).

To billionaire philanthropist Bill Gates, these sorts of questions are entirely beside the point. For it is precisely the prospect of "recognition" that drives the rich to give money to those in need. Recognition provides a "market-based incentive" for wealthy individuals and corporations to help the poor by enhancing the giver's reputation, thereby bringing together "self-interest and concern for others" in a mutually beneficial way (Gates 2008, 10–11). Seen from this angle, questioning Travolta's actions is an overly sentimental exercise in futility: there is no point in asking what things *might* have looked like had the resources been put to other uses, since it was only on the basis of Travolta's prospects for recognition that the funds were made available in the first place.

Gates's reasoning regarding "recognition," we would argue, is not entirely convincing. There is no inherent reason why the personal preferences and vanity of the wealthy should take precedence over considerations about how to alleviate human suffering in the most effective way. And yet, in many ways we would be among the minority, as the logic of his argument has increasingly become part of neoliberal common sense in much of North America and Europe. For a growing number of critical issues, it seems, people applaud celebrities for intervening and getting the "job done" without much interest in whether their actions are really making substantive differences for the better in the long term. While the "recognition" accorded to the good deeds of the powerful and wealthy, as Gates suggests, may have grown exponentially over the past decades, this has not necessarily been accompanied by a significant diminution of human suffering. In fact, the past decades have seen a historically unprecedented and widely documented escalation of social and economic inequality with severe negative effects for the poorest and most vulnerable globally (McNally 2010; Harvey 2005).

This book explores the possibility that the growing importance of powerful icons in structuring political debate in the public sphere is not a reflection of their practical and pragmatic ability to eradicate inequality and injustice, as their eager supporters would have it (Bishop and Green 2009; Kinsley 2008). Instead, we argue that the political power of today's icons is best understood as deriving from their ability to *suppress awareness* of the preponderance and roots causes of inequality and injustice. In addressing this general concern, the contributions in this book are centred on two main themes.

First, despite mounting evidence of a strong connection between neoliberal economic policies and growing inequality, discussed below, there remains a widely held sense of optimism in the West (certainly not among all sectors of society, as the recent Occupy Wall Street movement has powerfully revealed) about neoliberalism's ability to eliminate the very problems it helps to create. We argue that the power and pervasiveness of neoliberal optimism needs to be understood by recognizing not only Western capitalism's ability to commodify human relations and empty them of more meaningful and substantive content, but also through its ability to actively generate highly seductive images, discourses, and signs packed with intense emotional and psychological appeal. On this terrain, today's neoliberal icons stand equal to none.

Second, we argue that the immense power of Western icons can best be understood through a careful distinction between "idols" and "icons." Whereas the notion of "idol" tends to evoke a sense of inner emptiness and superficial connection, "icons" suggest something that is deeply interwoven with everyday life and embodies powerful emotions based on complex social connections. Neoliberal optimism's highly seductive appeal, we argue, is essential for understanding both the immense power of today's neoliberal icons – in commanding loyalty and expressing popular fantasies and desires – as well as the significant limits of this power, confined to the narrow boundaries of the neoliberal capitalist order upon which their iconic status depends.

Neoliberal Optimism

Neoliberal policies – centred on cuts to public spending, the privatization of public assets, and the removal of regulations limiting the flow of investment capital, currency exchanges, and trade – are central to the dominant political, economic, and ideological framework of our times. Beginning in the 1970s, neoliberalism rose to hegemony among the most powerful nation states and official international organizations, as well as a great many non-governmental aid and development organizations. Its rise brought an end to the varied and complex post-war era, dominated by a mixture of liberal international trade policies alongside an array of social interventionist models, including the Keynesian welfare state, economic nationalism, state communism, and a variety of international agreements to regulate financial flows and commodity prices. Drawing on classic liberal economic ideals, neoliberals are deeply opposed to state intervention in the economy for social ends, which they feel is bound to be inefficient, inaccurate, and biased towards the demands of specific "interest groups," such as unions or trade lobbies. In contrast, they argue that the competitive market serves as a "hidden hand" that responds efficiently and accurately to the actions of countless individuals through the undistorted market signals of supply and demand. Thus, while the state is depicted as choking individual liberty and initiative, causing economic waste and stagnation, the market, as summarized by David Harvey (2005, 20–1), is presented as "the best device for mobilizing even the basest of human instincts such as gluttony, greed, and the desire for wealth and power for the benefit of all."

One of the most significant social impacts of the past 40 years of neoliberal expansion on a global scale has been an ever-widening gap between rich and poor, a gap that has never been greater. A recent report by the International Labour Organization (ILO) (2008, 1) examining 73 countries concludes that "between 1990 and 2005, approximately two thirds of the countries experienced an increase in income inequality." Widening inequality is particularly evident between average workers and the super rich, especially in the United States where, in 2007, the average "US CEOs earned more than 521 times the average employee, as against 370 times four years earlier" (ILO 2008, 18).

Inequality between nations is also on the rise. The vast majority of middle- and low-income countries have experienced significantly reduced progress on economic growth and major social indicators (such as life expectancy, infant mortality, literacy) from the 1980s to 2005 compared to the decades of the 1960s and 1970s prior to the neoliberal era (Weisbrot, Baker, and Rosnick 2005). All the while, the gap between the richest countries and the poorest ones has grown considerably. In 1987, GDP per capita (in purchasing power parity, PPP) of the United States was 26 times that of the combined GDP per capita (PPP) of the least developed countries. By 2007, this gap had doubled to 53 times.[2] Globally, in terms of inequality between the richest and poorest people in the world, the statistics are even more shocking. The combined net worth of the world's 20 richest people is more than the total combined GDP of the world's 49 least developed countries and their 837 million inhabitants. Gates, currently the world's second wealthiest person, has a personal net worth of $53 billion, roughly equivalent to the *combined* GDPs of Kosovo, Rwanda, Malawi, Mongolia, Guinea, Barbados, Mauritania, Swaziland, Togo, Fiji, Central African Republic, Sierra Leone, Eritrea, Lesotho, Cape Verde, the Maldives, Belize, Burundi, Bhutan, Antigua and Barbuda, Djibouti, and Samoa (World Bank 2011; Forbes 2010b).

Interestingly, this historically unprecedented escalation of inequality has not yet resulted in the derailing of the neoliberal project in the West, even while it has sparked a degree of protest and disenchantment, as well as outright resistance, in the Global South, most notably by the rise of various "pink tide" countries in Latin America (Robinson 2007). In Western nations, however, despite signs of despondency and disappointment, what strikes us as most notable has been the continued pervasiveness of an intense spirit of optimism about the ability of neoliberal capitalism to create a world without poverty, disease, and suffering. It is not that public discourse has failed to register the existence of acute inequality, but rather that this fact and the social ills connected to it are typically portrayed not as something that neoliberal capitalism has caused but as something it has not yet resolved.

Following this logic, the editors of *The Economist* magazine, in the wake of the financial collapse of 2008, acknowledged the unprecedented amount of wealth being concentrated in the hands of a small number of rich "tycoons," only to assure their readers not to worry, because "in liberal democracies the powerful get on by pleasing others. In short, they work for us" (*The Economist* 2011b). The claim implicit in such formulations is that the core institutions of neoliberal capitalism are moving the world in the right direction but that much remains to be done to make their benefits universally available (Bishop and Green 2009; Kinsley 2008; Sachs 2005; Bhagwati 2002). Capitalism, in this way, is portrayed as an unwavering vehicle of historical progress for *all*, despite questions that might be raised by empirical investigation. What ultimately gets obscured is the relational nature of wealth: the fact that extreme riches do not exist on their own but are so often built on the poverty and exploitation of others.

Against a relational understanding of wealth and poverty, the proponents of neoliberal optimism offer unwavering confidence in the ability

of existing institutions to deliver universal inclusiveness and empowerment in the continuing struggle against major social problems, which
are assumed to be in the process of disappearing rather than becoming
worse. There is an element of near-religious faith in this devotion among
liberals who would otherwise insist on their claims to secularism and
sober pragmatism. While much has frequently been said about the neo-
conservative alliance of religion and big business in North America, less
has been observed about the kind of faith that hides under the claim to
progressive liberalism and the intense belief that neoliberal capitalism
is uniquely capable of delivering a universalism that is based not on a
concern with divine purpose but with mundane human needs. Neoliberal icons, we would argue, are powerful embodiments of this capitalist
faith in action, representing a potent mixture of hard-nosed realism (we
must work with existing institutions – giant corporations, the World
Bank, existing forms of government – to get things done) and uncompromising idealism (the individual *can* change the world, as long as she
submits wholeheartedly to the previous caveat).

The contributors to this book are sceptical about neoliberal optimism
and the assumption among much mainstream literature that the dominant trend in global capitalism is the gradual achievement of a more
just world. Reading the modern-day mainstream political economy
literature, one could be forgiven for thinking that the dominant trend
in global capitalism is the step-by-step eradication of injustice. The literature has become intensely concerned with the degree to which the
world deviates from an idealized picture of equal opportunity, even
though there is little evidence that this is a meaningful yardstick or that
the world is home to forces gravitating in that direction. The world is
considered as if it were not fundamentally structured by power and
control but by technical problems of logistics and coordination, with
power struggles merely localized disturbances in a fundamentally plu-
ralist, open-ended world. Robert Cox (1986) notably captured this trend
in terms of the tendency to privilege "problem-solving theory" over
"critical theory." While this argument has often been assailed for making an unwarranted distinction between the two, what he meant was
that there exists a strong tension between the ability to generate critical
insight and the focus on social problems *as these have been publicly identified and articulated*, after they have undergone a long process of editing
and sanitation.

For Cox, the primary responsibility of scholars is to investigate precisely how the public framing of social problems by policymakers,

politicians, and business leaders is often implicated in the maintenance
of much more fundamental problems, masking experiences of oppression that are deemed inappropriate for open articulation. Cox is critical
of those who devote too much of their time and energy thinking of
ways in which international institutions like the IMF and the World
Bank could ameliorate the global inequality it claims to be concerned
about, thus allowing their intellectual capital to become instrumental in
covering up the fact that these very organizations have been among the
main architects of present-day global inequality.[3] It is with this crucial
insight in mind that this book and its contributors offer a series of critical assessments of neoliberal icons. Rather than focusing on whether or
not icons can "fix" the everyday problems of neoliberal capitalism, this
books seeks to explore how icons work to reproduce neoliberal optimism, masking the manifold ways in which the social ills and inequalities of the current global order are not *accidents* of neoliberal capitalism
but rather *outcomes*.

Icons and Idols: A Critical Approach

This book seeks to critically explore the complex nature of today's neoliberal icons. To term these personas "iconic" is to emphasize the fact
that they are interwoven with the experience of everyday capitalist life
in complex ways and so embody powerful, highly seductive, emotions.
One way of approaching this argument is to consider the difference
between idols and icons. These terms are often used interchangeably,
but it is useful to draw a key distinction between them. Icons, we would
argue, express something in a way that is immediately obvious to us;
they are intuitively representative of the time and place that people live
in. In this sense they are quite different from idols, which may have a
strong subjective meaning but do not necessarily represent something
larger and complex. Some idols of course become icons, but this is not
necessarily, or even predominantly, the case. When one admires the image and persona of a certain musician, this fascination remains a largely
private affair, not necessarily organically bound up with social life as
it has been constituted in a particular historical period. Indeed, unless
over time the idol takes on iconic features, a fan may even end up feeling somewhat sheepish about things in the long run, left wondering
what it is they ever got out of the affinity to such an unremarkable
sign – "how could I have ever liked that singer?" one often wonders in
retrospect. Idolization tends to result in a sense of inner emptiness and

cultural alienation that has long been of concern to critical theory (Sennett 1974; Bell 1976; Lasch 1979; Adorno 1991).

The meaning of icons, however, is more deeply and organically interwoven with what concerns people in everyday life. While celebrity idols might rise today and fall tomorrow, successful icons, to borrow from Tiziana Terranova (2004, 59), "manage to engage the majority in a prolonged contract," one that often withstands empirical or reasoned appraisal. The promises made by icons go to the heart of the Western experience of life in the current era in a way that is not superficial and induces an experience that is somewhat different from the classic depiction of alienation. Icons capture the nature of modern life in a manner that appears non-reductive and does justice to life's complexity. Their universality – their status as general, readily recognizable social signs – is full rather than empty: they are fully connected to the substantive diversity and concrete complexity of life.

In this sense, icons bridge the divide between the public sphere and private concerns in a way that idols do not. Icons are public markers that readily command social validity and can count on immediate recognition; yet, at the same time their meaning is deeply personalized. They publicly figure some of people's most personal and intimate attachments – communicating concerns and affinities that are often deep and unconscious in complex and mysterious ways that often make them appear almost spectacular.

It is for these reasons that the perspectives advanced in this book are somewhat different from the analysis offered by media and cultural studies of entertainment celebrity, "its increasing purchase on our experience of everyday life and its implications in the construction and definitions of cultural identity" (Turner 2004, 21; see also Marshall 2006). One of the great strengths of this literature has been to develop an understanding of celebrity that runs counter to the dominant image in the mainstream media, which tend to focus on celebrities' seemingly astonishing individual powers to act, to persuade, or to lead. Critical celebrity theorists have argued that the power that celebrities appear to wield does not lie not within their own person but "is a product of media representation" rooted in a discursive regime organized around the celebrity. Key to this regime is the "pedagogy of celebrity" which serves as a template through which individuals learn to use consumer culture to "'make' oneself," something further enhanced in the world of online social networking through Facebook, Friendster, and Twitter. Celebrity studies analysts emphasize that this process it not just top-down, but rather one in which, states Marshall (2006, 10), "audiences matter in the construction and rearticulation of fame and celebrity" (see also Richey and Ponte 2011; Turner 2010, 2004; Brockington 2009; Marshall 2006; Rahman 2004).

A second strength of much of the celebrity studies literature has been to engage with the culture of celebrity in a manner entwined with questions of political economy, taking into account the wider social and historical context of neoliberal capitalism. The central focus of celebrity studies' engagement with political economy has been to point to the ways in which celebrity culture celebrates individualism and encourages commodification, weakening substantive social bonds and traditional communal institutions and replacing them with the impersonal market activities of a media economy based on the sale and consumption of celebrity images (Turner 2010; Marshall 2006; Turner 2004). This regime – involving the transformation of famous people into commodities "to be marketed and traded" by media and public relations industries, celebrating the ideology of individualism, and constantly reinforcing "that the individual has a commercial as well as cultural value" – is seen to be crucial in the legitimation of capitalism, as well as its expansion through the progressive commodification of an ever-wider range of cultural signifiers around identity, sexuality, gender, nationality, and race (Turner 2004, 8, 13, 25).

In this vein, a major contribution of celebrity studies has been to make explicit the powerful linkage between celebrity and the politics of consumption. While the mainstream media tends to portray Western celebrities in a relatively benign fashion, as famous people spending their wealth in sensational acts of consumption or charity, media and cultural studies have pointed to the manifold ways in which celebrities do not merely consume but are in fact lead symbols in the promotion of ever-greater levels of consumption for all. Consumption is at the heart of Western capitalism's seductions, and celebrities are at the forefront of encouraging acts of consumption without genuine self-reflection on their social and ecological impacts. In a cultural and ideological environment increasingly driven by multimillion-dollar branding and advertising campaigns, the "freedom to consume" has increasingly displaced political concerns about the meaning and nature of work and social relations into the sphere of individualized identity formation constructed around consumption (Marshall 2006; Turner 2004).

If one wants to stem the impact of climate change or fight poverty in Africa, an array of celebrity-branded products exist to divert energy and attention from more mundane acts of protest and politics into the spectacular world of consumption, one in which people exercise "consumer sovereignty," guiding corporate social responsibility from the comfort of the shopping aisle through the purchase of the right ethical, fairly traded, or eco brand. Against the powerful mythology around consumer sovereignty, critical thinkers have pointed out that consumers often lack basic and accurate information upon which to base their market decisions. Instead, they must engage the market under the coercion and manipulation of massive corporate advertising campaigns, totalling hundreds of billions of dollars a year, designed to engineer consumer choices before they ever even enter a store (Richey and Ponte 2011; Fridell 2007; Dawson 2003; Princen, Maniates, and Conca 2002).

Such perspectives are highly instructive and represent a core point of departure for many of the chapters in this book. At the same time, however, we would argue that the field of celebrity studies has tended at times to adhere to a somewhat reductive understanding of the signs in the capitalist public sphere, which tend to be conceived of as idols inserted into a logic of commodification and commercialization. In this sense, the celebrity studies literature is perhaps best understood as continuing in the tracks of earlier forms of cultural critique such as the Frankfurt School and the critique of the ungovernable subject formulated during the 1970s (Sennett 1974; Bell 1976; Lasch 1979; Adorno 1991). For Adorno (1991), the commercialized sphere of human culture offered little more than superficial signs that had a strongly homogenizing impact on the nature of social experience. Lasch (1979) conceived of the signs of the capitalist sphere as consumer fetishes whose worship allowed people to stave off more fundamental experiences of moral emptiness and disconnectedness brought on by the fragmentational forces of liberal individualism. As people become absorbed in passive, hedonistic indulgence, they become less attentive to the political dimensions of human interactions.

While there are important elements of truth here, we argue that this understanding of capitalist symbols does not fully capture the emotional dynamics of contemporary icons, which go deeper than the distractions offered by the culture industry. Criticism focused primarily on consumerist, apolitical submission often overlooks what is new and specific about the role of icons in neoliberal capitalism, namely, that contemporary capitalism, far from having become more individualized, fragmented, or anonymous, evinces an exceptional capacity to generate "social networks" by connecting people through cultural symbols that are ideologically charged in much more complex and profound ways than ever before. This cannot be entirely captured by situating celebrity culture in an economic "context," but must proceed from the notion that these signs are *themselves* "packages" of ideologically charged social relations (cf. Peck 2008, 8). That is what it means to call these signs iconic: they incorporate, embody, and express something complex in a very immediate, personal, and objective way.

The focus of the celebrity culture literature is on people who are "highly visible through the media" and whose private lives "attract greater public interest than their professional lives" (Turner 2004, 21). Of course, there can be little doubt that the achievements of many artists, politicians, and entertainers have become entirely overshadowed by interest in the details of their private lives, that this is one of the key drivers of Western commercialization, and that it fulfils an important ideological function: when people are voyeuristically absorbed in and entertained by the lives, wealth, and problems of others, they tend to lose sight of important political issues around their own lives and problems. This critique, however, applies more readily to idols than to icons. While it may be relatively easy to whip up a sudden mass interest in a particular individual – when properly marketed, a teenager can become a teen *idol* in a matter of months – being *iconic* is more elusive. Signs and images that accrue iconic features do so because they come to express something that people intuitively understand to be essential to the nature of their socio-historical time, undeniably real, and connected to intense pleasure or associated with indelible trauma.

In one sense, therefore, our conception of icon is more specific than the prevailing conception of celebrity: while celebrities fit well with the notion of idol, not all celebrities are icons. But in another sense it is much broader. It would be hard to claim, for example, that libertarian economist Milton Friedman is a celebrity in the conventional sense of the word, yet we can plausibly say that his name is iconically connected to the era of neoliberal capitalism. By following the media in focusing on those entertainers who are the most photographed, filmed, or talked about – that is, what Turner (2010, 13) critically refers to as a "limited pool of individual celebrities or celebrity-related media 'flashpoints'" – such approaches neglect more subtle iconic figures and images that are pivotal to Western social experience. Our focus in this book is on icons as a category that includes not only entertainment celebrities but also politicians, pundits, elite business people, policymakers, social institutions, and campaigns. While these figures and institutions are discussed in celebrity studies, this is generally only the case when they have at-tained celebrity status by having successfully adopted the style and performance methods pioneered by the entertainment industry – like Barack Obama or Tony Blair (Street 2006; Marshall 2006; Turner 2004).

But many iconic figures are not "famous" in the sense of being a household name and – contra the definition of "celebrity" – they may not draw nearly as much popular interest in their private lives as their public ones (such as Al Gore or Thomas Friedman). This is not to say that these icons do not engage in the production of celebrity, but rather that their iconic status is not strictly derived from their degree of ce-lebrity. Economist Joseph Stiglitz, for example, may carry some fame among policy advisors and politics junkies, but his celebrity is dwarfed by countless numbers of fly-by-night musicians and movie stars, and neither his economic ideas nor his private life are likely to be the topic of dinner conversation in any typical family. Icons are about more than celebrity in that they are culturally, politically, and ideologically charged social signposts for the age. People's interest in them is not related to what they may find by peeking into their lives but precisely to what they actively bear out and willingly display.

And this is precisely one of the novelties of neoliberal icons: they are not "covertly political" but precisely make conscious, purposeful claims to political significance. Contemporary icons are highly politi-cally charged, crucial points of social orientation, signposts on which people rely for direction and meaning. Few conversations about global inequality and poverty will conclude without referencing Bono; few people have done as much to shape the popular awareness of environ-mental problems in North America as Al Gore; and even philosophi-cally inclined discussions of how people should live and what kind of spiritual attitude to adopt in the Western world are likely to reference the insights of Dr Phil or Oprah. Bono reassures people that the institu-tions that presently exist can deliver universal freedom from want; Al Gore's campaign is motivated by a belief that the problems he diagno-ses exist primarily on the plane of confusion and misunderstanding, not power and interest; and the promise held out by Oprah and Dr Phil is that people can solve their personal problems by embracing more fully the neoliberal ethos of individual responsibility and self-help (Peck 2008). They project a fundamentally optimistic attitude to the institu-tions of neoliberal capitalism, enjoining people to trust that the latter are set up to advance everyone's interests – as opposed to the interests of millionaires and billionaires, a club to which icons frequently belong.

Distinctive of the neoliberal era is the fact that people's "sociological imagination" (Mills 1959) – their ability to connect personal experiences to wider structures of social power – has become increasingly mediated by the promises of these icons.

Contemporary icons do not promise people otherworldly bliss, but the perfection of life as it is: they hold out the promise that major social problems can be solved in this lifetime with the institutions that already exist. Icons are heavily rooted in everyday, commonly held assumptions and actions, but appear as if they stand above the messiness of everyday life as "heroic individuals" who nevertheless understand our lives and "feel our pain" (Goodman and Barnes 2011, 72; Littler 2008). People feel closely connected to icons, yet icons look far more dignified and powerful. Icons idealize capitalist life, put a spin on it, and reflect back something alluring and grandiose that people nonetheless immediately recognize. When Angelina Jolie and Brad Pitt delivered their first child in Namibia in 2006, the Western media had a field day with the imagery of daring, humbleness, and earthy engagement with poverty in "a world away from Hollywood" (Tauber and Wulff 2006). Of course, far from the typical Namibian experience (as well as that of many Americans), Jolie and Pitt stayed at an exclusive resort on the beach, surrounded by bodyguards and undercover police, with private medical care, and reportedly sold the first picture of the baby for millions of dollars, giving the proceeds to UNICEF and other African charities – travel and childbirth in Africa reflected back with hope and optimism.

The Politics of Icons

As celebrities have become increasingly visible in their direct involvement in humanitarian causes, several commentators have highlighted their political role. The most insightful works have drawn upon the celebrity studies approach, critically examining the ways in which celebrities play an ever-more-central role in mediating and representing the major political issues of the day – from saving the environment (Brockington 2009) to saving Africa (Richey and Ponte 2011) – commodifying themselves and the urgent crises they seek to remedy, channelling dissatisfaction, dissent, and desire to save the world into more and more "mundane consumption" (Brockington 2009, 130). Through this process, they argue, the complex social and historical roots of injustice and crisis become obscured, depoliticized, flattened, and simplified so that consumers become convinced that the solution lies not in less but more capitalism, more corporate involvement, and more shopping.

Others have taken a far more hagiographic approach to the role of icons in legitimating contemporary capitalism. Political scientist Andrew F. Cooper (2007) has examined celebrity activists, like Bono and Bob Geldof, viewing them as "ascendant diplomatic actors" who play an important role in addressing the crisis of legitimacy and efficiency of global institutions. Challenging conservative critics who see these celebrities as mere Hollywood radicals, Cooper argues that they in fact serve as a "filter or conduit between citizens and sites of authority" that helps to fill some of the "gaps" in global governance. To Cooper, celebrity diplomats play the role of NGOs in global negotiations, only with greater advantages in branding and popular appeal and individual talent, including Bono's ability to act as "master manipulator" whose "words can sooth but they can also sting" (Cooper 2007, 7–8, 17–19).

In a similar vein, economists Matthew Bishop and Michael Green's (2009, 2–3, 279) book *Philanthrocapitalism* presents a treatment of an array of philanthropic elites, from Bill Gates and Warren Buffett to Bono and Oprah, and their new approach to "businesslike giving," in which they work "to apply the secrets behind that money-making success" to solving the world's most pressing problems – from global poverty, to climate change, to genocide, to malaria and AIDS in Africa (see also Kinsley 2008). Whereas Cooper expresses some reservations about whether celebrity diplomacy can fully address issues of accountability and representation in global governance, Bishop and Green make no bones about their unwavering support for the growing power and prestige of philanthrocapitalists who "see a world full of big problems that they, and perhaps only they, can and must put right." While the state has a role to play in providing basic social services, only philanthrocapitalists can carry out the "risky innovations" required to address the world's major problems, because they "have no one to answer to but themselves" and are "'hyperagents' who have the capacity to do some essential things far better than anyone else" (Bishop and Green 2009, 3, 12, 283). Bishop and Green are confident that the world's richest can solve all major social and environmental ills, the only question is: "Will they stick at it when the going gets tough?" (Bishop and Green 2009, 8).

Such approaches to the politics of contemporary icons are incapable of looking past the deceptive appearance of things, dramatically overstating the degree to which these actors are capable of reversing structurally embedded trends towards commodification. It is of course not the case that, in countering the "hyperagency" assertion of iconic apologists, one can only adopt the position that icons are powerless. Individuals that come to occupy central positions in networks of human relations and so assume iconic qualities (e.g., Paul Hewson becomes "Bono") find their agency highly leveraged, even if this does not mean that it can be applied to purposes radically at odds with the processes through which it has emerged. Iconic agency remains oriented to the smooth functioning of the networks that constitute it, and yet the direction in which it tends and the interests it serves are still of immense political significance. The debate, we would argue, should not centre on *whether* Western icons matter, but *how* they matter.

The hagiographic literature on "celebrity diplomats" and "philanthrocapitalists" goes to great lengths to examine the leadership role of popular icons. But many icons are master leaders only in the sense that they epitomize conventional practices and iconically express hegemonic sentiments. In a July 2009 piece for the *New York Times*, Bono called for African leaders to "rebrand" the continent by dealing with corruption and political unrest and to demonstrate that "amid poverty and disease are opportunities for investment and growth." He encouraged U.S. President Barack Obama to "follow the impressive Bush legacy" and make clear to African leaders the dictate "Without accountability – no opportunity." Bono was particularly pleased that "United States aid dollars increasingly go to countries that use them and don't blow them" (Bono 2009). While much can be said about Bono's enthusiasm for U.S. debt relief – an enthusiasm that is not shared by major debt relief NGOs[4] – it is not the originality and inventiveness of these statements that stands out, but rather the opposite; Bono's apparent "leadership" emerges through his ability to re-spin old ideas that are cherished by the political establishment (Dienst 2011).

Of course, the fact that the practical commitments of contemporary icons are less politically revolutionary than their rhetoric might suggest has not gone entirely unnoticed. In 2006, Bono came under some criticism when it was revealed that his band U2 had moved part of their business out of Ireland to the Netherlands to avoid paying higher taxes, at the same time that he was demanding that the governments of Ireland and the rest of the world spend more public money on international aid. In response, Bono argued: "Ireland's prosperity is very much driven by tax creativity, inventiveness … It is completely in the spirit and letter of the law for U2 to be tax innovative. It's the culture. So, bollocks to those critics" (quoted in Bishop and Green 2009, 273). There is clearly nothing new about rich people avoiding taxes by moving their money abroad – but it is crucial to note that Bono is able spin his mundane ambition to augment his wealth as an exercise in social innovation that is part of a wider project of universal emancipation in a way that does not sound, to some, entirely ridiculous or implausible. Perhaps he overplayed his hand in this particular instance, but it is indicative of the power of icons to take popular sentiments and reflect them back with sparkles of optimism.

Western capitalism thus appears iconically as a world of endless opportunities. Rather than being the outcomes of the everyday operations of capitalism, social problems exist because people have "miss[ed] the benefits of the global economy," in Bill Gates's (2008, 9) words. From this vantage point, so willingly embraced by Bishop and Green, it makes perfect sense to focus on "problem solving" and how many resources an individual celebrity or philanthrocapitalist can accumulate for a certain cause. Bishop and Green give a Dickensian nod to class inequality – suggesting that the world's billionaires need to be more philanthropic to avoid "provoking the public into a political backlash against the economic system that allowed them to become so wealthy" – while at the same time going to great lengths to justify these very inequalities (Bishop and Green 2009, 11). Against those who criticize philanthrocapitalists for claiming to care deeply about the poor while spending lavishly on huge private estates, yachts, cars, sports teams, Bishop and Green reply that "rather than scold [rich tycoons] to refrain from pleasure, far better to encourage them to engage in helping poorer people in more constructive ways" (Bishop and Green 2009, 271). While they do acknowledge that some of the super rich have acquired their money in unfair and unsavoury ways, particularly in the case of the "wealthy oligarchs of the former Soviet Union," they state that: "All the giving in the world cannot wash away their sins. Yet perhaps some encouragement through the prospect of social redemption is in order, as it is surely better that they give money to the needy than use it to further inflate the bank balances of already wealthy soccer stars" (Bishop and Green 2009, 274–5). Michael Kinsley (2008, 2) puts forward a similar argument in his edited book *Creative Capitalism*, stating that while criticisms can be raised about the growing capitalist philanthropy movement, "Nevertheless, it is a trend that should be encouraged, don't you think?"

The political issues here, however, are far more complicated than whether one wants the rich to be charitable or not. In recent years, for example, global justice groups have pointed out that a significant amount of the key minerals (tin, tantalum, tungsten, and gold) used by the electronics industry to produce such things as personal computers and mobile phones are fuelling the ongoing conflict in the Democratic Republic of Congo, the deadliest since the Second World War, by providing hundreds of millions of dollars to armed groups.[5] Surely when computer giant Bill Gates or Bono calls on fans to buy electronic goods for "(Product) RED" to raise funds to fight poverty and disease in Africa, the fact that some of this wealth was acquired through a process that helps fuel the largest ongoing conflict in Africa – with over 5 million dead – is no small matter that can be easily brushed aside.[6]

Similarly, many people could readily agree that if they had some real influence on the way famous financial speculator and philanthropist George Soros spends his billions, they would likely encourage him to persist in and expand his philanthropic endeavours. But of course the problem for the vast majority is that they do not have this kind of ready access to the rich and powerful, and by actively seeking to bestow approval on Soros's philanthropic pursuits, they implicitly endorse and legitimate the kind of practices through which he has earned his billions. The effect is to lose sight of the prior question of how it is that people like George Soros have come to command such extraordinary resources. In the neoliberal cultural climate, the simple insight that wealth is built on exploitation is typically portrayed as motivated by envy, the kind of small-minded resentment of the powerless who seek to hold the powerful back from deploying the full extent of their capacities. "What is missing, invisible, off the agenda," states Richard Dienst (2011), reflecting on Bono's tireless philanthropic hobnobbing with the rich and powerful, "is any belief that economic development can be a mode of collective self-determination, opening up a realm of freedom for the poor beyond that envisioned for them by billionaires."

At issue here is the unseen violence of "social murder" (Chernomas and Hudson 2007), the systemic violence that remains hidden precisely because it involves the "often catastrophic consequences of the smooth functioning of our economic and political systems" (Žižek 2008, 1). Such structural violence is masked by the formalistic concern prevalent in the media and among political and economic elites for more "obvious" forms of violence such as crime, terror, civil unrest, international conflict. The philanthropic pursuits of contemporary icons ameliorate overt forms of violence in a highly selective manner, but – by downplaying issues of class and social power and by depicting violence, domination, poverty, and inequality as aberrations external to the operation of existing capitalist institutions – they play a central role in the normalization of the historically unprecedented incidence of systemic violence (Milonakis and Fine 2009; Žižek 2008; Lebowitz 2006).

From a positivistic, "problem-solving" mindset, structural violence is easily dismissed as obscure speculation and metaphysics. But surely few things are more incongruously speculative than the belief that people should look to billionaires for solutions to global inequality. To appreciate the role of contemporary icons in a critical way, therefore, we argue for the need to be alert to the layers of their meaning and the need to consider the operation of forces, feelings, and concerns that are not necessarily readily perceivable. As Žižek has argued, it requires reflection, holding off on action until a better sense can be garnered of what it is that needs to be done. Žižek (2008, 6, 16) takes particular aim at the "new liberal communists," like Gates and Soros, and their "court philosophers," like journalist Thomas Friedman, for projecting a "fake sense of urgency" that steamrolls over reflection and critical thinking in favour of solving the "concrete problems" of immediate crisis (famine, tsunami) and violence (genocide, war crimes): "There is a fundamental anti-theoretical edge to these urgent injunctions. There is not time to reflect: we have to *act now*" (Žižek 2008, 6–7). Through the unreflexive "fake sense of urgency," philanthrocapitalists, celebrity diplomats, and "court philosophers" obscure – and so enable the intensification of – deeper, systemic mechanisms of structural violence such as everyday forms of class or imperialist exploitation that take their tolls on the lives of millions every year (Brockington 2009; Richey and Ponte 2011).

If many contemporary liberal icons subscribe to Thatcher's conservative dictum that "there is no alternative," they do so in ways that she could only have dreamed of 30 years ago, embracing this belief with alacrity and buoyancy and enjoining everyone to do the same. Ironically, the most passionate critiques of "liberal communists" and celebrity diplomats have tended to come from right-wing populists and neoclassical economists, who accuse them of making "false accusation[s] about traditional capitalism" (Easterly 2008, 55; see also Posner 2008; Crook 2008, 111; Landsburg 2008; Chauvin 2008).[7] Responding to concerns that Bill Gates's philanthropic bent might suggest a lack of faith in capitalism, Bishop and Green (2009, 276) insist that, "Gates is into his capitalism just as much as his philanthropy." Gates himself has not neglected to clarify matters, pointing out that his vision of "creative capitalism" should not be taken as implying a critique of capitalism itself but precisely as a capitalist alternative to "some crazy sharing thing"

(Buffett and Gates 2008, 21). Progressives have been less forceful: even if the role of contemporary icons makes them feel uncomfortable, there is not much to be said about it because at least they are *doing something*.[8] This book seeks to break with this relatively uninspiring stance to ask just *what* exactly it is that they are doing.

The chapters that follow seek to shed light on these issues through careful examination of an array of neoliberal icons. Ilan Kapoor's chapter examines the role of entertainment celebrities in modern-day philanthropy. Through an analysis of the humanitarian activities of Bono, Bob Geldof, Angelina, and Madonna, he draws attention to the ambiguous nature and effects of their interventions, how they have legitimated the power structures responsible for the systematic production of the evils they combat, as well as the way in which their apparently selfless endeavours have been veritable career-boosters. The chapter by Janice Peck presents an analysis of Oprah, no doubt one of the most iconic characters of modern times. Tracing the close affinities of Oprah's discourse with the ethos of neoliberal capitalism, Peck questions the emancipatory potential of her self-help empire and humanitarianism and shows how her philanthropic pursuits serve to put a rosy gloss on some of the most oppressive aspects of neoliberal capitalism. Following this, Mike Goodman offers a series of reflections on the paradoxical nature of the modern celebrity politician – "*Celebritus politicus*" – who lays claim to the status of rebel while being at the heart of power, whose promises are often transparently fake yet command tremendous popular attention, and who epitomizes the neoliberal fantasy of all-powerful individuality while serving as the focal point of tremendous collective energies.

Kate Ervine interrogates the environmental campaign launched by Al Gore since retiring from the American vice presidency. She argues that Gore's willingness to bring "inconvenient truths" into mainstream political debate is in fact quite limited: the comforting promise borne out by Gore's environmental discourse is precisely that the course of environmental destruction can be reversed through modest personal efforts and without significant political change. An equally iconic global campaign is taken up by Colleen O'Manique and Momin Rahman who explore the dark side of (Product) RED: notwithstanding the welter of good intentions that have gone into its making, one of the main effects of (Product) RED has been to glamorize the business of fighting HIV/ AIDS and to make it an even more profitable business than it already was. They emphasize the inherent limitations of a market-based approach to fighting an epidemic that continues to claim millions of lives.

Turning the focus from politics to debates in the public sphere and the punditry that occupies such a central position in it, Feyzi Baban discusses the work of Thomas Friedman, one of the West's best-known public intellectuals. The chapter shows that Friedman's thought offers an uncritical cosmopolitanism that, due to its troubling lack of concern with difference, is characterized by a strong streak of orientalism. The popularity of Friedman's thought, he suggests, lies less in its intellectual force than in its ability to reduce complex configurations of political power to apparently simple problems with clear solutions. The chapter by Gavin Fridell explores the significance of one of the world's most unlikely icons, Joseph Stiglitz, who rose to fame as a critic of the excesses of neoliberal capitalism. He notes the paradoxical nature of this development – Stiglitz became seen as someone who could change the world from within the halls of power after he was unceremoniously removed from his job as Chief Economist at the World Bank for advancing modest criticisms – and identifies willingness to believe in the solutions held out by Stiglitz as above all driven by a "governance fantasy," the belief that, whatever their mistakes and misperceptions, the powers that be ultimately have everyone's best interests at heart.

Defying blatant and growing inequalities in a world besieged by global financial crisis, military violence, and imperial conquest and shadowed by the prospects of climate calamity, resource wars, and food emergencies, neoliberal optimism not only persists but thrives. Neoliberal icons offer ideological fantasies that penetrate deep into people's personal lives, offering up more of the same, in bigger doses, to explain what is happening and what the solution is. And their appeal only seems to grow amid constant failure to "deliver the goods." Reliance on Bono's (2009) attempt to "rebrand Africa" as a strategy to solve African poverty fails to make things better, and this gives only further impetus to a liberal sense of urgency, beseeching Bono to increase his efforts. Neoliberal capitalism becomes the solution to the problems of neoliberal capitalism. In these times, the need to understand iconic power and its astonishing ability to reproduce neoliberal optimism is an urgent task.

NOTES

1 To be sure, the final tally reveals that wealthy countries pledged far more material assistance in the immediate aftermath than has actually been delivered. Assessing relief efforts in Haiti 6 months after the earthquake, journalist Peter Beaumont (2010) points out that, "More than $5bn in aid

was pledged by the US government, the World Bank and the European Union among others. Only a fraction of this has been received so far."

2 In 1987, the GDP per capita (PPP) of the United States was $17,620 compared to $690 for the "least developed countries" (UNDP 1990, 131). In 2007, the GDP per capita (PPP) of the United States was $45,592 compared to $862 for the "low human development" countries (UNDP 2009, 171–4).

3 For well-known critical appraisals of hegemonic global institutions, see Soederberg 2007; Goldman 2006; Bello 2004; and George 2004.

4 The Jubilee Debt Campaign, an offshoot of the Jubilee 2000 group that Bono first became involved in debt relief with, has heavily criticized the major relief initiative targeting heavily indebted poor countries, which "whilst it has led to some crucial reductions in debt burdens ... is run by creditors, is open to too few countries, doesn't properly assess the need or justification for debt cancellation, and offers too little, too slowly, with harmful conditions attached" (Jubilee Debt Campaign 2009).

5 For more on this, see the website of The Enough Project: http://www. enoughproject.org/publications/comprehensive-approach-conflict-minerals-strategy-paper (accessed 16 August 2010).

6 Along these lines, Lisa Ann Richey and Stefano Ponte (2011) have recently argued that the emergence of the RED campaign marks a transition in "causumerism" from "conscious consumption" to "compassionate consumption." Whereas conscious consumption involves purchasing a product that claims to be produced in a more just manner than is typically the case, such as fair trade coffee or tea, compassionate consumption has severed the link between the product and the cause. It represents instead a new form of "disengaged" corporate social responsibility where one might buy a (RED) iPhone that promises to help fight AIDS in Africa, while obscuring and deflecting attention away from how the iPhone itself is produced.

7 Matthew Bishop (2008) comments on the defensive nature of the conservative critics of philanthrocapitalism, stating: "To Capitalism's Defenders: Don't Be So Defensive."

8 In this vein, Elizabeth Stuart (2008, 107), senior policy advisor for Oxfam International, comments that while there may be limits to Bill Gates's philanthropic vision of "creative capitalism," criticisms "shouldn't be used to dismiss what could be a great idea."

1

Humanitarian Heroes?

ILAN KAPOOR

Celebrity humanitarian work has become so pervasive these days. Whether in the form of mediatized events (concerts, awareness campaigns, product/campaign endorsements, travel to crisis areas), personal charity (donations, volunteer work, child adoption), or lobbying (i.e., pressuring political leaders), do-gooding is a virtual career requirement for the established or aspiring star. Almost every day, it seems, George Clooney is organizing a fund-raiser, Steven Spielberg is making a pledge, Scarlett Johansson is going on a mission, Jay-Z is touring Africa, a star like David Beckham is being appointed as UN Goodwill Ambassador, Roger Federer is playing a "Match for Africa," or *American Idol* is "giving back." Charity work has become so cliché, in fact, that even Brüno (aka Sacha Baron Cohen) sees it necessary to adopt an "African" baby to jump-start his Hollywood career!

I think it important to examine this phenomenon more closely, given that the pairing of humanitarianism with entertainment – commonly referred to as "charitainment," "politainment," or "philanthrocapitalism" – is a potent combination, bringing to development issues the enormous resources and reach of "star-power" and the media. I will focus primarily, although not exclusively, on the humanitarian work of Bob Geldof, Bono, Angelina Jolie, and Madonna. My purpose is to not to emphasize these stars' personal stories, motivations, or foibles, but to examine how their charity work helps illuminate key structural characteristics of our contemporary global economic and political system(s). In other words, the production of what I call "humanitarian heroes/heroines" says something important about both global capitalism and its accompanying political arrangement – liberal democracy.

My argument, accordingly, is that celebrity humanitarian heroes help legitimate late liberal capitalism and global inequality. Their outwardly "altruistic" and "heroic" humanitarianism is belied by several accompaniments: its tendency to promote both the celebrity's brand and the image of the "caring" (Western) nation; its entrenchment in a marketing and promotion machine that, willy-nilly, helps advance corporate capitalism and rationalizes the very global inequality it seeks to redress; its support to a "post-democratic" liberal political order that is outwardly democratic and populist, yet, for all intents and purposes, conducted by unaccountable elites; and its use and abuse of the Third World,[1] making Africa, in particular, a background for First World hero-worship and a dumping ground for humanitarian ideals and fantasies.

Celebrity Humanitarianism

Geldof has become much more famous as a global activist than as a rock singer and leader of the 1970s band, The Boomtown Rats. This is mainly because, benefiting from the onset of the global information industry in the 1980s, he pioneered the charity-rock-concert-as-global-media-event. Although his activism follows in the footsteps of such entertainers as Woody Guthrie, Paul Robeson, George Harrison, Audrey Hepburn, Joan Baez, Danny Kaye, and others, he is often credited with being the first to involve celebrities in large-scale global causes, thereby successfully galvanizing widespread public and media attention. Today, he has become a key player in global politics, especially concerning poverty, debt, trade, and HIV/AIDS. He is treated as political leader in his own right, benefiting from one-to-one meetings with the likes of U.S. President Barack Obama, British Prime Minister Gordon Brown, and Canadian Prime Minister Stephen Harper. In 2007, he persuaded German Chancellor Angela Merkel to include African development on the Heiligendamm G8 agenda, and he has been known to chide G8 leaders for not meeting their aid commitments, sometimes publicly shaming them into increasing their aid budgets. It is no wonder, then, that he and a few of his celebrity colleagues (Bono, Jolie) are labelled "celebrity diplomats" (Cooper 2007, 2008b), engaging in what he himself calls "punk diplomacy" (quoted in Hague et al. 2008, 11).

In 1984, responding to widespread news reports about famine in Ethiopia, Geldof co-wrote and recorded the song, "Do They Know It's Christmas" to raise funds for famine relief ("Band Aid"). It sold over 3 million copies and raised over £8 million (it was re-recorded and re-released in 1989) (BBC 2006). After a visit to Ethiopia in early 1985, and keen to keep the famine in the spotlight, Geldof organized "Live Aid," two live charity concerts in London and Philadelphia showcasing top musicians. The 16-hour concerts were broadcast in full on radio and TV channels in Britain and elsewhere. Dramatic video footage of the famine was aired, and public contributions were solicited. Watched by some 1.5 billion people worldwide, Live Aid raised over £110 million for famine relief in Ethiopia (BBC 2006).

A decade later, Geldof became the main organizer and de facto spokesperson of a broad-based global NGO effort (the Global Call to Action Against Poverty, represented in the UK by the Make Poverty History campaign, and in the United States by the ONE campaign) to compel G8 leaders to better address global poverty issues. A series of 10 simultaneous Live8 concerts was held across the globe. Eschewing fund-raising in favour of political lobbying, the intent was to help focus world attention on the Gleneagles G8 summit, and more specifically, to pressure G8 leaders into increasing Western foreign aid, reducing/cancelling the debt of the poorest countries, and improving the terms of trade for the South. The concerts were watched by some 3 billion people worldwide (Live8 2005), while at the summit itself, Geldof and Bono were received like political leaders, benefiting from exclusive meetings with George W. Bush, Tony Blair, and other G8 leaders.

Like Geldof, Bono (aka Paul David Hewson) has become a force to reckon with in the global anti-poverty movement, although unlike Geldof, he has successfully kept up his musical career as the frontman of the Irish rock band U2. His foray onto the global stage began mostly in the mid-1990s on questions of debt. In 2002, he established DATA (Debt AIDS Trade Africa), an advocacy association headquartered at Universal Studios in London and financed mostly by "philanthrocapitalists" George Soros and Bill Gates (Cooper 2008a, 51). In an effort to bring attention to some of the issues taken up by DATA, particularly HIV/AIDS, he convinced U.S. Treasury Secretary Paul O'Neill to accompany him on a tour of Africa. At the Davos World Economic Forum in 2006, he launched (Product) RED, which brings together corporate brands and consumers to raise funds for HIV/AIDS in Africa (see the O'Manique and Rahman chapter on "Glam Aid" for details).

Bono has collaborated closely with Geldof on a number of fronts, including, as just mentioned, the 2005 Live8/Make Poverty History campaign and the frequent lobbying of political leaders. Their joint efforts have also gone into publicizing development issues in the media: they have guest-edited several newspaper and magazine issues (mostly together), usually focusing on Africa – an issue of *The Independent* in 2006, *Bild Zeitung* and *Vanity Fair* in 2007, and *The Globe and Mail* in 2010.

Like Geldof, Bono has earned substantial credibility within global development circles. Bono calls Jeffrey Sachs, the Columbia University economist and ubiquitous "development advisor to the stars,"[2] his "mentor"; they have been frequent travel companions to Africa, especially on debt issues. He often uses the language of justice in his public forays on development and poverty, and frequently likens the experiences of colonialism, famine, and displacement of his homeland, Ireland, to those of contemporary Africa (cf. Cooper 2008a, 258). While ready to compromise on policy issues, Bono is no pushover: he has not hesitated to chide allies such as Canadian Prime Minister Paul Martin for not living up to aid commitments, and in 2007, when Martin's successor, Stephen Harper, said he was too busy to meet Bono at the G8 summit, the latter only had to publicly chide Harper for the lagging Canadian record on African aid before a meeting was hurriedly organized (Rachman 2007).

If Bono and Geldof are quite businesslike in their approach to global activism, Jolie and Madonna appear more empathetic and "caring," although no less media-savvy, in theirs. Jolie contributes significant personal time to her humanitarian causes, and often portrays herself as a "witness" to disasters, conflicts, and other people's suffering. She reportedly became interested in development issues while filming in Cambodia in 2000. Since then, she has carried out several missions across the Third World, from Chad to Darfur to Haiti, donating personal money for refugee causes and relief agencies (the Jolie-Pitt Foundation was established in 2006 to continue this charity work). She has put a lot of effort into volunteering for the UN High Commissioner for Refugees, and was named its Goodwill Ambassador in 2001.

But it is perhaps for her role as mother and transnational-adoptions advocate that Jolie is best known. In addition to her three biological children (including twins), she has three adopted children, from Cambodia, Ethiopia, and Vietnam, adopted to much sought-out publicity and fanfare. She has given several interviews advocating for transnational adoptions (cf. Davidson 2007), so much so that following her adoption of Zahara from Ethiopia in 2005, there was a reported increase in U.S. adoptions of African children, with one adoption advocacy spokesperson declaring that "After Angelina Jolie adopted a kid from Ethiopia, agencies got a spate of calls from parents wanting to know how to adopt a kid from Ethiopia" (quoted in Magubane 2007a, 3; cf. 2007b, 377; ABC

News 2005). Similarly, the birth of her and Brad Pitt's daughter in Namibia in 2006 attracted considerable media attention, with photographs of the baby and interviews sold to *People* and *Hello* magazines for millions of dollars (reportedly donated to charity). A similar scenario followed the birth of the couple's twins in France in 2008.

Madonna's charity work mirrors Jolie's, although it has been much less extensive, and has focused mainly on Malawi. In 2006, she travelled there to help fund an orphanage. Soon after, she proceeded to successfully adopt a boy, David Banda Mwale, surrounded by much media hype and controversy. In 2009, she decided to adopt again, this time a girl, Mercy James. While the adoption was initially rejected by a Malawian lower court, it was finally approved by the Supreme Court. Since then, Madonna has continued to visit the country for charity tours (often joined by Jeffrey Sachs), funding orphanages and building a school (the Raising Malawi Academy for Girls). The media frenzy over her adoptions and orphanage work has continued unabated, and she has often courted it, giving interviews and appearing on talk shows to defend herself and encourage adoption. Not surprisingly, news outlets such as the *Wall Street Journal* have reported that "international adoptions by Americans have been escalating with stars such as Madonna travelling abroad to adopt" (quoted in Magubane 2007a, 3; cf. 2007b, 377).

We thus live in an age – the information age – in which entertainment stars play a prominent role as "humanitarians" in world politics. Geldof, Bono, Jolie, and Madonna have significant access to the halls of power, and the ability to galvanize publicity on a global scale. They each have the clout to help fund-raise, increase audience awareness, and shape media perceptions on a range of global issues, from famine to transnational adoption. And much more than any mainstream politician or diplomat, they can connect with large and diverse audiences through a variety of media (news, MTV, blogs, Twitter, etc.). But how are we to assess this newfound power? How are we to speak truth to it, that is, to examine what it hides and excludes, for whom or what it speaks, and to what interests it is responding or beholden? These are the questions taken up by the next sections.

Self-Promotion

Despite being presented to us (or at least implied) as a selfless and altruistic philanthropic act, celebrity humanitarianism is notably tarnished: it is deeply invested in self-interest and promotion, and in this post-Fordist industrial age, it is particularly invested in the creation and marketing of the celebrity "brand." Today's stardom and celebrity "heroism," after all, is manufactured, backed by a massive marketing machine that includes management and talent agencies, entertainment lawyers, and advertising and public relations firms, each often tied to larger corporate media and entertainment interests. The integration of celebrity philanthropy and branding has enabled the creation of a brand-identity (the "humanitarian-celebrity-as-hero"), with widespread and instant recognition that sells not just a product but also a lifestyle, value, aspiration. Thus, just as Nike is associated not merely with shoes but "transcendence," Benetton not just with clothing but "multicultural diversity," and Starbucks not just with coffee but "community," so stars such as Jolie or Bono are associated not just with entertainment but "caring," "compassion," or "generosity."

It is for this reason that humanitarian celebrities (and their marketing backers), capitalizing on the apparent insatiable demand for celebrity stories, are keen to solicit media coverage that can show them "up close," so they can "confess" to really caring about global poverty, refugees, or orphans. It is also for this reason that they often rely on a slew of philanthropic advisors and "cause marketing" firms that counsel them on which humanitarian causes are worthy and saleable (cf. Drake 2008; Littler 2008).

Espousing humanitarian causes allows celebrities to build their brand image in several ways. It can increase their profile by widening their media exposure and allowing them to remain in the public eye. It is surely no accident, for instance, that the Madonna and Jolie-Pitt adoption stories were repeatedly leveraged in the media; it helped keep them in the news even when there was no CD or movie to promote, while also marketing the image of the multicultural brood as trendy, sexy, or "good looking" (the fact that Jolie and Pitt are frequently voted the "most beautiful" and "sexy" in the world only adds to their brand mystique, helping differentiate them from other stars).

Charity work aids in humanizing the celebrity, too: it can soften the image of crassly mainstream and commercial entertainers, helping to make them compassionate and sympathetic. In some instances, philanthropic work can divert attention away from the more embarrassing or lurid elements of celebrities' lives – in the case of Madonna, her serial marriages and affairs, racy videos, or "material girl" reputation; in the case of Jolie, her "wild child" past, or her reputation as a marriage wrecker (i.e., for allegedly having an affair with Pitt while he was still married); and in the case of Geldof, his foul-mouthed character, or his troubled marriage and child-custody battles.[3]

The branding of celebrity humanitarianism also brings significant economic returns to both the celebrities and the entertainment industry that supports them. First, before even engaging in humanitarian work, there are significant tax benefits to derive from establishing a charitable foundation such as the Jolie-Pitt Foundation (in the United States and elsewhere, charitable gifts are tax-exempt for non-profit foundations). Then, there are the professional benefits to be drawn from carrying out the actual charity work. Jolie, for example, who can earn some $15 million per film, saw her "Q score," a Hollywood quotient that measures a star's likeability, almost double between 2000 and 2006, due at least in part to her "good works" (Swibel 2006, 118). Similarly, Geldof, while not performing at his live charity concerts, has nonetheless profited from them: he has rereleased the entire back catalogue of his former band, The Boomtown Rats, and even attempted to resurrect his solo musical career with a British tour (*New Internationalist* 2006). And in 2006, riding high in the pop-music charts and from Bono's notoriety as global humanitarian, U2 moved part of its corporate base away from Ireland to the Netherlands after the Irish government ended the tax exemptions that allowed the band to collect royalties tax-free, which angered many in Ireland (Dieter and Kumar 2008, 263).

But probably the most pertinent example here is that of Live8. Billed as the "greatest show ever" in support of global humanitarianism, it was produced, as mentioned earlier, as a massive media event that sloganized and logo-ized debt and poverty (e.g., the "Make Poverty History" advertising campaign) and served as marketing platform for several corporate sponsors (AOL Time Warner, BBC, Nokia). It also provided "unpaid" artists with wide global exposure, and subsequent rises in music sales. Thus, for example, the HMV and Amazon album sales of Live8 artists Pink Floyd, The Who, Annie Lennox, Sting/The Police, and Madonna increased by between 150% and 3600% in the week following the concerts (BBC 2005).[4] By any measure, this was indeed the "greatest show ever," although not for poverty so much as self-promotion.

Complementing the economic benefits are the symbolic returns of celebrity humanitarianism. Talking about Live8 in a *Guardian* interview, Bono declares, for instance, that "[t]his is show business ... Years ago we were very conscious that in order to prevail on Africa, we would get better at dramatising the situation so that we could make Africa less of a burden and more of an adventure" (Bunting 2005). He admits that drawing attention to "Africa" requires dramatization through show-business-as-adventure; but what he shies away from is that such dramatization often ends up centring the star, not Africa. So when Jolie speaks about Africa on CNN (as she did in 2006), for example, the story ends up being not about Africans, but mostly about her – *her* experiences travelling there, *her* guilt, *her* sympathy.

A similar scenario unfolded as the Gleneagles G8 summit drew to a close, with several NGOs criticizing Geldof for misrepresenting the summit's accomplishments: keen to make the Live8 pressure on the G8 leaders look fruitful, he boasted to the press about "mission accomplished," declaring it was "a great day for Africa," and giving British Prime Minister Tony Blair a "10 out of 10" for his leadership and the G8 an "8 out of 10" for debt relief efforts (*The Guardian* 2005). Yet, many NGO leaders who had worked hard on the Make Poverty History campaign were much more critical, with one spokesperson declaring that "Bob Geldof's comments after the G8 were very unhelpful, because they made people think everything had been achieved" (Dave Timms quoted in Littler 2008, 243; cf. Hague et al. 2008, 6).

Such celebrity urges to sensationalize, declare premature victory, or show moral outrage are all self-centring and hero-producing strategies aimed at promoting their own brand image. The unfortunate casualties are the humanitarian causes being espoused, often resulting in drowning out dissenting voices instead of heeding them, simplification instead of considered examination, razzle-dazzle instead of content.

Success, though, may not be the point at all; failure may in fact be fine, as long as the philanthropic effort comes off looking good. Thus, Band Aid/Live Aid raised significant funds for famine relief in Ethiopia, which was marketed as an outward success. Yet, some 1.2 million people still starved to death in the 1984–5 famine (BBC 2006), and the indiscriminate supply of aid may have helped prolong the civil war in 1991, with allegations of some aid being diverted to buy arms and a few aid agencies acting as accomplices to the crimes committed under President Mengistu Haile Mariam (de Waal 2008, 52; BBC 2010a, 2010b).[5] As Alex de Waal states, "the rush was *to be seen* to deliver food. The public and politicians demanded visible action to salve their consciences. The pressure unleashed by Band Aid debased the currency of humanitarianism ... advertising went up and quality went down" (2008, 52, italics in original; cf. Cooper 2008a: 64).

The same is true of Live8, which the above NGO criticisms of Geldof were alluding to: while the concerts garnered enormous public and media attention, the development outcomes were dismal (belying Geldof's sounding of victory). The 0.7% aid target has not been reached by any G8 country, and may have actually declined in real terms if debt relief is excluded (World Development Movement 2006). The promise to cancel or reduce debt, especially for the poorest countries, has not materialized, with only some 10% of pledges met a year later, much of this coming from already committed bilateral and multilateral aid (Shah 2006; Eurodad 2006, 4; World Development Movement 2006). Furthermore, the G8 commitment to greater trade justice has all but vanished in the face of the European Union's refusal to reduce farm subsidies, which bar agricultural exports from the South. Meanwhile, the G8 leaders, along with Geldof and his celebrity allies, have all emerged as heroes, announcing aid pledges and debt reduction schemes to much fanfare, and successfully spinning the failures as success – proving once again that what really matters is optics and image boost. Some have argued, in fact, that the entire Live8/Make Poverty History campaign was a losing proposition from the start, because it chose to work with institutions dominated by the rich and powerful states of the North that have a continuing interest in the status quo (Monbiot 2005a; Nash 2008, 176–9).

Consequently, celebrity humanitarianism's presentation of itself as benevolent and successful is severely tainted. Although outwardly other-regarding, its first duty is to itself, helping to advance the stars' brand image and allowing them to accrue spectacular economic benefits. The stars' personal "heroism" is hardly what matters. Backed by the power of corporate entertainment and media, their humanitarianism is choreographed and staged, so that it is not necessarily achievement that is rewarded, but presentation, uniqueness, sexiness, saleability, spin, and continuous media exposure. This is not to say that their charity work is only about marketing and branding: as the cases of Geldof, Bono, Jolie, and Madonna illustrate, stars often do have some knowledge of the issues they espouse, putting in resources, time, and effort, and undertaking field missions to gain on-the-ground experience. Michael Goodman puts it this way: "We, as the audience, need to be convinced to some degree they, as the celebrity, do indeed know what they are talking about in order to be taken somewhat seriously and, thus, the celebritization of development is not just *simply* about marketing-driven photo-shoots designed to up the celebrity's exchange value" (2009, 13). True, but it must not be forgotten that their knowledge of development issues (like their public display of "caring") is not pure or neutral, but motivated and invested; it is anchored in the expectation of generous economic and psychic/symbolic returns.

Promoting the (Western) Nation

A distinguishing feature of any nation is the way in which it builds its unique identity through festivals, sports, holidays, myths, and the like. Celebrity philanthropy is a case in point, since it allows Western nations to construct political community around a heroic figure in the person of the humanitarian celebrity. When Jolie and Madonna donate large sums of money to charities, when Geldof is repeatedly considered for the Nobel Peace Prize, or when Bono is chosen as *Time* magazine's 2005 "Person of the Year," the nation – in these cases, the United States, Great Britain, and Ireland – feels and looks good. Celebrity humanitarianism is thus bound up with nationalist/occidentalist discourse, since it helps produce a generous and benevolent national community or Western identity, building unity and pride. It is no wonder that politicians are keen to heroize the likes of Geldof by knighting them, or that in 2005 Tony Blair and Gordon Brown were eager to position themselves as the champions of the Make Poverty History campaign, promoting Britain as a "great nation" that stands for cosmopolitan and humanitarian values (Nash 2008, 175). Their euphoria was supported and echoed, in turn, by celebrities such as Coldplay's Chris Martin, who during the same G8/Live8 spectacle was quoted in *The Mirror* as saying, "Britain is amazing – it really cares about this stuff [i.e., debt cancellation, more foreign aid, etc.]" (quoted in Nash 2008, 176). Such mutual self-congratulation and gratification is intoxicating, so much so that Western countries may well have become hooked on it, giving new meaning to the term "aid dependency": as I have suggested elsewhere (Kapoor 2008, 89–90), it is not just that parts of the Third World may have become dependent on humanitarian aid, but also that the First World may be addicted to it because of its potent psycho-symbolic returns.

But several problems ensue. Heroization means that people identify with their national myths and heroes/heroines without really knowing or understanding them. We feel so proud and ennobled by our national icons, it's as if we *do* know them intimately; we are willing, then, to overlook their imperfections, either through blissful ignorance or disavowal. Celebrity humanitarianism thus appears pure, altruistic, courageous, heroic – and it is advertised as such by entertainment stars and Western national leaders alike. What tends to get buried in this melee is the careerism and profiteering done in its name.

Another concern is the nationalist/occidentalist attitude towards the "outside." The construction of humanitarian icons is a way to make the country unique and recognizable – in the manner of the "compassionate" nation, for example. Humanitarianism allows the Western nation to gloat vis-à-vis its neighbours and competitors, or lord it over its aid recipients (i.e., the Third World), a point I will return to later in this chapter.

A notable feature of nationalist discourse is its preoccupation with gender, particularly the symbolic importance given to mothering and childbearing, something Jolie and Madonna's humanitarianism aligns itself with. In fact, the philanthropic causes they have espoused appear stereotypically gendered, equating femininity to motherly caring and transnational adoption.[6] Such gendered humanitarianism mirrors idealized nationalist (and Christianized) notions of womanhood, wherein mothers are entrusted with ensuring the stability of home and hearth and with the preservation and reproduction of family and kinship. Indeed, in the United States during and after the Cold War, to adopt a child was to serve the nation and its national security/foreign policy priorities, especially in the aftermath of the Korean and Vietnam wars (cf. Eng 2003). Madonna and Jolie may thus be said to be continuing this U.S. national tradition: their transnational adoptions aid the nation by encouraging others to adopt, while also constructing themselves (and other adoptive parents) as saviours of orphaned Third World children. To echo Gayatri Spivak (1988), it's another case of white women saving coloured babies from coloured (wo)men, in the service of the nation.

But in addition to being a symbolic support, Madonna and Jolie are also a material support to the (Western) nation: their example as transnational adoptive parents helps address critical bottlenecks in Western country demographics and labour markets. Declining birth rates (themselves the result of such factors as improved health and the increasing presence of women in the workplace) and the rising labour requirements of ever-expanding economies translate into the need for greater immigration and adoption. Not surprisingly, Western governments have been quick to encourage international adoptions, many of them providing tax incentives. In the United States, for example, adoptive parents can claim up to $10,000 in tax credits (cf. Saunders 2007, 8; Eng 2003, 10). As a result, some 50,000 transnational adoptions happen globally every year, most in the United States and Europe (Saunders 2007, 2).

Far from yielding a multicultural brood (à la Madonna and Jolie-Pitt), transnational adoptions have been gendered (most adoptees tend to be girls) and highly racialized. In the United States, for example, the first main wave of adoptions was Asian children, in the aftermath of the Korean and Vietnam wars. But after the collapse of the Soviet Bloc, there was a significant rise in adoptions from such countries as Romania and Russia, with a corresponding decline in adoptions from Asia: "as soon as white children were available, prospective international adopters opted for race over all other considerations" (Gailey 2000, 5). Even when Third World children have been adopted, there is a noticeable hierarchy of babies, with those from China, for example, being preferred over those from "Africa."

It should be noted that there appears to be a marked preference for transnational over domestic adoptions. In the United States and Canada, black and aboriginal children are over-represented in the welfare system,[7] yet most adoptive parents favour adopting from abroad. As Ortiz and Briggs suggest (2003, 40, 181; cf. Waldinger and Lichter 2009), this is due partly to the pathologizing of black and aboriginal "welfare mothers" and "crack babies," partly to rescue fantasies and the sentiment that foreign babies can be more easily transplanted and moulded to suit the new nation/home, and partly to the more complex legal environments in the West that make it more difficult to adopt at home (i.e., more strict eligibility criteria, the risk of custody battles, etc.). The consequence is a racialized discursive practice of transnational adoption.

Aided and abetted by celebrity humanitarianism, transnational adoption is therefore nothing short of neocolonial. When privileged white Western parents deracinate Third World children, deprive a country of significant social/intellectual life-potential, select the most "desirable" children (based on race, health, ability), all the while failing to address the root causes (inequality, social strife, high birth rates), we have relations of domination and dependency.[8] It is for this reason that critics such as Twila Perry have argued that "rather than transferring the children of the poor to economically better-off people in other countries, there should be a transfer of wealth from rich countries to poor ones to enable the mothers of poor children to continue to take care of their children themselves" (quoted in Eng 2003, 10). At first glance, Madonna and Jolie may be considered to be doing some of this by their funding of orphanages in Ethiopia and Malawi, for instance; but their efforts still remain largely piecemeal, addressing individual issues and pet institutions rather than broader structures and causes.

Celebrity humanitarianism is thus at the service of the (Western) nation. It helps construct the image of national beneficence, singling out the nation as unique, while also setting it apart from its Others. It aids in strengthening nationalist/occidentalist and racialized discourses on mothering and childhood. And in the form of transnational adoption, it facilitates the West's economic/labour agenda, organizing the nuclear family "as a supplement to capital" (Eng 2003, 12), often at the expense of the Third World. Far from being altruistic and pure, then, celebrity humanitarian heroes are once again blighted, by their collusion with nation ... and capital.

Promoting Capitalism

Celebrities' dalliance with capital has already been alluded to above, but I want to develop the point further in this section. I will argue that celebrity humanitarianism isn't just entrenched in capitalism, but actually promotes it, thereby rationalizing the very "poverty" that such humanitarianism seeks to redress.

Celebrities are already tied to the corporate world through their professional work (commercial, film, and TV, music industry, sports corporate sponsorships, PR and marketing firms, etc.), earning some of the highest incomes globally, as reported by the likes of *Forbes* magazine (2010), for example. They also profit tremendously from their brand image, a point I underlined earlier. In the movie industry, whereas stars used to be tied exclusively to the studios, they (like most entertainment celebrities) now legally own their own image or "publicity rights," which function like a trademark or copyright (Drake 2008). This means they have a monopoly over their brand image and can control who profits from it, including the studios when the latter do movie promotions or DVD releases. Philip Drake puts it this way: "[T]he political economy of celebrity is one that firmly favors the rights of celebrities over their fans. Celebrities propertize themselves by drawing upon a discourse of achievement associated with traditional notions of the hero, in order to exclusively claim the intellectual property of their images, extending a former privacy right (available to all) to a property right (the right of publicity, available only to the famous)" (2008, 450). It is these exclusive intellectual property rights that enable celebrities to take advantage of corporate product endorsements, lending their name and image to a corporate brand for a fee that can amount to several million dollars. Thus, even a brief Google and YouTube search reveals the following endorsements by various humanitarian celebrities: Geldof – Kleenex, Telstra, Wilkinson Sword; Bono/U2 – BlackBerry, Apple iTunes, Skol; Jolie – St. John Knits, Shiseido, Arnette, Louis Vuitton; Elton John – Coke, VISA, Verizon, Cadbury's, Orange; George Clooney – Toyota, Nestlé, Martini, Fiat, Emidio Tucci; and Madonna – Pepsi Cola, Mitsubishi, The Gap, Versace, Panasonic, H&M, Shochu.

Of course, some humanitarian celebrities are entrepreneurs in their own right. Bono, for instance, owns a luxury hotel and is the managing director and co-founder of Elevation Partners, a private equity firm with some $1.9 billion of capital invested in intellectual property and media, including shares in the conservative business-publishing conglomerate Forbes (Dieter and Kumar 2008, 262–3). Jay-Z owns and manages a billion-dollar empire, including an urban clothing brand (Rocawear), a stake in a beauty products franchise (Carol's Daughter), a global investment firm (Gain Global Investment), luxury hotels, and real estate (Curan 2010). For his part, Geldof co-owns a TV production company (Planet 24) and a media/publishing firm (Ten Alps).

Significantly, humanitarian celebrities bring their business acumen and experience to their charity causes, which is well in keeping with their adherence to "creative capitalism" or "philanthrocapitalism." This was already the case in 1985 when, organizing Live Aid, Geldof is reported to have declared, "the more multimillion record selling acts the better" (quoted in Hague et al. 2008, 10). In this sense, as Hague et al. argue, "his role was not that of the perceptive artist shaping popular sensibility, but rather of enterprising entrepreneur staging events to raise cash. He was branding and marketing a cause" (2008, 10). The same commercial branding was visible 10 years later during Live8, with its logo-ization of poverty ("Make Poverty History") and its corporate sponsorships (as outlined earlier). Bono describes himself as an "adventure capitalist" (quoted in Bunting 2005), and in a *New York Times* article, entitled "Citizen Bono Brings Africa to Idle Rich," he goes further, advertising Africa as business opportunity in the manner of an agent of capital: "One of the things I have learned of in Africa is the crucial role that commerce will play in taking its people out of extreme poverty. Everyone talks about China being the next big thing, but if you spend any time in bars or hotels in Africa, you see a lot of Chinese doing deals there. There is tremendous opportunity there ... Africa is sexy and people need to know that" (Carr 2007; cf. Magubane 2007a). Therefore, not only are humanitarian celebrities deeply immersed in capitalism, but their charity work is entangled with it and even promotes it unconditionally. Yet, what they fail to realize (or admit) is that it is this very capitalism that is so often the root cause of the inequality they seek to address through their humanitarianism. It is beyond the scope of this chapter to demonstrate this link; others have done so in great detail (e.g. Wallerstein 1974, 1980, 1989, 2004; Harvey 2006). Suffice it to say that the historical development of global capitalism has produced abundance alongside deprivation, and capital dispersal and concentration alongside inequity and unevenness. In its latest "neoliberal" phase (mid-1980s onward), supported by market and trade liberalization regimes, capitalism's unquenchable thirst for surplus value and new markets has meant the super-exploitation of labour reserves (e.g., sweatshops, primarily composed of women) and the exclusion of social groups from accessing socio-economic and environmental resources, particularly in the Third World.

It is important to note that several of the multinational corporate firms that humanitarian celebrities are associated with have contributed directly to social marginalization and exploitation. Of the celebrity-endorsed firms listed above, for instance, a few are worthy of mention: Nestlé is famous for its baby-formula fiasco in the 1970s–1980s, and is also reputed as one of the worst violators of labour rights, ranging from its use of child and forced labour on cocoa farms in West Africa to its mistreatment of workers and union busting in Colombia (Curtin 2005, 164); Coca-Cola also has a questionable labour record in several countries (including Colombia), and has contributed to global water depletion (e.g., in India) through its overuse of groundwater and its drive towards water privatization (Killercoke 2010); and finally, Gap is well known to have sold products produced in sweatshops (e.g., in Cambodia and India) (DeWinter 2001). To add insult to injury, Jeffrey Sachs ("development advisor to the stars"), rather than being critical of certain corporate labour practices in the Third World, has defended them, declaring in the *New York Times* that his "concern is not that there are too many sweatshops but that there are too few" (Myerson 1997).

What is troubling is that the humanitarianism of celebrities proceeds as though equality/justice can be achieved without confronting power, including their own. Their production as heroes/heroines feeds into the neoliberal ideology of personal initiative and individual (heroic) effort and empowerment as a panacea for structural problems. Such depoliticization is evident in the fact that rarely do they implicate their own privilege and authority in their work. Nickel and Eikenberry write, for example, that Jolie's "story [of humanitarianism] is fiction ... because she has not actually challenged the power dynamics that made her story possible in the first place" (2009, 983). Moreover, celebrities almost never do challenge capital (at most, Bono and Geldof will decry Third World debt, but they refrain from criticizing the IMF or other banking capital that underwrites it).[9] Ostensibly, this is because they are leery of alienating their audiences, but mostly it is because they have little incentive to confront the corporate power they so profit from. Yet, it is this depoliticization of capital that causes its presence to be unspoken and taken for granted.

Promoting a "Post-Democratic" Order

The rise of humanitarian heroes is emblematic of what Slavoj Žižek and Jacques Rancière have termed a "post-political" or "post-democratic" order. The terms describe our current capitalist liberal democratic landscape, in which "all parties are known and ... everything is on show, in which parties are counted with none left over and ... everything can be solved by objectifying problems" (Rancière 1998, 102). This is a world where all is ordered and given a place (Rancière 1994, 173). Democracy is reduced to periodic elections, and people choose between mostly politically indistinguishable parties/platforms. The liberal democratic regime is accepted as given without any fundamental rethinking or critique, so that political change actually means the status quo. Politics becomes what Žižek calls "the art of the possible" (1999, 199).

The post-democratic state is a mostly managerialist one: technocrats, expert policymakers (polling specialists, economists, scientists), and corporate oligarchs interpret people's demands and translate them into practical policy decisions. "Good governance" replaces politics through the use of expert analysis and "enlightened" policymaking. The phenomenon is particularly acute in supranational bodies such as the WTO, IMF, UN, or World Bank, where administrators and legal experts, who claim to be doing what's best for everyone, can override national sovereignty and decide what member states should do, or can be used by the member states themselves to get around the will of the people to achieve the government's desired policy priorities (Rancière 2006, 81–2).

Politics, in this state of affairs, is really the lack of it, with disagreement and dissent foreclosed. Enemies, outsiders, "fundamentalists," and radicals are vilified, and state power is used with impunity to neutralize them by resorting to the declaration of emergencies and the suspension of the rule of law, which can subsequently become the norm (i.e., what Agamben calls the "state of exception"). With dissension and conflict defused, political regimes can afford to engage in "consensus building," outwardly including and valuing "all" points of view. For Rancière, such consensual politics, is the hallmark of the post-democratic order: "Consensus refers to that which is censored ... there is no contest on what appears, on what is given in a situation and as a situation ... Consensus is the dismissal of politics as a polemical configuration of the common world." (2003, paragraphs 4–6). Consensual politics is mediated not through party politics as much as the corporatized and technocratic state managers. As a result, the state becomes a kind of "police agent servicing the (consensually established) needs of market forces and multiculturalist tolerant humanitarianism" (Žižek 2006a, 72; cf. 1999, 198). Indeed, neoliberalism and multiculturalism are the order of the day: the former enables late global capitalism to proceed without disruption or upheaval; and so does the latter – it accedes to the individualized cultural demands of various groups, but is careful to prevent the universalization of any emancipatory or economic claims so as not to obstruct the smooth circulation of capital (cf. Žižek 2006b, 151ff.).

Humanitarian celebrities strengthen, and fit well into, this post-democratic order. Advised by managerial experts such as economist Jeffrey Sachs, they have become, as emphasized earlier, the pundits of global altruism and "go-to" people on global-policy questions ranging from debt and HIV/AIDS to adoption and famine. They command exclusive access to the global corridors of power, with the ability to influence G8 leaders, U.S. Congressional representatives, captains of industry, or senior policymakers from the World Bank or IMF. In their capacity as "celebrity diplomats" they serve as a support to the work of state technocrats, purporting to represent popular consensus and dispensing "enlightened" policy.

The rise of celebrities as policymakers can be seen, for example, in Live8, which was framed as though Bono and Geldof, along with the G8 leaders, were the exclusive representatives and change agents on such causes as debt and poverty, in spite of the fact that the Make Poverty History campaign was a primarily NGO effort. It can also be seen in the well-known Sharon Stone incident at the Davos World Economic Forum in 2005: after the Tanzanian president had expressed the need for mosquito nets because people were reportedly dying from malaria, Stone rose up and pledged $10,000, challenging other business and political leaders in the audience to match her pledge. Over $1 million was eventually pledged, but only a portion was actually honoured, with the UN having to step in to make up the difference (Littler 2008, 242–3). As a result, several observers questioned Stone's and other celebrities' legitimacy and credibility as policymakers, asking how celebrities can determine on what the likes of the UN should be spending their limited resources. The issue, as Littler explains, is that "the power of celebrity can pull aid towards a particular cause that appeals to them and away from others" (2008, 243).

The Stone incident is characteristic of the elite political landscape of post-democracy. In this age of neoliberalism and widespread belief in the merit-rewarding society, it underlines the heroization and "hyperindividualisation" of humanitarian celebrities (Littler 2008, 246). Backed by powerful interests (corporate, nationalist), celebrities are positioned to act as political brokers and decision-makers, and feel entitled to do so under the guise of well-intentioned altruism, despite their lack of accountability. As Hague et al. argue, "the logic of ... [celebrity humanitarianism] echoes post-democracy in that, despite the rhetoric of populism, it is elite-focused. The emphasis ultimately is not on mass public action but on elite action" (2008, 19). Meanwhile, as audience members, we become the means by which celebrity charity work is legitimated, acting as witnesses to such celebrity media events as Live8. Politics thus becomes mediated spectacle, with citizens transformed into fans, consumers, and bystanders.

Using and Abusing Africa/the Third World

I have already underlined how celebrities act as direct or indirect agents of capital. Whether through their professional work (in music, film, sports), product endorsements, or personal business ventures, they help advance global corporate power, including in the Third World. In reference to the film industry, Lee Barron points out that "studios do not merely transmit film product to the 'south' ... but also use Southern countries to make their films. For example, Jolie's *Tomb Raider* ... which was shot at the Angkor Wat temple in Cambodia, opened up the country to numerous subsequent productions that took advantage of the lower costs of filming there" (2009, 223).

But such economic imperialism is complemented and supported by cultural imperialism, with the Third World being used by celebrities as both cultural backdrop and dumping ground. Despite best intentions, celebrity visits to the South on observer or philanthropic missions are most often self-promoting and voyeuristic endeavours: as journalists look on and cameras roll, the spectacle of smiling/suffering children or thankful/crying mothers serves as excuse to showcase the celebrity's do-gooding. Africa, in particular, is constructed as desperately in need (of philanthropy). With the celebrity as the audience's hero and guide, the "dark continent," bedevilled by "poverty" and corruption, becomes a museum or tourist attraction and, to recall Bono's earlier-quoted remark, "less of a burden and more of an adventure." The narrative here tends to reproduce the stereotypical hero-tale: the compassionate and wise celebrity-hero/heroine confronts obstacles, triumphs over adversity, and delivers African victims from their plight. Sometimes, such instrumentalization is plainly crass. For example, Madonna has used images of AIDS-stricken African children as a backdrop for her concert performances. Commenting on such a practice, the *New York Times* opines that she "has always known how to spot a trend. And much as it may strain the limits of good taste to say it, Africa – rife with disease, famine, poverty, and civil war – is suddenly 'hot'" (Williams 2006; cf. Magubane 2007b, 376–7; 2007a).

If the Third World serves as background for the purposes of instrumentalization and appropriation, it also acts as dumping ground for a range of First World fantasies. There are, to begin, the rescue fantasies we touched on earlier, which produce the West as dominant and Africa, in particular, as an aberrant space – a construction which conveniently mobilizes a rationale for (heroic) external intervention in the form of charity, aid, adoption, guidance, etc. These celebrity fantasies are not much different from the colonial "white man's burden" or the missionary visions of salvation of yesteryear; indeed, they can even be tinged with a Christianized message of deliverance, as witnessed by Geldof's famine relief song, "Do They Know It's Christmas."

And then there are the strong celebrity tendencies to romanticize the Third World. In her travel writings, for example, Jolie declares she is in "awe of these [African] people" and proclaims she "loves" her very simple and basic travel lodgings (2003, 37). Similarly, in his 2005 BBC TV series, Geldof pronounces Africa to be "quite simply the most extraordinary, beautiful and luminous place on our planet," and depicts "Africans" as having a "captivating grace of elegance and gesture" (2005). Yet, while outwardly sympathetic, such romanticized and aestheticized fantasies about the Other mask a colonizing gaze: they aim, first and foremost, at consolidating the Self by ingratiating the celebrity to the audience and rationalizing her/his humanitarianism. They also aim at managing the Other, by exoticizing it, and where necessary, passing judgment on it to put it in its place. Thus, even as she strives to come across as empathetic to Africa and Africans, Jolie records her indignation towards the use of the burka (2003, 164), saying that it allows for "no individuality ... I bought one and tried it on. I felt like I was in a cage. They are horrible" (2003, 220; cf. Barron 2009, 221). Likewise, having pronounced Africa to be a "luminous place," Geldof feels entitled to proffer a slew of orientalist characterizations such as "conflict bedevils Africa" or Kinshasa is the "capital of chaos" (2005).

Therefore, just as the Third World already serves as a dumping ground for hazardous materials and e-waste, or for dangerous products such as milk substitutes and contraceptive implants, so it serves as disposal site for self-promoting and colonizing fantasies that cover up or disavow the celebrity's power and privilege (cf. Kapoor 2008, 65–6, 72). The problem, however, is that in this process, the Third World is rendered silent. As self-declared global representatives of famine victims, poor people, orphaned children, and the like, the stars end up speaking *for* the Third World/subaltern. Thus, Jolie has no compunction about going on CNN to comment on "Africa" in an hour-long program in which not a single member of the African public is heard. In her 2006 interview with Anderson Cooper, she states that the "borders were drawn in Africa not that long ago. These people are tribal people. We ... colonized them. There's a lot we need to ... understand and be tolerant of, and help them to do. They have just recently learned to govern themselves" (quoted in Magubane 2007a, 6). And such orientalist constructions are reproduced time and again. In *Geldof in Africa*, which aired on TV, Geldof is present in almost every frame, either visually or verbally through his (paternalistic) voice-over commentary, opining about poverty and conflict (Geldof 2005). Yet once again, very few Africans are actually interviewed, and when they are, it is mostly cute children, or quaint or "exotic" hunter-gatherers and village elders. Missing in this idealized and sentimentalized account are any contemporary urban people, as though the whole of Africa is stuck in some ancient rural backwater.

The exclusion of Africans pervades many of the celebrity-organized charity programs and institutions as well. For instance, most Southern NGOs refused to join the 2005 Make Poverty History campaign because it was so dominated by Geldof and Northern NGOs (Hague et al. 2008, 20). They were not wrong, as it turned out, since the concerts themselves included practically no African musicians, with Geldof justifying his decision by asserting that "African acts do not sell many records" or have much "political traction" (quoted in Hague et al. 2008, 16; and Magubane 2007a, 6). Even Bono, who has explicitly tried to forge close links with African musicians, is not immune here: his organization, DATA (Debt AIDS Trade Africa), has exclusively Anglo-Westerners on its board, and only one of five of its offices is located in Africa (Dieter and Kumar 2008, 263); and the board of the ONE campaign, with which he is closely associated, is conspicuous by the absence of any Africans (cf. Cooper 2008b, 271).

Celebrity humanitarianism thus constructs the Third World, and Africa in particular, as voiceless and invisible. Because Africans are shown to be passive, without knowledge or agency, the stars can ventriloquize and paternalize them. The ideological resort to stereotypes – "Africans" are simple, noble, tribal, incompetent, politically naive – aims at fixing and naturalizing them, diverting attention away from the real nexus of problems (i.e., inequality, domination). The employment of the term "Africa"[10] attempts to elide or homogenize the continent's complexity and difference in order to contain it, to make it manageable.

All of these are deeply depoliticizing ideological moves. They try to keep the Third World, particularly Africans, subordinate and submissive in the global economic and political system. This is not to say that such strategies necessarily succeed, or that Africans do not actually resist or have agency (cf. Kapoor 2008, ch. 8). But it does point up the dominant position of the humanitarian celebrity; the psychic, cultural, and economic resources s/he draws on; and the hegemonic relations of power that African subjects are pitted against.

Conclusion

I have argued that celebrity humanitarianism is an ideological phenomenon of the times: one way in which late capitalist liberal democracies rationalize their structural tendencies towards domination and inequality is through celebrity charity work, which is sold as a solution to addressing Third World poverty, debt, famine, etc. Relying on their star-power, celebrity humanitarian heroes draw significant public attention to development problems, but their tendency to individualize and isolate such problems means that their own socio-economic complicity, as well as broader issues of political economy and cultural imperialism (what Žižek (2008, 2) calls "objective" violence), is glossed over or depoliticized.

Perhaps the most depoliticizing move here is that, by trying to cure the symptom rather than the cause, the current global discourse on humanitarianism ends up prolonging inequality. The remedy itself becomes part of the problem because, rather than making inequality impossible, it merely tries to keep "poor" people alive, by enabling them to survive through charity (cf. Žižek 2009). By framing the problem through the depoliticized lens of poverty (rather than inequality), it strives to bracket out the notion that inequality is unjust (cf. Manji 1998). Thus, Žižek (2009), drawing on Oscar Wilde, argues that the worst slave owners were those who were "kind," because they ended up rationalizing slavery under the pretence of their enlightened goodness, but in so doing may have helped prevent the politicization of the slaves and prolong the very institution of slavery.

One last point: despite indications to the contrary, the current pervasiveness of celebrity culture prompts many to wonder whether some humanitarian celebrities are "better" (i.e., more critical) than others. Andrew Cooper contends, for instance, that Bono is a significant actor on the global policy stage, and in many respects "far more astute" and effective than Geldof, who sometimes lacks charm and diplomacy (2007a, 7, 18; 2008b, 269; cf. 2008a, 36ff., 52ff.). Zine Magubane takes a similar tack, although she argues against Bono in favour of Oprah, mainly because Oprah challenges racism and the prevailing stereotypes of black people (2008, 11; 2007b, 374). The latest assessment comes from William Easterly (2010): he sides with Lennon against Bono, because the former was a rebel who challenged power, whereas the latter is a conformer, interested more in technical and policy solutions than political activism. What these analysts conveniently sideline is that all their heroes[11] are deeply entrenched and invested in late capitalist liberal democracies, which as I have argued, severely taints their humanitarianism or indeed rebelliousness. Can one really separate the stars' branding functions (and the entire marketing and media machine that accompanies it) from their humanitarian work? Are these stars' newfound roles in dispensing moral outrage or "enlightened" global policy democratically legitimate? And can humanitarianism qualify as dissident when it is so entrenched in dominant material and symbolic systems? I think not.

Therefore, my short answer to the question as to whether some celebrities are "better" than others is this: it seems improbable, since to be a "celebrity" is already to be invested in dominant power structures. But much more important, I claim, is that it is a mistake to seek a redemptive or radical politics in "good" celebrities when it is the broader structures which produce celebrity culture that require scrutiny and dismantling.

NOTES

1 I use the term "Third World" well aware of its pejorative meanings. But given that the mainstream discourse of development and its accompanying terminology is so problematic, I find the term the least of evils. I prefer it because of its anti-hegemonic connotations and origins – it became popular after the 1955 Bandung meeting of non-aligned countries, at which Third World leaders attempted to chart an alternative course to either the capitalist West or the communist Soviet Bloc.
2 In addition to being an economist at Columbia University, Sachs is closely associated with the United Nations, having been its Director of the Millennium Project (responsible for the Millennium Development Goals). He has often advised Third World and Eastern European "transition" governments on issues of market liberalization and structural adjustment. He was the main advocate of the disastrous "shock therapy" in Russia's transition to capitalism, and although he appears to have repackaged himself as a populist and "advisor to the stars" since the 1990s, he still advocates a version of shock therapy for Africa: the need for massive aid infusion and debt reduction, big development projects, and more trade (Sachs 2005). Ironically, his earlier structural adjustment policies are the very ones that contributed to the current debt problems of much of sub-Saharan Africa.
3 None of these traits are necessarily lurid or embarrassing, but mainstream Western society appears to think so, and the media profits from fetishizing "deviations" from the norm, which is why celebrities and their PR machines must ultimately find ways of either compensating or conforming.
4 As far as I can tell, only two Live8 performers (Paul McCartney and Pink Floyd guitarist, Dave Gilmour) committed to giving the revenues from the increased music sales to charity (BBC 2005).
5 While the BBC claimed repeatedly that resources raised by Band Aid were used to buy arms (2010a), it has subsequently withdrawn these reports and issued an apology (2010b).
6 Arguably, Geldof and Bono's humanitarianism is also gendered, fitting well the masculinist role of super-organizers and super-managers of large events such as Live8, for example.
7 The United States and Canada (as well as Australia) have a deplorable history of the treatment of indigenous/aboriginal children, many of whom were forcibly separated from their families, sent to "reform schools," and

placed with white families, and this throughout the twentieth century, until as late as the mid-1990s.

8 One has to be careful not to take this argument too far afield though, as some nationalist leaders have marshalled eugenic arguments to stop international adoptions, claiming they deplete a country's gene pool (cf. Saunders 2007, 11–12).

9 George Monbiot (2005a) asks, in this regard, "Where, on the Live8 stages and in Edinburgh, was the campaign against the G8's control of the World Bank, the International Monetary Fund and the UN? Where was the demand for binding global laws for multinational companies?"

10 Of course, I, too, am using the term "Africa," even as I warn against its use. This contradiction speaks to the very limitations of language – of never being able to step outside of language, of enjoying no access to any privileged place outside it, and hence of having to critique language through language itself. But there is a crucial difference between my use of "Africa" and the celebrities': unlike them, at least I use it aware of the risks of homogenization and exclusion of difference.

11 These analysts' own role in seeking to champion (and heroize) one celebrity over another is to be questioned, as it risks reproducing celebrity culture and "post-democratic" politics.

2

The "Oprah Effect":
The Ideological Work of Neoliberalism

JANICE PECK

It's what this show is all about, and has been about for 21 years, taking responsibility for your life, knowing that every choice that you've made has led you to where you are right now. Well, the good news is that everybody has the power, no matter where you are in your life, to start changing it today.

– Oprah Winfrey, *Oprah Winfrey Show* (2007b)

From the 1800's treatise *Self-Help* by Samuel Smiles to *The Power of Positive Thinking* by the Rev. Norman Vincent Peale, politicians, business executives, and millions of other Americans have gravitated to the message and messenger who tells them that the proper state of mind can produce physical, material and spiritual treasure.

– Karen DeWitt, *New York Times* (1995)

When Oprah Winfrey threw her support behind Senator Barack Obama's quest to secure the Democratic presidential nomination, hosting an extravagant fund-raiser at her vast California estate and stumping with the candidate in Iowa, New Hampshire, and South Carolina, media worldwide speculated whether her "magic touch" would extend to electing a U.S. president (Jones 2007). That question was to be expected, a *Christian Science Monitor* article observed, because Winfrey is no mere celebrity: rather, she is "a social icon, an earth mother, a television priestess" and "one of the great marketing machines of history" (Marks and Vanek Smith 2007). Such hyperbole has long been standard in the media's treatment of Winfrey; over the years she has been anointed a "prophet," an "inspirational phenomenon" (Avins 2000), and "almost a religion" (Lebowitz 1996). The "synergy" of her talk show, book club, website, magazine, radio channel, personal growth tours, YouTube channel, Facebook page, and, most recently, TV network has made Winfrey not just one of the "most trusted brand names" in America, but "The Queen of All Media" (Feeney 2000; Forbes 2009).

Winfrey did not always enjoy such positive press. Although her talk show was an immediate success from its national debut in 1986, by the early 1990s she and the swelling ranks of talk-show hosts were targets of public condemnation of the genre as "talk rot," "trash talk TV," and worse. In 1994, with criticism of talk shows escalating and her own ratings slipping against competition from new shows, including *Ricki Lake* and *Jerry Springer*, Winfrey announced she would stop focusing on "dysfunction" and start emphasizing "positive" topics (*Oprah Winfrey Show* 1994). By the end of the decade, she had not only survived the "talk show wars" and maintained her program's top-ranked spot, but had become a fabulously wealthy media tycoon and "cultural icon of mainstream America" (Brown 2002, 242; see also Grindstaff 2002; Peck 2008). In 1999, *Time* magazine included Winfrey in its inaugural list of the 100 most influential people in the world. She has since appeared every year on the "Time 100" list – more often than any other person (*Time.Com* 100, 1999; Donahue2010).

Winfrey's political clout has grown accordingly. In 2000, Vice President Al Gore and Governor George W. Bush eagerly appeared on her show in their run for the White House, and some have credited her with helping boost Bush's vote count (Mitchell 2000; Skinner 2000a, 2000b; Millman 2000). The same year, a wing of Ross Perot's Reform Party floated the idea of making her its presidential candidate ("President Oprah" 1999). A writer for *American Prospect* suggested in 2003 that Winfrey seek a U.S. Senate seat representing Illinois – a possibility that would later be entertained by soon-to-be-deposed Governor Rod Blagojevich as he looked to fill Obama's vacated Senate position (Jones 2003; Mooney and Goldman 2009). In 2004, film-maker Michael Moore created a "Draft Oprah for President" petition on his web page, arguing that she "represents the interests of the American people" (Moore 2004; Jicha 2004), and in 2008, a website was dedicated to "Oprah for President" (Dreammagic.com 2008). Winfrey has so far declined all invitations to public office. As she stated in a 1995 interview, "I think I could have a great influence in politics, and I think I could get elected ... But I think that what I do every day has far more impact" (Adler 1997, 246; also *Deseret News* 2003). She reiterated that message 15 years later to a reporter covering the impending launch of the new Oprah Winfrey Network (OWN). Asked of her political aspirations, Winfrey said: "I just feel like there's so much more ability for me, personally, to be able to effect change and to be able to influence through stories and ideas than I could ever do with politics" (Elber 2010).

In a piece about Winfrey's endorsement of Obama titled "The Audacity of Oprah," *Nation* columnist Patricia Williams (2007) referred to the pair as the "Double O's" and argued that their "particular form of raced celebrity enshrines the notion of American mobility." Obama "radiates a kind of hope that crosses the immigrant epic with a romantic desire for rainbow diversity," while Winfrey, who "reinvented herself by sheer will and rose against all odds to the very top of … the entertainment industry," personifies "the black, female, Horatio Alger, rags-to-riches story of our day." When Obama emerged as a front runner for the Democratic nomination, *New Republic* editor John Judis (2008) opined that the candidate's "hope and change" message tapped into one of the founding articles of American faith – the capacity to "wipe clean the slate of history and begin again from scratch" – and evoked the biblical figure of Adam, "the only person … to have lived unburdened by what came before him." This "Adamic" myth, which is premised on the intertwined principles of self-creation and self-determination, animates the creed of American exceptionalism and its companion, the "American Dream." If Obama's rise is a testament to "the American craving for an Adam figure" (ibid.), Winfrey's ascent to cultural iconicity is rooted in the powerful "bootstraps" narrative with which she paints herself as proof of the "American Dream."

Given her career trajectory, it is not surprising that Winfrey has been dubbed "both kingmaker and rainmaker" and credited with helping put the first African American in the Oval Office (Barboza 2010; Garthwaite and Moore 2008; Vedantam 2008; Forbes.com 2010). Her legendary ability to push products, ideas, causes, and people has been condensed in the now ubiquitous phrase, the "Oprah effect" (Kinsella 1997; Max 1999; Ulrich 2006; Marks and Vanek Smith 2007; *Oprah Effect* 2009; Hornbuckle 2009; Barboza 2010). This chapter is centrally concerned with the "Oprah effect" – the historical ground, political-economic conditions, and cultural tensions out of which it developed and from which it derives its ideological power.

Theorist Raymond Williams urges analysts of media and culture to look for the "indissoluble connections between material production, political and cultural institutions and activity, and consciousness"

(Williams 1977, 80). Attention to complexity and synthesis also defines the approach Douglas Kellner terms "diagnostic critique," which grounds media texts and institutions in a socio-historical context with the goal of comprehending "the defining characteristics, novelties, and conflicts of the contemporary era" (Kellner 2003, 27). Fredric Jameson proposes that the power of popular cultural texts – a category applicable to the entire output of Winfrey's media empire – lies in their "transformational work on social and political anxieties and fantasies" generated by "concrete social contradictions" that deny easy solution in reality (Jameson 1992, 25). Cultural texts both acknowledge and manage those contradictions through a process that "strategically arouses fantasy content within careful symbolic containment structures which defuse it, gratifying intolerable, unrealizable, properly imperishable desires only to the degree to which they can be momentarily stilled" (ibid.). This "management of desire" is accomplished by "the narrative construction of imaginary resolutions and by the projection of an optical illusion of social harmony" (25–6).

A successful narrative – and Winfrey's "bootstraps" biography and positive thinking mantra is surely one – accurately identifies an audience's fears and desires and offers satisfying responses to the tensions it has provoked. The challenge for the analyst engaged in "diagnostic critique" is to keep sight of both the utopian and the ideological dimensions of a given cultural text so as to grasp its complex relations to the fundamental contradictions of its era. The aim of such an analysis, which tacks back and forth between "text" and "context," is to provide a "diagnosis of contemporary pathologies, anxieties, political contestation, and ambiguities" (Kellner 2003, 28) that might allow us to gauge the difference between "what is" and "what might be." Paul Jones, writing of Raymond Williams's work, describes this approach as "emancipatory ideology critique" that sets its sights on the "contradictory tension of actual and possible" (Jones 2004, 67).

Applying this critical analytical method to the "Oprah effect" involves situating Winfrey and her enterprise within the socio-historical and political-economic processes that have made her a cultural icon, spiritual guru, and media mogul. Winfrey's core message is relatively simple, as exemplified in this promotion for one of her Personal Growth summits: "You only have to believe that you can succeed, that you can be whatever your heart desires, be willing to work for it, and you can have it" (Roeper 2000). But its simplicity is belied by the depth of its appeal, which issues from powerful currents in American political-economic, cultural, and religious history. If, as Roland Barthes contends, myth freezes history and makes it partially mute – giving mythical speech "its benumbed look" so as to "transform it into 'Nature'" – the practical efficacy of myth is necessarily historically conditioned (1972, 112, 116). For anthropologist Maurice Godelier, the power of myth does not issue from what it *is*, but from "what it *gets done*" – specifically, from its ability to "explain the order or disorder reigning in society" and thus "facilitate effective action upon the problems connected with the maintenance of this order or with the abolition of this disorder" (1986, 186).

Winfrey's status as a cultural icon is intimately bound up with her image as a spiritual leader/healer and her representation of her media enterprise as a mission "to transform people's lives, to make viewers see themselves differently and to bring happiness and a sense of fulfillment into every home" (Fitch 2000). In his study of the history of psychotherapy, Philip Cushman (1995) observes, "Every era has a particular configuration of self, illness, healer, technology; they are a kind of cultural package … when we study a particular illness, we are also studying the conditions that shape and define that illness, and the sociopolitical impact of those who are responsible for healing it" (7). This invokes the question of what Winfrey, by means of her public persona and sprawling media empire, "gets done" in contemporary society. What is the nature of the societal affliction to which she ministers, and of the cure that she prescribes? To what strains of societal "disorder" does her rags-to-riches biography – and requisite prescription of self-invention – propose itself as a solution? To answer these questions we must locate Winfrey's journey from talk-show host to cultural icon within larger historical developments that have made the narrative of self-invention, which she seeks to personify, rhetorically powerful and ideologically effective.

Those developments include the dramatic "growth of therapy as an institution and industry in American culture" over the past century (Epstein and Steinberg 1998, 84); the eclipse of the political project of second-wave feminism and its subsumption by the depoliticizing force of "postfeminism" (Stacey 1990); the proliferation of New Age spirituality, whose commitment to individualized "spiritual growth" has its roots in nineteenth-century religious movements (Roof 1999, 7; 1993; Albanese 2007); and, conditioning all of the above, the rise in the 1980s and triumph in the 1990s of "neoliberalism" – understood as an interlocking economic, political, and ideological project to establish a new set of rules for governing the functioning of capitalism. This chapter focuses primarily on these last two developments, which constitute the religious and political-economic foundations of Winfrey's enterprise.

Neoliberalism as Winfrey's Defining Context

Confronted with mounting debt from the Vietnam War, competition from the recovered economies of Europe and Japan, and political challenges from Third World national liberation movements, the United States by the early 1970s was losing the competitive advantage it had enjoyed for more than two decades. Thus began the shift from the post–Second World War "long boom" to the "long downturn" that continues to the present (Brenner 2006). The neoliberal project, which emerged with the elections of Ronald Reagan in the United States and Margaret Thatcher in the United Kingdom, can be understood as a particular political response to this constellation of challenges to American capitalism's global political-economic supremacy. That response was a dual "makeover" – first, of the economy, by means of deindustrialization, growth of the service sector, and shift of investment from goods to finance, and second, of the role of government within the economy, through tax reductions for corporations and the wealthy, deregulation, privatization, and dramatic cuts to public infrastructure and social programs (Pollin 2003; *Harvey 2005*; Irvin 2008).

Reagan's economic policies (aka "Reaganomics") constituted a dramatic restructuring of U.S. economic policy, including cutbacks to social programs, increased military expenditures, aggressive deregulation (e.g., airlines, utilities, telecommunications, finance), major tax cuts for corporations and the wealthy, and high interest rates benefiting banks and speculators. These policies accelerated trends that had started in the late 1970s: the export of jobs in search of cheap labour from the unionized "frostbelt" to the union-weak "sunbelt" and to developing nations with low-cost, non-unionized labour and minimal regulation; a shift from relatively high-wage factory work in heavy industry to low-wage service occupations; growing dependence on part-time and temporary employment; and a large-scale movement of women into the workforce to offset declining household incomes. The tensions generated by this climate of scarcity exacerbated polarization "not only between classes, but *within* classes," providing a rich medium for backlash politics, in which women, people of colour, and the poor could be blamed for the financial hardship and individual and social problems resulting from those same economic policies (Davis 1986, 178).

Although Reagan's presidency is associated with the birth of U.S. neoliberalism, it is crucial to recognize that what David Kotz (2003, 15) terms "neoliberal restructuring" was always a bipartisan enterprise. In 1977, faced with political pressure to reduce inflation, the Jimmy Carter administration and Democratic-controlled Congress imposed a freeze on social spending, raised interest rates, and over the next two years reduced the domestic budget, abandoned health care and labour law reforms, and curtailed urban jobs programs. Reagan's victory in 1980 was therefore not so much a radical reversal of Democratic policy as an acceleration of pre-existing developments. A similar assessment can be made about Bill Clinton's continuation of the policies and politics of his Republican predecessors. One of Reagan's most important accomplishments, according to Doug Henwood, was "the transformation of the Democratic Party" (1997, 161) – a project that began in 1985 with the creation of the Democratic Leadership Council (DLC) by a group of conservative, mostly southern Democrats (among them, Bill Clinton and Al Gore). Reagan and, in his wake, George H.W. Bush secured and consolidated Republican power by forging an alliance of the rich, the white professional middle class, and significant blocs of the white working class, especially those living in sunbelt state suburbs, and did so by explicitly capitalizing on race and gender divisions and anxieties. The DLC's founding strategy was to woo white voters from the professional, middle, and working strata, recoup the party's losses in the South, and return "Reagan Democrats" to the fold.

Arguing that the "traditional liberalism" associated with the Democratic Party from the New Deal through the 1960s was no longer relevant or politically viable, the DLC proposed a "New Liberalism," which espoused "mainstream moral and cultural values" (Galston and Kamarck 1989, 4) and eschewed "special interests," that is, labour, poor people, minorities – especially African Americans – women, gays, and lesbians (Henwood 1997; see also Reed 1999). Combining savvy use of media and generous funding from the energy, health care, insurance, pharmaceutical, retail, and tobacco industries, the DLC embarked on an ideological battle with liberal/left Democrats with the aim of pushing the party rightward. Those efforts were rewarded. By the end of the 1980s, the group's New Liberal agenda would "dominate Democratic Party politics and discourse" (Klinkner 1999, 12). In 1992, that agenda supplied Clinton, the DLC's first presidential contender, with a ready-made platform and campaign organized around the tropes of opportunity, responsibility, and community. In effect, Democratic New

Liberalism validated Reaganism's diagnosis of what ailed America (swollen government, bad values, lack of personal responsibility and individual enterprise) and adopted Reaganomics' prescription for curing the patient (small government, privatization, deregulation, slashed social spending). The success of the right turn orchestrated by the DLC is demonstrated by the fact that every Democratic presidential candidate since Clinton, including Barack Obama, has had the organization's blessing (Horowitz 2008; Dixon 2009). Thus, the neoliberal project has been driving the ideas, policies, and priorities of both major political parties in the United States for the past three decades.

In addition to economic policies aimed at redistributing wealth upward, neoliberalism entails political practices devoted to a "deep reshaping of social relations and ideas" (Leys 2001, 2) and "the valorisation of free market transactions of commodities as the best way of ordering society" (Dovey 2000, 175), as well as ideological practices that cultivate forms of subjectivity compatible with that order. The instantiation and extended reproduction of the neoliberal political-economic order has depended in part on forging semantic unity among the concepts of a "free market," unfettered entrepreneurship, "personal responsibility," and individual "empowerment." Winfrey's enterprise can be understood as a site of that ideological work through its role in producing and valorizing reliable neoliberal subjects.

The Power of the "Power of Mind"

In February 2007, Oprah Winfrey introduced her talk-show audience to "The Secret," a DVD/CD/book created by an Australian reality-TV producer promising health, wealth, and happiness to those who master the principle of the "Law of Attraction" (condensed in the slogan "Ask, Believe, Receive"), a force that governs our existence as inexorably as the law of gravity. Winfrey explained that "The Secret" proves we "create our own circumstances by the choices that we make and the choices that we make are fueled by our thoughts." It thus follows, she said, that "everything that happens to you, good and bad, you are attracting to yourself. It's something that I really have believed in for years, that the energy you put out into the world is always gonna be coming back to you. That's the basic principle" (*Oprah Winfrey Show*, 2007a). Winfrey was primed for "The Secret" because its mind-over-matter message has informed her enterprise from the beginning. As she remarked in introducing the first "Secret" episode, "it's what this show is all about, and

has been about for 21 years." Her relentless repetition of that message
has been central to forging her public persona as a "black, female Horatio Alger" and elevating her to the status of cultural icon.

A *Los Angeles Times* story in 2000 hailed Winfrey as a "teacher sent
to Earth to spread the word" and an "inspirational phenomenon" who
had "synthesized ... Eastern and Western philosophy and the gurus of
New Age enlightenment" (Avins 2000). Winfrey's message is not new,
however. It is steeped in the peculiarly American synthesis of capitalism, religion, and the therapeutic enterprise that took root in the late
nineteenth century during a period of religious turmoil. Variously
called mind cure, New Thought, positive thinking, and abundance
therapy, all strands of the new religion renounced "negative thinking"
and promoted the distinctly "American conviction that people could
shape their own destinies and find true happiness" (Leach 1993, 227).
This ensemble of religious/spiritual movements developed and proliferated in the United States during a period Martin Sklar (1988) identifies as "the passage of capitalism from its proprietary-competitive stage
to its corporate-industrial stage" (3). That shift fostered the "rise of a
professional, managerial, and technical middle class" (3, 441) and facilitated a dramatic expansion in the production of commodities, which
would require a corresponding increase in consumption. This societal
transformation included the cultivation of a new kind of social subject for whom commodities might represent fulfilment, self-worth, and
identity, as well as the elimination or reinterpretation of values that
were at odds with such an equation.

The success and longevity of mind cure issued from its ability to adapt
religious themes and practices to the evolving priorities of the developing corporate capitalist order and to speak to the experiences and values
of a key class stratum within it. The new theologies emerged out of, took
root in, and flourished within the rising middle class, whose members,
already comfortably removed from the realities of material deprivation,
could easily imagine their material comfort as the natural result of their
correct thinking. Significantly, mind cure exerted a particular attraction
for white middle-class women – it was even referred to on occasion as
the new "woman's religion" (Satter 1999, 240). Women comprised the
majority of students and followers of the various branches of the movement (e.g., Christian Science, Divine Science, Spiritual Science, Mental
Healing, Mind Cure) and were prominent as leaders, healers, teachers,
and authors. The appeal of these new spiritual systems, Cushman argues, rested on their ability to explain people's psychological distress,

to offer prescriptions for easing it, to "further construct and guide the self most in synch with that system," and to do so "without overthrowing, or even upsetting, the social and political structures that caused the suffering" (1995, 131). For middle-class women, mind cure was seductive because it took into account and provided meaningful responses to the "emotional and cultural tensions" of the patriarchal order that confronted them in Victorian America (Satter 1999, 240).

Mind cure proliferated in the late nineteenth century, Cushman says, because it offered "a compensatory political solution ... for the moral and economic problems of the times. Its discourse and practices were a response to the emotional and social consequences of a political system – industrial capitalism – that was gaining preeminence and creating a great deal of human wreckage in its wake" (1995, 131). In the late twentieth century, Winfrey encountered the wreckage of "post-industrial" capitalist society and responded with her latter-day technology of healing built on mind-cure principles. As was the case for her nineteenth-century antecedents, the primary market for Winfrey's thought-as-power credo is white middle-class women – some 73 to 78 per cent of the audience for her program, magazine, and website is female, 80 per cent of her show's viewers are white (Anburajan 2007), more than half are college educated, most are homeowners, a majority are employed, and advertisers line up to reap the rewards of the "Oprah effect" on her educated, upscale demographic (Peck 2008; Quantcast 2009).

Although Winfrey's appropriation of mind-cure cosmology has important parallels with her nineteenth-century counterparts, the explanation for this continuity must be sought in the character of our own times – hence the need to situate her enterprise historically in relation to the social values, political commitments, and economic priorities of neoliberal restructuring. Although Winfrey has been reciting the mantra "You are responsible for your own life" since 1986, her decision to accentuate the positive in the mid-1990s marked a significant career turn. From the mid-1980s through the early '90s, the *Oprah Winfrey Show* epitomized the "therapy talk show" format. Focused on issues of interest to women, who comprise the majority of the talk-show audience and the clientele for the therapeutic industry, the therapy talk show format relies on psychological concepts and terms, uses guest experts from the mental health industry, and offers solutions framed through a self-help ethos (Shattuc 1997; Peck 1995). Winfrey's show was specifically refracted through the tenets of the "recovery movement" – an amalgam of therapeutic practices, self-help groups, publications, mental health policies, and treatment programs that by the mid-1980s had become "a near universal way of thinking about human troubles in the larger society" (Rapping 1996, 77). Organized around the principles and practices of the 12-Step model of addiction, the recovery movement aims at healing the damaged self that it sees as the necessary by-product of the near universal "dysfunctional family."

A key effect of the proliferation of the recovery model in the '80s – thanks in part to its widespread dissemination in popular culture and media – was to transmute social and political issues into personal and psychological problems. A significant consequence of that transmutation was to undermine the powerful insight of second-wave feminism – that the "personal is political" – by reducing it to the idea that the political is ultimately only the personal. This transmutation goes to the heart of the ideological work of the therapy talk show: by corralling topics within the domain of the personal and subjective, it circumvents an interrogation of the objective conditions and structural relations of power within which personal experience is constituted (Lerner 1990; Tallen 1990; Krestan and Bepko 1991; Peck 1995). The upshot of that ideological move is to depoliticize public issues and social problems. Feminist psychologist Harriet Lerner has argued that the rise of the recovery model in the 1980s contained and managed the feminist critique of women's unhappiness: it was, she said, "a sort of compromise solution" that "teaches women to move in the direction of 'more self' while it sanitizes and makes change safe," because the existing gender order "is not threatened by sick women meeting together to get well" (Lerner 1990, 15). Winfrey's program was an ideal medium for this message, beginning with her enthusiastic endorsement in 1986 of Robin Norwood's best-selling *Women Who Love Too Much* (1985), which viewed all of women's difficulties with men through the lens of addiction and masochism – and thus unrelated to gender inequality. From its first season through the early 1990s, the *Oprah Winfrey Show* provided a dependable platform for an assortment of recovery movement experts and diagnoses (Travis 2009).[1]

For Winfrey, the recovery model offered a popular, non-threatening framework of intelligibility for talking about women's problems at a time when the right-wing political backlash against feminism was in full swing, including campaigns against the Equal Rights Amendment, women's reproductive rights, affirmative action, and gender pay equity (Faludi 1991). Further, her program's endless examples of the damage inflicted by the "dysfunctional family" (and the reification of its elusive "functional" counterpart) had parallels with Reaganism's defence of

the equally reified "traditional family." The guiding precepts of the recovery paradigm shifted all responsibility for individual suffering and
social disintegration onto the "dysfunctional family" and its corrupted
values – a logic eminently compatible with the ideological agenda of
Reaganism, which blamed the objective decay of the social fabric on the
subjective failure of irresponsible individuals and families bereft of values. Casting social problems caused by deepening economic inequality
as moral problems caused by individual and familial pathology could
then serve as justification for the state's abandonment of responsibility for social welfare in the name of restoring "personal responsibility"
(Rapping 1996; Peck 2008).

Jimmie Reeves and Richard Campbell argue that the proliferating
"discourse of recovery" in the 1980s was directed at "the psychic repair
of the bourgeois soul" (1994, 40). By the early 1990s, as an unlimited
supply of dysfunctional souls was making Winfrey vulnerable to the
charge that talk shows were little more than a "parade of wackos," she
was ripe for a public-image makeover (Mair 1998, 214). Winfrey's decision in 1994 to replace the recovery movement's "dysfunctional self"
with the "enchanted self" of "mind cure" – with the aid of "spiritual
psychologist" Marianne Williamson – provided the road to respectabil-
ity she craved. This turn to "positive programming" and message of
empowerment through positive thinking from the mid-1990s onward
has been crucial to elevating Winfrey from mere talk-show host to "almost a religion." It facilitated the makeover of her public persona as
well as the formal revamping of *The Oprah Winfrey Show* in 1996, which
included the creation of the phenomenally successful Oprah's Book
Club and extended her reach to an upscale market. It provided the basis
for her openly New Age "Change Your Life TV" season in 1998 and laid
the foundation for the creation of the "Oprah brand," which was built
on strategic business partnerships with ABC/Disney, Hearst and the
Oxygen cable network, and the expansion of platforms within her media empire. And it is the guiding principle of the fusion of commercial
calculation and spiritualized self-healing – which Kathryn Lofton refers
to as the "spiritual practice of capitalism" (2006, 599) – that character-
izes Winfrey's entire enterprise.

The Class Politics of the Empowered/Enterprising Self

Bill Clinton's New Liberal presidency provided the political-economic
context for Winfrey's makeover and her ascent in the 1990s to "prophet"
status. The New Liberal conception of human subjects had significant

affinities with Winfrey's revamped configuration of an empowered, enchanted self. Both were organized around a doctrine of "personal responsibility," a belief in the power of individual will to overcome material obstacles, a vision of community that rejected social division and conflict, and commitment to growth and consumption. In other words, both were built on what Nikolas Rose (1998) terms the "enterprising self," celebrated by neoliberalism. Rose proposes that neoliberalism should be understood not only as a rightward reconstruction of "macroeconomic policy, organizational culture, social welfare, and the responsibilities of citizens" (150), but as a medium for cultivating an "enterprise culture" that "accord[s] a vital *political* value to a certain image of the human being" (151). The ideal neoliberal subject "makes an enterprise of its life, seeks to maximize its own capital, projects itself a future and seeks to shape itself in order to become what it wishes to be" (154). Like the "empowered" subject invoked by Winfrey, the enterprising neoliberal subject takes personal responsibility for her life, eschews dependence, invests in her human and social capital, discovers her desires, and seizes her opportunities.

As I argued in the opening of this chapter, unravelling the appeal of the "enterprising" self, the resiliency of mind-cure cosmologies, and the longevity of the Adamic myth requires an investigation of the political-economic conditions that have endowed them with explanatory power. The decades straddling the turn of the twentieth century, when mind cure took root, and those leading up to the twenty-first century, when it experienced a broad rebirth, were marked by significant political-economic change. The first period witnessed the passage of U.S. capitalism from its competitive to corporate stage, while the second saw the replacement of a Keynesian model of the government/economy relationship with a neoliberal model (Pollin 2003; Kotz 2003). That the mind-cure theology suffusing Winfrey's enterprise originated in the former period and that her journey from talk-show queen to cultural icon/media mogul paralleled the rise and triumph of the latter period are of central importance in a diagnostic critique of the "Oprah effect."

It is no accident that the original Gilded Age linked to the rise of industrial capitalism in the United States and the "new gilded age" (Uchitelle 2007) associated with the deindustrialization of America over the last quarter century brought growth and expanded opportunities to a specific sector of the middle class. Variously labelled the professional managerial class, the upper middle class, and the new petty bourgeoisie, and identified with law, education, business, science and engineering, medicine, social services, and media, this class stratum strives to advance and maintain its social power by valorizing higher education, credentials, and specialized knowledge. The dominant values of the new petty bourgeoisie include competitive individualism – stemming from the isolated nature of professional labour – and a commitment to meritocracy. As a class, it tends to favour expanded decision-making and opportunities for promotion, but it is less inclined to support major structural transformation of society. As political theorist Nicos Poulantzas puts it, the new petty bourgeoisie "does not want to break the ladders by which it imagines it can climb" (Poulantzas 1975, 292).

What has been happening over last quarter century that might help us understand the appeal of Winfrey's mind-cure message for the professional managerial class – as well her particular attraction for women? Women have played an important role in the shift from Keynesianism to neoliberalism. The end of the long post-war boom in the United States and resulting stagnating wages from the 1970s onward brought an end to the "family wage," making it increasingly necessary to have two (or more) incomes to sustain a household (MacLean 2002). As women poured into the workplace out of necessity, they encountered an expansion of low-wage, high turnover, part-time jobs and saw their participation in the workforce grow from 34 per cent in 1960 to over 60 per cent in 2005 (Eisenstein 2005, 491). Women's mass movement into the paid labour force created a need to replace their unpaid labour at home, leading to commercialization of personal services in the form of low-paying service jobs – which were filled primarily by other female workers. At the same time, deindustrialization and the pursuit of cheap labour relocated manufacturing work from unionized to non-unionized provinces, nations, and global regions. The resulting creation of export processing or free-trade zones in the global South accompanied moves to cut production costs in the North by means of immigrant labour and automation – with both developments relying heavily on female labour.

Further, over the past three decades an increasing number of women in the United States have entered higher education, earned degrees, and joined the ranks of professional/managerial employment. According to the U.S. Bureau of Labor Statistics, the percentage of women in managerial and professional jobs grew from 26.1 per cent in 1980, when Reagan was elected, to 51.4 per cent in 2010 (Rosin 2010). A 2010 article in *The Atlantic* with the hyperbolic title "The End of Men?" observed that "for the first time in American history" women occupy "a majority of the nation's jobs," "dominate today's colleges and professional schools" (three women earn bachelors' degrees for every two men), and predominate in thirteen of the fifteen job categories expected to grow over the next decade (ibid.). In contrast, more men are finding themselves outside the workforce, whether involuntarily or by choice. In 2010, one in five men in their prime employment years was not working; in 1950 in the long boom's heyday, that ratio was one in twenty (ibid.). Such statistics suggest that across classes women are shouldering more and more of the economic obligations in their households – a responsibility that may heighten their susceptibility to "thought-as-power" cosmologies.

In addition, mind-cure theology has always spoken with a middle-class accent. In the late nineteenth century, it appealed to educated middle and upper-middle classes because it "offered peace of mind and emotional tranquility to those already on the way up" (Quebedeaux 1982, cited in Roof 1999, 140). At the end of the twentieth century, these same class strata were facing mounting economic insecurity, thanks to neoliberal restructuring. Corporate downsizing, the expansion of contingent labour, cutbacks in the public sector, and the outsourcing of jobs have presented serious challenges to the 30 per cent of the U.S. population identified as the college-educated middle class – a group that also represents a key target market of the Oprah brand (Uchitelle 2006, 66). Particularly troubling are the collapse of job security – between 1984 and 2004 at least 30 million full-time workers were laid off (5) – and the dramatic decline of "good jobs" paying at least $17 an hour with employer-paid health care and retirement benefits (Schmitt 2005, 4). As the "family wage" and the dream of a comfortable middle-class existence became harder to realize in the 1980s and '90s, competition for the dwindling number of good jobs grew fierce. In such a climate, we might expect people to be more vulnerable to anything that promises the "secret" to escaping the brute logic of the cut-throat marketplace in what Louis Uchitelle calls the "go-it-alone world" of neoliberal capitalism (Uchitelle 2006, x). Hence the allure of the makeover, particularly when dressed up in the rhetoric of empowerment by a figure whose professed mission is to empower women and who has come to represent the personification of the empowered woman herself.

Meanwhile, it is important not to lose sight of neoliberalism's bipartisan support. If, as economists Gerard Dumenil and Dominique Levy argue, the neoliberal revolution in the United States began with a quest by a sector of capitalist owners to regain "power and income after a setback of several decades" (2002, 53), the success and sustainability of neoliberalism has depended on its ability to "establish a new social compromise in an environment of rising inequality" by "associating a broader social strata to the growing prosperity of the few, really or fictitiously" (45). At root, neoliberalism is a class-based political project to achieve a dramatic upward redistribution of wealth (Harvey 2009). This is the basis of its continuity from Reagan to Clinton and beyond to Obama. Surveying the results of Clinton's two terms, economist Robert Pollin concluded that "Clintonomics" amounted to "down-the-line neoliberalism: global economic integration and fiscal austerity, with minimum interventions to promote equity in labor markets or stability in financial markets" (Pollin 2003, 75). The main beneficiaries of the Clinton era were those at the top, for whom "wealth exploded" in the second half of the 1990s (ibid.). The primary engine of economic growth during Clinton's second term was a "debt-financed consumption boom" fuelled by a dangerously overheated stock market (65), with nearly all of this consumer activity occurring among the richest 20 per cent of households (67). Meanwhile, the majority of Americans coped with economic stagnation or decline as wages "remained below their level of the previous generation" (75). In fact, average wages for non-supervisory workers and the earnings of those in the bottom 10 per cent "not only remained well below those of the Nixon/Ford and Carter administrations, but were actually lower even than those of the Reagan/Bush years" (42–3). The economy's putatively "exceptional" performance in Clinton's second term, Federal Reserve Chairman Alan Greenspan told Congress in 1997, was largely due to "a heightened sense of job insecurity and, as a consequence, subdued wages" (53). That amplified sense of job insecurity, Pollin says, "lies at the very foundation of the Clinton administration's economic legacy" (54).

Depoliticization and the Oprah Effect

Mike Davis argues that the restructuring of the U.S. economy since the end of the 1970s reflects the bipartisan political strategy of "mobilizing the mass middle strata" by "expanding its claims to the national income" (Davis 1986, ix). In his analysis, "Democratic neo-liberalism as well as Reaganism asserts that the first function of the state is to provide welfare to the well-to-do and preserve a dynamic frontier of entrepreneurial, professional and rentier opportunity." The reinvention of the Democratic Party in the 1990s made it increasingly indistinguishable from its Republican counterpart – so much so that Gore Vidal (2004) would characterize the United States at the end of the twentieth century as governed by "one political party, the Property Party, with two right wings, Republican and Democrat." Starting from an understanding of politics as "a constant struggle over who has the right to rule whom" carried out by historically specific political subjectivities (Wang 2007), the erosion of meaningful political differences reflects a crisis of party politics that has traversed Western democratic states over the last quarter century (Wang 2006a, 2006b; Russo 2006; Boggs 2000). With the globalization of the neoliberal order, political parties have shed their identification with and representational commitments to specific class-based constituencies while increasingly converging around "broad macro-economic consensus" (Wang 2006a, 32). Such "depoliticized politics" are the hallmark of neoliberalism. In the United States, this process of depoliticization is evident in both the Democratic and Republican parties' eagerness to identify government as the chief cause, and the market as the preferred solution, to nearly every societal problem.

This is the context in which Oprah Winfrey attained the status of world celebrity and cultural icon. Her mind-cure enterprise can be understood as an ensemble of ideological practices that help legitimize a world of growing inequality and shrinking life possibilities for the majority of people by promoting a configuration of self compatible with a "go-it-alone world of personal responsibility" (Uchitelle 2006). Reaching back to the nineteenth century New Thought movement (which played a central role in the formation of the middle-class American self) while embracing neoliberalism's triumphal present (in which the steady upward transfer of wealth, institutionalization of layoffs as standard management practice, and decimation of the welfare state have left us with little more than our "personal responsibility" to protect us from the vagaries of the market), Winfrey's healing technology conserves the American religion of positive affirmation from which it descends and provides tutelage in building the "enterprising self" with which it is contemporaneous. A conspicuous beneficiary of the neoliberal order – in 2010, she was 130th on Forbes' list of the 400 richest Americans with a net worth of $2.7 billion and earnings of $315 million, while paying income and social security taxes at the same rate as those making $50,000 to $75,000 a year (Forbes.com 2010; Tabb 2007, 40) – Winfrey has played an important role in promoting, validating, and exporting its values at home and around the world.

Thanks to the parallel expansions of her media empire and her philanthropic activities, Winfrey is now a global cultural icon. By its 2011 finale, *The Oprah Winfrey Show* was airing in 150 countries; the *Oprah. com* website had become an international gateway to the Oprah brand; and the South African edition of the phenomenally successful *O, The Oprah Magazine* was carrying out its mission "to help women become more of who they are" (Carr 2002). Through funding from her namesake foundation, money from her fans channelled through Oprah's Angel Network, partnership with the Save the Children, support for fellow celebrities' causes (e.g., Bono's (Product) RED campaign, which had its U.S. debut on *The Oprah Winfrey Show* in 2006; Alicia Keys's Keep A Child Alive project), and endorsement of microcredit (e.g., Grameen Bank), fair trade, and social entrepreneurship, Winfrey has had a powerful hand in valorizing and legitimizing neoliberalism's ideological and political practices.

South Africa, in particular, has played a starring role in Winfrey's philanthropic enterprise, beginning with a 2002 "Christmas Kindness" party for 50,000 South African orphans. Oprah's Angel Network money paid for 18,000 school uniforms and funded an elementary school in the largely black and poor province of KwaZulu-Natal (Oprah's Angel Network Fact Sheet 2009), and 2007 marked the opening of the Oprah Winfrey Leadership Academy for Girls, an exclusive $40-million boarding school intended to replicate her own "up-from-the-bootstraps" trajectory and turn poor girls into future "leaders" of Africa (Gien 2007, 156). All of these philanthropic activities are predicated on the economic polarization, hollowed-out state, and withered public sector that are the hallmarks of neoliberal restructuring. As ideological practices, they help legitimize a political-economic order that favours private initiative and individual self-improvement over public funding and collective responsibility for societal needs. In the process, these practices personalize – and thereby depoliticize – what are profoundly inequitable geopolitical power relations.

The collapse of the housing bubble and ensuing financial meltdown in 2008, which set off the worst economic downturn since the Great Depression of the 1930s, elicited widespread speculation as to whether the reign of neoliberalism – including the "market fundamentalism" on which it is based – was coming to an end (Stiglitz 2008, 2010; Harvey 2009; Pollin 2009; Gumbel 2009). Barack Obama's election that year conjured dreams of a return to Keynesian policies, including extensive financial regulatory reform and state expenditures for infrastructure and job creation (Rothschild 2009; Davidson and Blumberg 2009; Stiglitz 2010; Reich 2010). Had such a political-economic turnaround occurred, Winfrey's mind-over-matter project might have found itself in unfamiliar ideological terrain. But rather than a break with neoliberal restructuring, the Obama era has proven to be more a continuation of those policies and politics, and thus as compatible with Winfrey's message as were those of administrations from Reagan onward (Peck 2010, 231–63).

A favourite of the Democratic Leadership Council since the genesis of his Senate career, Obama shared his affinity for market fundamentalism in a 2008 interview: "I am a pro-growth, free-market guy. I love the market" (Klein 2008; also Street 2009a). Since taking office, Obama has populated his administration with architects of neoliberalism and denizens of Wall Street, spent billions in public money to bail out Wall Street with no strings attached, advanced a health care bill that lines the pockets of the insurance and pharmaceutical industries, abdicated his campaign promises to organized labour, agreed to continue George W. Bush's tax cuts that overwhelmingly benefit the wealthy, continued and expanded U.S. military operations around the world, and carried on Bush's education policy – under a new name – that favours school privatization and blames public education's problems on unionized teachers (Street 2010). Indeed, Obama has played a powerful role in legitimizing and advancing the attack on teachers' unions; in this he replicates Bill Clinton's assault on welfare in the 1990s. In both cases, a Republican administration would have encountered major resistance from Democratic opponents and constituents. Just as it took a Democratic president to "end welfare as we know it," it may take a Democrat to bring down organized labour in the public education sector. Significantly, Oprah Winfrey was as vocal a champion of "welfare reform" during Clinton's reign as she is of "education reform" during Obama's (Alter 2010; Gabriel and Dillon 2011).

Although the National Bureau of Economic Research announced in September 2010 that the Great Recession in the United States had officially ended in June 2009 (Lee 2010), the unemployment rate was then still hovering between 9 and 10 per cent, as it had been since May 2009. Federal Reserve chief Ben Bernanke disclosed in early 2011 that "even in an ideal world," it would "take years" before unemployment approaches "normal" levels in the United States (Derby 2011). Although those in the lower rungs of the economic ladder have been hardest hit by job and housing losses, the college-educated are also feeling the bite of this latest "jobless recovery," with the unemployment rate for Americans with a bachelor's degree climbing to 5.1 per cent, the highest in 40 years (Irvin 2008, 138; Davidson 2010). The economic havoc and human misery wrought by the recession led Robert Pollin in early 2009 to declare that "neoliberal capitalism – whose defining features were Wall Street and big business domination of government policy-making – is dead" (2009). Such pronouncements proved premature as the neoliberal project demonstrated remarkable resilience. Economist Paul Krugman observed in 2009 that although Reaganomics had "failed to deliver what it promised," Reaganism had managed to live on as a "zombie doctrine" (2009). The following year, he lamented that even as the "free-market fundamentalists have been wrong about everything ... they now dominate the political scene more thoroughly than ever" (Krugman 2010). The durability of neoliberalism is directly related to its bipartisan backing. That support is apparent in Obama's 2010 address to the U.S. Chamber of Commerce, where he raised the issue of a "widening chasm of wealth and opportunity," identified the deficit as the cause and "entitlements spending" (i.e., social security and Medicare) as the driver of the problem, and offered as his solution "that we freeze annual domestic spending for the next five years, which would reduce the deficit by more than $400 billion over the next decade, and bring this spending down to the lowest share of our economy since Eisenhower was president" (Ford 2011).

As Obama's first year as president drew to a close, *New York Times* media columnist David Carr, writing of the approaching launch of the Oprah Winfrey Network, asserted: "It could be argued ... [that] without Oprah Winfrey, there would be no Barack Obama. Not because she endorsed him, but with her message of bootstrap accountability, she not only empowered black people, she empowered white people" (Carr 2009). Formidable as the "Oprah effect" may be, the relationship between Oprah Winfrey's rise to cultural icon and Barack Obama's ascent to head of the most powerful state in the world cannot be reduced to direct causality or simple personal influence. Rather, as I have argued, the accomplishments of the "Double O's" must be situated within the larger historical context of the triumph of neoliberalism over the past three decades. While the Adamic myth of self-invention and reinvention is deeply rooted in U.S. history and imagination, it has been particularly vigorous during the expansion of the neoliberal political-economic project, which so adroitly deploys the language of reinvention, self-fashioning, innovation, and transformation. This is where the intersection of "text" and "context" do their ideological work – where the "particular form of raced celebrity" represented by the "Double O's" embodies and valorizes "the notion of American mobility" (Williams 2007).

In late 2010, Winfrey was reported to be approaching "the pinnacle of her career" (Goudreau 2011; see also Goudreau 2010) with the impending launch of the Oprah Winfrey Network (OWN). Devoted to "positive thinking and self-betterment" (Weiss 2011), the network was the logical extension of her mind-cure enterprise/media empire. In late Victorian America, according to Steven Starker, New Thought literature "told readers in effect to close their eyes and wish very, very, hard, and all would be granted" (1988, 39). More than a century later such magical thinking and the mythology of self-creation have not lost their grip on the American imagination. During an era when people's real power over the material condition of their lives has dramatically declined while the power of capital has expanded exponentially (Irvin 2008, 29), Oprah Winfrey has soared to the position of global cultural icon by telling us we can do anything if we only put our minds to it. This is a promise not unlike that of the lottery. Both are forms of wish fulfilment that owe their allure to the harsh reality of a "go-it-alone world," and both are ideological practices that help legitimize and reproduce the neoliberal order and forms of subjectivity appropriate to it.

Despite their seductions, those promises do nothing to change the facts that since the peak of the housing bubble in 2007, the median household in America has seen a 36.1 per cent drop in its wealth (Wolf 2010), that some 44 million Americans (one in seven people and one in five children) were living in poverty in 2009 (Eckholm 2010), or that in 2010, one in ten families was receiving food stamps – the highest percentage on record (Yen 2009) – while 50.7 million people had no health insurance (Wolf 2010).

Political theorist Kees Van Der Pijl observes that neoliberal restructuring gradually removed the "structure of solidarity on which the welfare state is based," and in its wake, "the only aspiration meaningfully entertained is that of individual improvement, placing each and every citizen in the position where he or she must ask, How will I achieve this? What are my chances? Religion certainly gravitates back to centre-stage as a consolation prize" (Van Der Pijl 2006, 28, 30). Oprah Winfrey's "thought-as-power" cosmology can be understood as one such consolation prize. Its promise that through the power of mind we can bring the external world into accordance with internal desire is readily attached to notions of class mobility, meritocracy, individual achievement, and the "American Dream." In the process, it carries out the ideological work of legitimizing, by sacralizing, the neoliberal political-economic order.

NOTE

1 Among the recovery experts who appeared on *The Oprah Winfrey Show* from 1986 to 1993 were Melody Beattie, John Bradshaw, Janet Woititz, Claudia Black, and Sharon Wegscheider-Cruse.

3

Celebritus Politicus, Neoliberal Sustainabilities, and the Terrains of Care

MICHAEL K. GOODMAN

It is safe to say that in many countries around the world celebrity politics has become more than a fringe phenomenon. Nor is it likely to be an ephemeral one. It is inextricably tied to the late-modern constitution of the public sphere and it is therefore here to stay.

(Marsh et al. 2010, 16)

Jim Carrey concerned about Third World sustainable rice production. Demi Moore and Ashton Kutcher focused on sex trafficking and global prostitution networks. George Clooney as the "face" of Darfur and Sean Penn that of Haiti. Lindsay Lohan tweeting about child labour in India. Kim Kardashian and Naomi Campbell raising awareness about "conflict" diamonds. And Scarlett Johansson, Helena Christensen, and Kristin Davis – all as Oxfam's global ambassadors – writing an open letter to the UK's *Guardian* newspaper about their hopes for the Cancun climate conference. From the perspective of these examples, the contemporary icons of development, human rights, and the environment are undergoing makeovers of spectacular proportions.[1] Relatively gone or at least in the process of being overtaken are the old images of drowning polar bears, starving, fly-covered African children, and even the well-branded human-rights NGO Amnesty International in favour of those images and media formulations of the "caring" and "politicized" celebrity. Indeed, evolving out of this growing confluence of care, politics, foundations/charities, activism, NGOs, media, popularity, and stardom – as encapsulated in Littler's (2009) quip that compassion is now part of the job description of the contemporary celebrity – is what I like to now think of as a novel "species" of celebrity called *Celebritus politicus.* This is the increasingly stable figure of the rich and famous who are more and more fronting various causes that work for broadly defined progressive improvements in the multitudinous environment- and development-related problems across the globe. In this, the rise and evolution of *Celebritus politicus* is working to change the nature of celebrity, fame, and expertise (e.g., Goodman and Barnes 2011; Richey and Ponte 2011) but also seeming to shift the cultural politics of environment and development as they become more deeply celebritized (Boykoff and Goodman 2009; Goodman 2010; see also Brockington 2008, 2009; Ponte et al. 2009; Richey and Ponte 2008).[2]

As the opening quote by Marsh et al. (2010) alludes to, celebrity politics are quickly becoming much more than a privileged few pronouncing on the poor state of the environment or the state of the poor through these growing ties of celebrity politics to what they call the "late-modern constitution of the public sphere." Yet, as I argue in this chapter, we need to consider the processes and impacts of celebrity politics even *further* than Marsh et al. give them credit: more than just contributing to the production of the public sphere (how and in what ways?), celebrity politics in the body of *Celebritus politicus* have been situated and also have worked to situate themselves as a stylized form of the neoliberalized governance of the problems of environment and development. In short, drawing on but also contributing to the moral authority of a hegemonic market-led governance of sustainability, this "celebrity governance regime" works to produce a kind of economy of care and responsibility that goes right to "the people" in the form of fans designed to circumvent the slow politics of states, policy, and government regulations. Thus, in a way, this chapter builds on Illouz's (2007) fascinating work on what she calls "emotional capitalism":

> Emotional capitalism is a culture in which emotional and economic discourses and practices mutually shape each other, thus producing what I view as a broad, sweeping movement in which affect is made an essential aspect of economic behavior and in which emotional life – especially that of the middle classes – follows the logic of economic relations and exchange ... In fact ... market-based cultural repertoires shape and inform interpersonal and emotional relationships, while interpersonal relationships are at the epicenter of economic relationships. More exactly, market repertoires become intertwined with the language of psychology and, combined together, offer new techniques and meanings to forge new forms of sociability. (Illouz 2007, 5)

The results here, then, with *Celebritus politicus* are a sort of neoliberal form of sustainability politics: on the one hand, the "heroic individualism" (Boykoff and Goodman 2009) of celebrities and these new fans of "enviro-" and "poverty-tainment" are called upon to solve current and ongoing world crises directly through this market in emotions. On the other hand, these same individual responses are collectivized into markets for and of care through the bodies of celebrities, their foundations/ charities and their access to powerful decision- and other market-makers. However, given the attention economy embedded in the spectacles of *Celebritus politicus*, the "natural selection" of causes, attention, care, and resources is similarly embedded in and constructs the very boundaries of what it is we should be caring about and how we should go about doing this caring in an increasingly unequal world.

Through the sections of this chapter, I hope to produce an initial exploration of the ways in which *Celebritus politicus* act as an embodiment of neoliberal sustainabilities. In this, my arguments are diffusely based on interviews, conversations, and reflections over the last two years with a number of progressive UK NGOs about their engagements with and uses of celebrities in their campaigns, as well as a kind of reflexive participant observation emersion in the television, newspaper, and online media related to celebrity politics and activism. More specifically, though, I want to first establish what I mean by celebrity governance regimes and how they draw on but also contribute to "neoliberalized sustainabilities"[3] and the wider cultures of neoliberalisms that circulate in contemporary post-industrial societies. And, while this is merely one possible interpretation of many of the characteristics, impacts and a/ effects of celebrity politics (e.g. Brockington 2009; Bunting 2010; Cooper 2008b; Marsh et al. 2010; Marshall 1997; Street 2004), the point here is to open up further and wider questions about the relationalities of *Celebritus politicus* and the cultural political economies within which they are embedded.

Second, this chapter focuses in on the processes by which this celebrity governance regime works, namely through the "fame-seeking" and "fame-utilizing" behaviours of celebrities to bring attention to their various causes; the ultimate goal, I would argue, is to create new fans of development and/or environmental causes and concerns, whose concerns are then, through this poverty- and enviro-tainment, collectivized through the bodies, foundations, and access of *Celebritus politicus* to the halls of power. In this, the heroic individual in the figure of *Celebritus politicus* acts as the mechanism through which to collectivize this market in existing and new fans' emotions and care as a way to further the particular causes she or he is concerned about. As such, one of the key tensions of *Celebritus politicus* is expressed: In order for them to generate the emotional capital and monetary value for various causes and concerns, they must work to shed their (commodified) skins as consummate commodities to instead present to audiences their ordinary personhood as caring individuals willing and able to do something about suffering, environmental damage, and human rights abuses. The relationalities between and among the commodity-ness and non-commodity-ness of the caring commodities of *Celebritus politicus* are embedded at the very core of their species-media-being. Here – and I am unable to do full justice to this in this chapter – the paradoxes, contradictions, and somewhat awkward nature of *Celebritus politicus* come to the fore: at one and the same time, their very individualized, commodified nature circulates and mitigates against their non-commodified, 'fan-collectivizing' function that, in turn, works to mitigate against and circulate in relation and opposition to this individualized, commodity-ness. In the words of Žižek (2008), they, as "liberal communists" (13) who are the "true citizens of the world" (17) working to create their very own "Porto Davos"[4] (14), are able to unsteadily embody market and social responsibility side-by-side through their "neutral, non-ideological, natural [and] commonsensical" (31) approach to poverty and environmental destruction. Indeed, as he puts it further and in no uncertain terms,

> In liberal communist ethics, the ruthless pursuit of profit is counteracted by charity. Charity is the humanitarian mask hiding the face of economic exploitation. In a superego blackmail of gigantic proportions, the developed countries 'help' the underdeveloped with aid, credits and so on, and thereby avoid the key issue, namely their complicity in and co-responsibility for the miserable situation of the underdeveloped. (Žižek 2008, 19)

Finally, the chapter briefly concludes with questions about the competitive political economies, many of them tied to the psychologies and personal concerns of particular celebrities and their potential to garner media coverage, related to the natural selection of not only celebrities but of their causes. It is my hope that this chapter works to provide an initial assessment and set of questions surrounding the possibilities and also problematics of *Celebritus politicus* – somewhat beyond Žižek's (2008) rather crude (but somewhat justified) indictment of liberal communists and charity ethics – as a way to more fully bring into sharp relief the rich ironies of working to reduce global inequalities and environmental problems through many of the same neoliberal governmentalities that have had a hand in creating and facilitating them in the first place.

Neoliberalized Celebrity Governance Regimes

It is pretty safe to say we in the post-industrial North – if not most of the globe – are governed in various and multitudinous ways and means by the precepts, materialities, and ideologies of neoliberal capitalism. Privatization, marketization, commodification, entrepreneurialism, freedom of choice, individualization, competition, consumerism, anti-regulation, and voluntarism seemingly rule much of the political and cultural economics of the day. And, yet, as most geographers and many others will argue, the reach and actual impacts of neoliberalism are uneven, incomplete, shifting, and indeed contested (e.g., Harvey 2005; Smith 1984; Gibson-Graham 2006); this is especially true when it comes to the commodification, privatization, and marketization of nature (Mansfield 2008; McCarthy and Prudham 2004; Castree 2003). Indeed, debates are now centred around exploring and uncovering "actually existing neo-liberalisms" (Castree 2005) and also engaging with contestations within neoliberalism through the use of market-based forms and tools (Ferguson 2009) in the pursuit of "diverse economies" (Gibson-Graham 2006). Yet, even with the unevenness of the roll-back of the state and roll-out of neoliberal political economies, the hegemonic *cultural politics* of neoliberal capitalism seemingly remain, endure, and, if the newly elected Conservative government in the UK and the back-in-power (Tea Party) Republicans in the United States are any indication, are set to expand to an even greater extent (cf. Goodman and Boyd 2011).

One of the areas in which neoliberal capitalism is particularly ascendant is in the realm of how to fix environment- and development-related problems. As Micheletti and Stolle (2008, 750) put it in the specific context of the politics and materialities of the anti-sweatshop movement, "capitalism is helping capitalism to develop a face of social justice." In the realm of environment politics, McAfee (1999) has astutely called this "greening of capitalism" (Bakker 2010) the "selling of nature to save it." Here, in more general terms, the tools of privatization, commodification, and marketization are deployed to create new markets in sustainable or environmentally-, development- and/or human rights-friendly goods for ethical consumers to purchase. Or, in parallel, complete markets like those for carbon offsets are created in order to turn whole economic sectors green. Called everything from "natural capitalism" (e.g., Hawken et al. 1999) to social entrepreneurship, green capitalism, caring capitalism, to the triple bottom line, these neoliberal sustainabilities work on and through *values* to create and extract conservation and development *value* through markets for sustainable natures and developments. While neoliberal sustainabilities have been subject to a number of critical academic treatments of late (e.g., *Antipode* 2010; Bakker 2007, 2010; Castree 2003; Fridell 2007; Prudham 2009; Rutherford 2007; see also Escobar 1995), I have argued in particular that neoliberal sustainabilities work to, on the one hand, not only marketize and commodify care and caring across space – the most obvious example of this being the purchase of "care" off the supermarket shelf through fair trade products – but also responsibilize consuming publics with the task of making the choice for sustainability in the products they buy (cf. Guthman 2007). On the other hand, counter-arguments see these "ethical consumption singularities" (Clarke et al. 2007; Clarke 2008; see also Barnett et al. 2010) as the empowerment of caring consumers in the processes of social change through their "everyday" and "ordinary" acts of choice that then, in turn, work to similarly empower development and environmental NGOs who do the hard work of civil society lobbying for progressive change in the name of these ethical consumers. Here, NGOs work to collectivize these individual purchases into a monetized but also socially responsible market of caring emotions, which, if this market is large or influential enough, is able to garner media attention as well as access to policymakers. How this all plays out on a vastly unequal playing field remains to be seen, but if the success of the fair-trade movement and market in the UK – at over £1 billion in 2010 and potentially recession-resistant (Fairtrade Foundation 2011) – is any proof, then neoliberal sustainabilities can be quite successful, compete with capital to a certain extent, but also have far-reaching implications for livelihoods and environments in those markets *that are successful*. The wider point is this however: neoliberal sustainabilities draw on but also contribute to the political, cultural, and moral authority of neoliberal capitalism and so seem to further embed it in civil society, our everyday lifestyles and livelihoods, and, of course, the natural environment.

But what, you might ask, does this have to do with *Celebritus politicus*? Well, for me, the figure of *Celebritus politicus* is fundamentally situated in, draws on, and also contributes to these hegemonic cultural politics of neoliberalism and of the neoliberal sustainabilities that define this particular historical moment. More specifically, the processes surrounding and constructing *Celebritus politicus* are entrenched in the implicit and/or explicit moral authority of the neoliberal ways of doing things in, for example, how *Celebritus politicus* creates media-ted and competitive markets for various causes and concerns (more on this below). And while, like any species, the individualized behaviours at any one time might be quite different for various members of that species, there are generalizable trends, if not "genetic markers" that lend themselves to categorization and comparison within and across these trends. Put another way, while there are different specific processes, characteristics, and outcomes for different celebrities and different celebrity-fronted campaigns, there exists here what I am calling a *celebrity governance regime* that works to emulate, take guidance from, and contribute to the processes of neoliberal sustainabilities.

I want to turn now to sketch the outlines of this celebrity governance regime by exploring how it expresses and embeds key aspects of neoliberalism/neoliberal sustainabilities as the morally "right" and/or "good" way of going about doing development, conservation, or human rights. Be aware, however, that more is going on here as these governance regimes have, across their diversity, made neoliberal sustainabilities very much in their own complex and even sometimes paradoxical image; these sustainabilities cross the boundaries of media-tion, personas and personalities, fans, audiences, emotions, tastes, and knowledges in addition to the complicated and slippery politics surrounding causes, charities, and relief efforts. Indeed, the various discourses and material processes that create these celebrity governance regimes through their own internal differences and dynamics work to lend credibility to the arguments that there are multiple cultural and political economies of neoliberal-*isms* (cf. Castree 2005). In this, these neoliberalisms circulate in and out of celebrity governance regimes to discipline and also reward those operating within them and their moral framing about what *does* and *should* count as progressive development and environmentalism through the figure of *Celebritus politicus*.

In order to explore celebrity governance regimes in more detail, I have divided their main aspects and characteristics into several descriptive and analytical categories that, while separated out for effect, are very often (yet also differentially!) connected across these regimes.

Heavenly Bodies and (Media) Market Competition

The first point to make here is that celebrity governance regimes are fully market-oriented and -coordinated both metaphorically and in actual practice. Market-led competitive relationalities define most aspects of *Celebritus politicus*: from competition by causes for A-list or hot celebrities, to competition by these celebrities for media face time for their causes, to that among celebrities for the emotions and (very often) donations by caring audiences. Moreover, *Celebritus politicus* is in fundamental competition with all the other messages, marketing, knowledges, and imaginaries transmitted by media "out there" in wider mediascapes. Here then is a market created by and for the "fame game" in which (some) celebrity sells (Pringle 2004), the marketing and sales pitch of which is for attention – and often, ultimately donations, purchases, and revenues – for progressive causes. Indeed, it might be argued that through the use of some of the top A-list celebrities such as Angelina Jolie, Beyoncé, and Matt Damon, causes and concerns gain, at least for a short time, the exposure and access to media power often only reserved for the likes of large corporations.

Yet all of this competition among *Celebritus politicus* and within the celebrity governance regime is situated within the competitive markets for media more generally. Thus, the power of *Celebritus politicus* is fully mediated by the powerful markets – but more often monopolistic power (McChesney 2008; see also Marshall 1997) – of media outlets as well as their own internal political and cultural economic logics. And, while buffers against these media monopolies are being created through the growth of Internet media in general and the growing number of online celebrity gossip and news websites[5] in particular, the goal for much of *Celebritus politicus* is to explicitly make it *into* more mainstream news and media outlets to gain the greatest amount of coverage. Indeed, simply in terms of exposure, and in what might seem like a heretical statement, for *Celebritus politicus*, media monopolies are actually a "good" thing for those who can, indeed, make it into the mainstream in efforts to further the awareness of particular causes. Nevertheless, the mediated power of celebrities works to create distinct winners and losers in the competitive, marketized fame game embedded in celebrity governance regimes, but so too does the power embedded in and wielded by the distinctive political economies of the media landscape. Thus, the outcomes of these markets are a result of the competitive logics, relationalities, causes and concerns, and tensions of *Celebritus politicus*, and of the political and cultural economies of the media. The neoliberal tendrils embodied in *Celebritus politicus* have long and winding networks that reach not only into and out of the marketized competition for and of celebrity, causes, and audiences, but into the highly mediated realms of profit- and audience-seeking media organizations, and their editorial boards and board rooms.

Part of this competition means that *Celebritus politicus* and the progressive organizations they are involved with must be particularly entrepreneurial across all media in order to maximize exposure or develop exposure in the first instance. This entrepreneurialism is needed specifically to creatively and decisively cut through both the signal and noise of the wider media landscape, and so is expressed in what celebrities are matched up to what causes, how they go about gaining exposure, and/or what types of media are used to develop concerned fans and followers. One of the contemporary hallmarks of this entrepreneurialism is the growing use of social or new media such as blogs, Facebook, and Twitter.[6] Examples here might include Ben Stiller tweeting that "People in Haiti need our help and attention right now" immediately after the disaster and George Clooney's "Not on Our Watch" Darfur Facebook page, which has now morphed into his star- and corporate-studded "Satellite Sentinel Project" designed to be an "Antigenocide Paparazzi" (Benjamin 2010).[7] Indeed, given the overt obsession of the current "mainstream" media about the simple use of new media by campaigns of all stripes, many activists are merely counting on the fact that they simply *use* Facebook and Twitter as a way to get traditional media exposure, regardless of the campaign, the celebrities, or the contents of their posts. But of course, the type of and/or need for entrepreneurialism is differentially situated across the various actors involved in celebrity governance regimes. So, for example, those already on the A-list or those organizations like WWF with a well-established brand and media profile need to seemingly work much less hard for media exposure than do other celebrities and organizations. Rather, A-listers and established environment and development NGOs work at new ways in which to harness the media and develop or sustain new campaigns. The real work of the entrepreneurial spirit comes in with less well-known campaigns and celebrities who need to develop new and more creative ways of making it into the media. In either case, though, the point still stands: entrepreneurialism here is about the creativity and inventiveness in both the use of celebrities by campaigns but also about the ways that *Celebritus politicus* wield their celebrity in new, interesting, and sometimes shocking (think PETA here) ways to garner attention from media and audiences both new and old.[8]

"Stars – They're Just Like Us":[9] *A/Effective (Non)commodification and the Economies of Hope*

Commodification, one of the cornerstones of capitalism and not just its neoliberal variants, is also rife in celebrity governance regimes in a number of interesting, complex, and even contradictory ways. Here, celebrity-driven campaigns are very often focused around the purchase of socially responsible goods, be they Product (RED) lattes from Starbucks, hybrid cars, sustainable fish, or fair-trade coffees and other goods. Through these mechanisms, celebrities lend their elevated voices, media-generated credibility, and expertise in all things environment and development related to the credibility of these goods but more fundamentally, to the commodifying processes behind them. Their authority and exposure feeds into the authority, power, and "correctness," "goodness," and "rightness" of the commodification of care and responsibility for Others and the environment, as well as feeds into the wider moral authorities of neoliberal sustainabilities. This, to me, is one of the furthest reaching implications of the celebrity governance regime and *Celebritus politicus*: given their seemingly increasing power to market to us the "right" pathways and products to deal with global inequalities and environmental concerns, they fundamentally strengthen the cultural and economic hands of consumerist capitalism as a specific tool for more sustainable and "caring" societies.

Attached to the above, there are also other processes of commodification, or at least commodification by proxy, through a further key component circulating in celebrity governance regimes: the monetary contributions made by the public as cajoled by *Celebritus politicus*. In this, care and emotion are monetized and set at a particular price, the amount depending on what a particular person is willing to voluntarily give or pay, to then be collected into the total amount given. Then, these monetized acts of care are more fully (re)commodified into the goods provided to the poor/environment at the other end of the networks of *Celebritus politicus*: they are turned into conservation habitats, mosquito nets, anti-viral drugs, disaster relief, food aid, and sometimes local labour, used to rebuild war- or disaster-torn places, landscapes, cities, and homes. Thus, along with the deployments of socially responsible goods for consumption, through their extensive focus on donations and giving, the celebrity governance regime has developed a heavy reliance on growing and sustaining these commodified and monetized forms of care politics that further flesh out the moral authority of neoliberalized sustainabilities.

In celebrity governance regimes, there is also a kind of reverse or relational commodification of care, emotion, and responsibility: here, the politics and ethics of care become part of or at least intimately related to the commodity form of *Celebritus politicus*. This then translates into a "de-differentiation" of consumption (Bryman 2004), whereby there is increasing slippage among the purchase of the more normal outputs of *Celebritus politicus* in their albums, movies, cookbooks, and television shows and a buying-in to them as caring celebrity subjects and an equal (but potentially more distant) buying-in to the caring campaigns they are associated with. Thus, *Celebritus politicus* are not just like any celebrity commodity – of which they very much still are, *politicus* or not (Turner 2004, 2010) – but also, they are commodities that are now even more fully embedded with meanings related to care, politics, and emotion. The most obvious instance of this reverse commodification is where celebrities expressly do things (e.g., appearances, shows, competitions, etc.) for charities or causes or where part of the value created by their normal outputs in albums, books, clothing lines, and perfumes might go towards charities, causes, or foundations. Here value and values in their multiple forms flow and circulate in a number of interesting ways: by using their celebrity value as a commodity and cultural icon, celebrities add value to campaigns through exposure and/or increasing the monetary value of campaigns. But this can also flow the other way: care as a value works to contribute to the value of celebrity brands and commodities as well as their own subjectivities as caring individuals with elevated voices bent on – as Bono has put it – spending their "currency" of celebrity on good and worthy causes (Boykoff and Goodman 2009). Care has thus also become a "currency" of a kind that can work to add meanings and values to the celebrity commodity brand in its more normal and non-*Celebritus politicus* state (cf. Littler 2008).

This growing currency of care is briefly but incredibly well-illustrated by the recent moves of the former Pussycat Doll Nicole Scherzinger, who

> ... announced her forthcoming debut solo album or, as she put it, "a miracle of Haiti's disaster": She had met the album's producer at the recording of a charity single for Haiti. "The one good thing to come from that tragedy,"

she suggested, "was my music" which will doubtless come as considerable comfort to the relatives of the 316,000 people who died, the 1.6 million
left homeless and the 3,500 affected by a subsequent outbreak of cholera.
Obviously they're suffering, but with the news that Scherzinger['s] got a
"raw, soulful and funky" solo album out of it, at least their suffering isn't
in vain. (Petridis 2011)

Not surprisingly, many critics have quickly jumped on instances like
these and worked to articulate the much more cynical position that caring celebrities are either working to plot the further elevation of their
brand or some sort of comeback for those either knocked off the A-list,
on the B-list anyway, or undergoing some sort of media/tabloid scan-
dal. The question is of course one of the weighing up of authenticity by
audiences: Where does the caring versus commodity-ness of *Celebritus
politicus* begin and where do they each end? This clearly depends on
the specific celebrity and/or campaign in question, but this is also partially about our *hope* that celebrities might be as authentic and altruistic
as they seem, especially given their power to articulate the politics of
development and the environment. In short, we (or at least I!) have
a deep-seated hope that our contemporary politicized glitterati actually *really* do care about the climate (DiCaprio), "clean" diamonds (Kardashian), water (Damon), sustainable housing (Pitt), women's rights
and refugees (Jolie), exploited children (Lohan), hunger in the United
States (Affleck), and AIDS and global poverty (Lennox), among the
other quickly growing bevy of celebrity-fronted causes and concerns.
Or, maybe a better approach here is to simply collapse the caring- and
commodity-nature present in *Celebritus politics* and their "terrains of
care" to suggest that they are *themselves* – much like socially responsible consumer goods – "caring commodities" that utilize their elevated
voices to articulate to us what they want us as publics to do about underdevelopment and environmental problems.

Yet, from a different perspective, this is also about celebrities working to *de-commodify* themselves and appear to be coming from a more
normal subjectivity of ordinary personhood. Here the task is to slip
out of the bounds of their superstardom to engage with us as regular
people: celebrities cannot only take our phone calls in charity drives,
set up tent villages in places of disaster or crisis, write letters extolling
our political leaders into action, but they can seemingly bear witness
for us by engaging with, walking among, and being filmed in the presence of the poor and deteriorating environments (Goodman and Barnes

2011; see also Nunn and Biressi 2010; Chouliaraki 2008). What we need to see, hear, and read about is Matt Damon's trip across Africa for the ONEXONE's clean water campaign, Jim Carrey joking with locals in the midst of rice fields, and David Beckham laughing as he plays a round of "footie" with poor African children. This is a very important point as it introduces one of the key paradoxes that circulates and makes up celebrity governance regimes: *Celebritus politicus* work to generate monetary value and emotional values out of their commodified *and also* non-commodified, ordinary forms, seemingly both for the campaigns/ causes they contribute to and also for their own brand value. And the motivations behind all of this are also potentially paradoxical: the currency of celebrity can be spent to invoke care and care in others for Others and for the environment but at the same time this care is its own currency that can be spent to much more cynically invoke the care by publics, consumers, fans, and audiences for the more quotidian products of celebrities and so expand their own personal values, media values, and brands.

Publicizing Private Politics and the New Responsibilization

Finally, in celebrity governance regimes, privatization (from politics, care, and giving, all the way to private enterprise and the private sector) is extolled and/or implied as the way to go about solving underdevelopment, dealing with disasters, or confronting environmental problems. And here this privatization of care falls across a number of the ways and means of *Celebritus politicus*. First, as both rhetorically applied or implied more diffusely, privatization is set up as the "right" and "better" way to perform these things as states and governments are constructed as too slow to respond, corrupted, captured by other (often corporate) powers, misguided, not flexible, and generally as having failed the development and environmentalist project. This sense of failure on the part of states – and in particular, the failure of states to take care of their own people and environments – figures very large here and so the alternative of extolling the virtues of private individuals and the private sector, as well as the private politics of *Celebritus politicus*, has been put forward in celebrity governance regimes as the way to very often do development and conservation. Much like NGOs and other movements, celebrities have stepped into the gap of the growing democratic deficit both nationally and globally and attempted to fill this up in very interesting, private-led, "collectivized" ways.

Furthermore, however, the private politics and care emotions of celebrities go public to implore us to also take our own private donations, purchases, and emotions public in the form of help for those less fortunate than we. And these connections – brokered by the private/public emotions of *Celebritus politicus* and their own connections to foundations, NGOs, and relief organizations – can take the form of us as private citizens emotionally and materially connecting to Others or specific species "over there" to broader connections between our private selves, our private lives, and media audiences to Other civil societies and/or forms of nature in need. Here, it might be argued that the figure of *Celebritus politicus* is in the very real business of fostering and creating, through private donations and the collecting and connecting up of private emotions and care, a more aware, political, and active "global citizenship" that might stand in distinction to or at least outside of neoliberalism's penchant for hyper-individualism. Much more needs to be made theoretically and empirically of the relationalities between and among the functioning of the private/public politics of *Celebritus politicus* and the private/public subjects and objects of individuals, civil societies, the public realm, and global citizenship. Suffice it to say here, however, much of the celebrity governance regime calls on us, one way or another, as privatized subjects and calls on the private sector to act in ways very often contra the state, to confront underdevelopment and environmental crisis.

Tied very much to this penchant for privatization in celebrity governance regimes is that of both the volunteerism and the responsibilization of individuals and of *Celebritus politicus*; both this voluntary regulatory approach and that of the responsibilization of individuals further embed the moral authority of the privatized, individualized, choice-based politics that are at the veritable core of not only neoliberal sustainabilities – especially in the form of progressive food politics (Guthman 2007; Johnston 2008) – but also neoliberalisms of all stripes. In celebrity governance regimes, then, donations, contributions, and the purchase of socially responsible goods are voluntary and so become yet another version of this choice-based politics, but one that works through the imploring media exposure of the volunteered philanthropic and emotional politics of celebrities. Celebrity-driven campaigns can also be seen to work to responsibilize consumers and audiences as the agents of change through their targeting of audiences, publics, and private individuals; this often elides or wilfully ignores the offending structures, corporations, and/or other actors involved in underdevelopment, poverty, and environmental destruction. As articulated in more dire and uncompromising Žižekian (2008) terms, the distracting "bait-and-switch" of this "objective violence" in the spectacularized images of celebrity-fronted campaigns seems to work quite well to actively cover for the wider processes of "subjective" or capitalistically induced violence they are consciously or unconsciously part and parcel of.

Here, through *Celebritus politicus*, audiences are asked to choose among worthy celebrities, campaigns, petitions, corporations, and products as *the* force for "good," outside the power and agency of (failed) states and governments. Yet, this is also about and works on the empowerment of audiences through the words, images, and power of *Celebritus politicus*. In some ways similar to ethical consumption (Clarke et al. 2007; Lewis and Potter 2010; Littler 2009), having these particular choices of doing good through donations, charity, and ethically branded products in celebrity governance regimes – in an era where too much information or the democratic deficit seemingly disempowers people or at least gives them the impression nothing can be done – works to empower individuals to donate or shop for social and environmental change. This of course says little about *who* has the resources to donate/shop and then be/feel empowered, but it is most often triggered through the discourse that comes from *Celebritus politicus*, like "your donation will ..." or "simply sign this petition ..." or "please give what you can to ...," and also through the abilities of celebrities to lead by example as heroic individuals, the closer examination of which I turn to now.

Fame Matters: Heroic Individuals That Create Collectivized Caring Markets

Much more than the other characteristics of the celebrity governance regime described above, it is the neoliberal cultural economic figure of the individual that reigns supreme here. Celebrities are a kind of "ultimate" or "uber" neoliberal individual: through their own meritorious or media-generated power, their very individuality in the form of their individual personhood comes to represent a commodified brand in and of itself but also represents the apogee of what an individual can and should be. As Marshall (1997, 17; see also Marshall 2010 and Boykoff et al. 2010), drawing on Dyer (1979), puts it: "the star is universally individualized, for the star is the representation of the potential of the individual." By the power of who they are individually, through their image, name, words, or action, they sell and endorse themselves and, equally, their campaigns, causes, and politics. They are the heroic individuals who use their fame for good causes but who are also the self-same heroic individuals we are inspired to be, whom we aspire to be, or at least whom we aspire to be related to through our own heroically individual relief-fund donations and socially responsible purchases.

But there is much more going on here: while neoliberalism works to empower individualism, it also, through its discourses and the materialities of consumer purchases, works to empower markets as well. Here, in economic theory at least, rational, consuming individuals are collectivized into markets that can be used to speak for and about markets in this or that, but these markets can also be used as forms of power by corporations wishing to "speak" for and in the name of these markets of collectivized individuals. Similarly, as in ethical consumption networks, neoliberal sustainabilities work in very much the same way: individual progressive consumption choices (for example, fair trade goods) are collectivized by NGOs who then gain political power by speaking for and through these markets for ethical goods or contributions from members (Clarke et al. 2007). In many ways this is also happening here in celebrity governance regimes: *Celebritus politicus* as individuals work to collectivize us/publics as individuals and our singular emotional responses through progressive campaigns and their individual actions as the voice for various causes. In their recent book "Brand Aid," Richey and Ponte (2011) show the propensity for this – or at least for politicized celebrities to *believe* this propensity – in stark relief through the words of Bono:

> The reason why politicians let me in the door, and the reason why people will take my call is because I represent quite a large constituency of people. Now, I do not control that constituency, but I represent them in a certain sense, even without them asking me to, in the minds of the people whose doors I knock upon. That constituency is a very powerful one, because it is a constituency of people from eighteen to thirty, who are the floating vote ... They're the most open-minded, and that's why politicians pay attention to what's going on in contemporary culture and what a rock star might have to do with all of this: because of the people I represent. (Richey and Ponte 2011, 36)

In a sense, *Celebritus politicus* is at the epicentre of the creation of novel markets in care and emotions; they mobilize these markets through and for donations, Internet campaigns, and the like, and they then also

speak for them when writing letters, talking to the media, and/or engaging with those in power in the context of their politicized concerns.
The key here, though, and somewhat contra neoliberal sustainabilities
and neoliberalism more broadly, is that these are markets that are importantly made up of fans of *Celebritus politicus*, and so, much beyond
the more traditional markets made up of monetary donations, charity
giving, and petition signatories, these new parallel markets in emotion
are created but also fundamentally bounded by issues of taste, media
exposure, personality, and the fans' relationalities to *Celebritus politicus*. So, increasingly important in celebrity governance regimes are the
number of Facebook friends or Twitter followers – an equally increasingly important way for celebrities to gather, speak to, and speak for
their fans (Marshall 2010) – for both *Celebritus politicus* and the causes
they are associated with as social media too is now part of the collectivized market for which they speak to and from and from which they
draw their power and elevated voice.

In order to create these markets, *Celebritus politicus* and the celebrity
governance regime work principally through two types of celebrity behaviours. The first involves those fame-utilizing behaviours to bring
awareness to campaigns through the already-accreted fame of a particular celebrity and the second includes those fame-seeking behaviours
that work to publicize campaigns through celebrities working to up
their brand by association with particular causes. In short, both behaviours try to raise the awareness of already-existing fan bases as well as
bring in new fans to either the celebrity or the cause or both such that
the focus here is on the development of more fans of what might be
called poverty- and enviro-tainment. In this, these markets of emotion
and care come into their own: *Celebritus politicus* is used to sell causes,
contributions, concerns, and socially responsible consumerism through
a competitive market for poverty- and enviro-tainment designed to develop, capture, and "use" the fans of this poverty- and enviro-tainment
towards progressive ends.

An Ending as Beginning: The Psycho-political
Economies of *Celebritus Politicus*

By way of a conclusion to this chapter – which is actually more of a
beginning into what needs to be a much more sustained exploration
into the worlds, networks, and relationalities of *Celebritus politicus* and
its celebrity governance regimes – I want to make several observations

as well as offer some key questions for further work. First, poverty- and enviro-tainment are the growing end results of the celebrity governance regime and one of the major ways we engage with disasters, crises, underdevelopment, and threatened natures now. Structured by celebrity governance regimes – which, if my analysis holds any empirical water, take on and contribute to the trappings and moral authority of neoliberalism/neoliberal sustainabilities – poverty- and enviro-tainment are as much structured by the political economies of media as they are real and authentic needs. But, very importantly, poverty- and enviro-tainment are not only shaped by the political and cultural economic networks they are situated in, but also structured by the powerful psychologies, personal experiences, and emotions of *Celebritus politicus*. In many ways, it is these caring (non)commodified politicized media figures who are now very much in the (actual) business of relating to audiences/publics what is wrong with the world today, what to do about it, and in what ways to go about doing this. The psycho-political economies that shape the who, what, and how of *Celebritus politicus* and, in turn, their shaping of poverty- and enviro-tainment are working to not only structure the bounds of our understandings of and solutions to underdevelopment and environmental destruction, they are fundamentally shaping the much wider cultural and political economies of the terrains of care that circulate in contemporary societies. Moreover, and in a final nod to Žižek's (2008) bleak take on all of this, there comes with *Celebritus politicus* a kind of "plausible deniability" – similar to what Max Boykoff and I have called "conspicuous redemption" in the context of climate-change celebrities – that gets turned into a kind of "caring deniability" designed to set loose the philanthropic sensibilities and materialities of *Celebritus politicus* that very often work to hide the systemic and subjective violences upon which neoliberal capitalisms are based.

Second, through this, more power has been ceded to and collected by already fabulously powerful individuals. Here, through *Celebritus politicus*, the generic power of celebrity and media-generated fame is extended even further into our daily lives and the public realm through the "do-goodingness" of celebrities, their pedagogical functionality, and the often extended media coverage this all continues to get. More importantly, though, in the context of this chapter, celebrities have been granted but also have seized the power to define for us what is important (or not) to fix and save and how to specifically govern these social and environmental problems (or not). From the psycho-political economies surrounding the cultures of *Celebritus politicus*, celebrities are our contemporary muses revealing what is wrong with key aspects of the globe and what approaches to take to deal with these crises of underdevelopment, poverty, and threatened natures. Thus, the markets in emotion created in and through *Celebritus politicus* create winning and losing causes, concerns, and solutions that, when on the winning side like Hope for Haiti in the United States ($57 million), Comic Relief in the United Kingdom (£74 million in 2011), and the global success of (Product) RED ($160 million by 2011), can generate millions in donations/purchases, or, when on the losing side, may not even make it much, if at all, into the consciousness of the public sphere (cf. Marsh et al. 2010).

A number of important questions and issues remain in the context of this flourishing of poverty- and enviro-tainment. For example, how might celebrity governance regimes and *Celebritus politics* change or add to our understandings of how fandom is created and experienced now? Similarly, what are the actual, material impacts of new media such as Facebook and Twitter on the constitution as well as outcomes of campaigns fronted by *Celebritus politicus*? In short, what does the growing importance of the number of Facebook friends and Twitter followers mean, beyond the arguments put forward here, for the ways activist campaigns are carried out, for the ways *Celebritus politicus* gets their work done, and to the ultimate success of creating a better, more caring and more progressive set of global politics? Moreover, how do *Celebritus politicus* and the celebrity governance regime – and in particular their inclusion of the subjectivities and objectivities of "fans" into these stylized markets for care – challenge the development of new theorizations around the growing discussions of ethical consumption (Barnett et al. 2010; Lewis and Potter 2010), new forms of (elite?) global citizenship, and the new spaces of care emerging in the post-industrial, globalized world? Furthermore, how do the paradoxical trends and momentums of individualization versus collectivization, superstardom versus normalization, and commodification versus non-commodification play out in the specific instances of the practices of *Celebritus politicus*? In other words, how do all of these seemingly contradictory cultural political economies and materialisms work to construct *specific* instances and cases of (un)successful campaigns and the progressive politics of the day? Finally, much more critical light needs to be shed on the kinds of social, political, cultural, and economic inequalities that are paradoxically somewhat challenged by but also further entrenched in celebrity governance regimes and the figure of *Celebritus politicus*. In other words, *who is* and/or *what politics are* collectivized in the individualized embodiments of *Celebritus politicus* and the (current) terrains of care they are in the processes of creating, and why might this be the case in different spatial, cultural, and temporal contexts?

Otherwise, poverty- and enviro-tainment might simply be (re)creating a novel cultural and economic spectacle of hegemonic neoliberalist capitalism in a world seemingly in need of something much different and/or alternative. And, while it remains to be seen if some of the world's most rich and powerful individuals in the form of *Celebritus politicus* can usher in a new era of a globalized terrain of care across the political economic geographies of difference, it is these sets of contemporary icons who will be the public voices of environment and development for much of our near and continuingly celebrity-focused – and celebrity-governed – future.

NOTES

A hearty and heartfelt thanks to Andrew Brooks, Cheryl Lousley, Julie Doyle, Lisa Ann Richey, Dan Brockington, and Max Boykoff for suffering through earlier versions of this chapter; thanks also to the participants at Dan's "Capitalism, Democracy and Celebrity Advocacy" symposium and particularly to the unrelenting critiques of Mark Wheeler, Scott Prudham, Ilan Kapoor, and Cheryl. Many thanks to Gavin and Martijn for vastly improving this chapter through their keen and supportive editorial efforts.

1 Indeed, at the time of the writing of this chapter, the earthquake and tsunami had just hit in Japan, and a number of celebrities, like P. Diddy and Khloé Kardashian, immediately jumped up to "help" through Twitter. As a *Guardian* newspaper blog post rather cynically put it: "say what you will about the world's celebrities, they're nothing if not redoubtable in a crisis. No sooner had the Japanese earthquake struck than they sprang into action, immediately using their fame to offer the most effective and practical form of help imaginable: better than urging their fans to donate money to Red Cross efforts, better even than donating themselves. They mounted a hashtag campaign on Twitter suggesting people should pray ... 'Let us pray!!!!' offered P. Diddy. 'Praying hard' added Khloé Kardashian" (Petridis 2011).

2 One particular aspect to the fascinating history of the rise of *Celebritus politicus* in the form of "celebrity diplomats" is described in Cooper (2008b).

3 For more on this see part four in Goodman et al. (2012).

4 This is Žižek's mash up of Porto Alegre, the meeting place of the "who's who" of global social movements, and Davos, the yearly meeting place of the "who's who" of global capitalism.

5 There are now several dedicated websites, such as looktothestars.com and ecorazzi.com, specifically devoted to the media surrounding these stars and their politicized doings.

6 Twitter in particular has been used for *Celebritus politicus* to announce support for certain causes, or for causes to either demonstrate their connections to celebrities or launch and/or maintain existing campaigns.

7 Satellite Sentinel uses satellite mapping to publicize conflict and military/militia movements in Sudan; for more, see www.satsentinel.org.

8 While not explored specifically here, entrepreneurialism is also involved in celebrity governance regimes in the more traditional sense: social businesses like (Product) RED (see Richey and Ponte 2011), or at least stumping for these social businesses, are quickly also becoming part and parcel of the job description of *Celebritus politicus* as well as more "progressive" business and civil society leaders; Porto Davos (Žižek 2008) indeed.

9 This is the byline from the ongoing featured section in the American "star-gazing" tabloid *Us Weekly* that works to show just how "like us" real people megastars actually are through candid photos of them bike riding with their children, buying coffees at Starbucks, and wearing "relaxing" clothes on the weekends.

4

Al Gore as Carbon Warrior:
The Politics of Inaction

For many, the emergence of modern-day environmentalism represented the ultimate embodiment of Western society's countercultural desires, a radical divergence from the everyday, and a movement within which the seeds of a new, green world order could be envisaged. Indeed, the realization of our environmental imaginaries demanded a fundamental reconfiguration of our "modern" existence, away from the false promises of mass consumption in favour of lifestyles capable of foregrounding the natural world as central to our very existence. While not without its problems, early environmentalism was at least willing to name the dystopian reality that is late capitalism; today this is no longer the case. Indeed, one of the central arguments of this chapter is that Western environmentalism has undergone a cultural overhaul – not simply a change by degrees but a change in kind (Finn 1999), whereby its mainstream manifestations appear strange and foreign, embodying "unnatural combinations" that unify the problem as solution, capitalism as saviour.

This metamorphosis is revealed perhaps most spectacularly in the person of Al Gore and in his work on global warming. As the high priest of the modern environmental movement, mainstream recognition of Gore's message is unrivalled: in 2006 his documentary *An Inconvenient Truth* received two Oscars; in 2007 he received the Nobel Peace Prize for his efforts to spread the global warming message; and his work helped to popularize "carbon neutral" as the Oxford Dictionary 2006 word of the year. As popular icon, Gore embodies the crystallization of our deepest discontents and fears, and thus hopes and dreams. But what is particularly worthy of examination in relation to Gore is not the success with which his message has been embraced, but the absence of a critical self-reflexivity on the part of his followers that sets as its task an interrogation of Gore's apparently self-evident prescription for green deliverance. Indeed, for Gore, deliverance will be attained not through a radical reorientation of Western lifestyles and political economic structures, but through the promise of the "offset" whereby we – Western governments, businesses, and citizens – can continue to produce and consume a disproportionate share of the world's resources, comfortable because someone else, typically in the South, will now pay for our carbon sins (Spash 2010).

The purpose of this chapter is to explore the cultural politics of Gore's carbon neutral vision in order to understand the contradictory imbroglio that is contemporary mainstream environmentalism. In particular, it will examine the mechanisms through which carbon offsetting's "politics of inaction" has garnered such widespread popular appeal, arguing that the answer is to be found, in part, through an understanding of offsetting as a psycho-social device that sanctions one's impulse to take flight in the face of looming ecological crisis. By employing Bruno Latour's insights on the contested meaning of modernity in light of proliferating environmental decline, which point to a destabilization of the historical union of modernity with progress and enlightenment, this chapter demonstrates how carbon offsetting, as central to Gore's carbon neutral plan, ultimately reconciles modernity's obvious contradictions. Indeed, through offsetting, denial dons the mask of action, reassuring us that something is being done. The value-added return on offsetting is that it simultaneously promises both pleasure and self-satisfaction. Indeed, rather than demand the austerity typical of traditional environmental agendas, carbon offsetting, through its neoliberalized individualism, suggests that we might keep on consuming; in fact, the more consumption the better, since offsets offer the valued-added benefit of a "development dividend," "solving" poverty in the South as the ultimate act of altruism. Overall, capitalism is re-signified as green liberator, while our faith in modernity is restored.

The Problem

While predictions of a warming earth attributable to anthropogenic activities such as the burning of fossil fuels were made throughout the twentieth century, it was not until 1988, the hottest year on record at that point, that the issue garnered widespread public attention (Weart 2010). As a specific issue, global warming belongs to a longer genealogical history of scientific research on global environmental crises, with the 1970s marking a watershed decade in the evolution and acceptance of the predications made within this tradition. In 1972 the Club of Rome published its seminal *Limits to Growth*, which, while decidedly Malthusian in its orientation,[1] called for an overall reorganization of the predominant economic model of growth and consumption patterns in order to prioritize environmental and human needs over those of profit. Importantly, its critique of the temporal limitations of neoclassical economic theory, with its emphasis on short-term individual benefits as indicative of progress, led the authors to call for a global redistribution of wealth and the adoption of a steady-state economy (Meadows et al. 1972; Randers and Meadows 1973).While not without its problems, and detractors, especially within the economics profession given its interrogation of economic orthodoxy which insists on continuous economic growth, *Limits to Growth* signalled an emerging discontent among the environmentally inclined who increasingly believed that, through industrial society and its mode of production, a "dystopian" rupture had emerged upon the fabric of presumed progress and enlightenment that was late capitalism (Smith 1998).

Fast-forward to the present, with 2010 confirmed as the hottest year on record since data collection began in 1880 (Emspak 2011), this brand of critique has all but disappeared, with Western society's collective faith in the power of capitalism to reverse such trends more entrenched than ever. While all indicators point to a rapidly deteriorating global ecosystem, this in spite of two decades of concerted global action on the environmental front, we seem content to accept that business as usual will free us from the noose that is tightening around our necks. In order to identify meaningful paths to change, then, we must first identify from where this contradiction has emerged. What factors have led to our collective denial?

While this chapter does not wish to suggest that nature's general, though constructed, ontological status in Western society pre-exists and has thus predetermined the technologies and economic strategies that have been harnessed to change that very nature, it does contend that coming to terms with this nature as *social identity* must be a priority in understanding the social and political paralysis that has enveloped strategies intended to mitigate global warming. As human beings defined by the social meaning that we ascribe to the world around us, we have centralized nature in a particular narrative of *who we are*. In Western society in particular, this has entailed the separation and purification of an apparently ontologically distinct nature – that is, nature is what we are not (Gregory 2001; Castree and Braun 1998; Cronon 1995; Latour 1993; Smith 1984). Within this narrative, historically nature and its overwhelming power to shape the possibilities of human survival came to represent that which must be tamed, dominated, and controlled, should we succeed in casting off the shackles of our early oppression. Subordination and exploitation concurrently transformed nature into the foundational building block upon which industrial society would eventually emerge. In this way, nature has been "simultaneously central to society and marginalized. It appears as the 'outside' of society" (Beck, Bonss, and Lau 2003, 4). Such positioning relied on the collective capabilities of capitalism, science, and technology, all deeply interconnected and mutually constitutive, to underwrite nature's transformation. Indeed, it is in part through each and their particular treatment of nature that in the West we have come to define ourselves as *modern*.

But as Bruno Latour and others have noted, the emergence of environmental crises of limitless range and intensity strikes at the heart of our own self-identification as modern and emancipated, and as the product of the linear march of progress (Giddens 1999; Beck 1999; Latour 1993, 8–12). Citing Ulrich Beck's work on "risk society," Brian Kean contends that "industrial capitalist society manufactures and generates its opposite," risk in the form of disease, ecological collapse, economic insecurity, and so forth (2006, 37). While assured that capitalism and techo-science can simultaneously remedy such risks, Westerners nevertheless have begun to lose their "self-confidence" in the face of this reality. Nature, rather than passive object to be subsumed under and according to our desires, appears as active agent capable of rejecting our interventions, thus calling into question the very substance of *who we are*. Perhaps "we've never been modern," if one of the central hallmarks of modernity has been our perceived control and domination over nature, delivered through the mainstays of industrial society (Latour 1993).

The implications of this ecologically induced identity crisis are many. On a personal level, our surroundings are no longer familiar and safe, or capable of inspiring confidence in who we are and why we do what we do as a society. In a 2008 study in the United States by Kellstedt, Zahran, and Vedlitz, it was found, quite remarkably, that increased personal informedness regarding global warming led to a decrease in concern for the problem, coupled with a sense of less rather than more personal responsibility (2008). What explains such results? Recent work in psychoanalysis offers some clues. In a 2008 article for *The Ecologist*, scholar Renée Lertzman asks: "Is it possible that our anxieties about ecological problems, and the existential dilemmas they raise regarding how we are to live, can be so great as to be unmanageable or unthinkable? Might we unconsciously deny what is staring us in the face because what is at stake is too painful to consider?" (2008). Lertzman's use of psychoanalytic theory to understand responses to challenges like global warming suggests that when confronted with problems of such deep magnitude that not only impinge on our own personal identity but simultaneously threaten the very life-support system that sustains us as a species, the individual may be induced to take flight. Denial, dissociation, and repression, understood in psychoanalytic terms, are common defensive responses to the painful reality, allowing us to maintain the illusion of normalcy despite the mounting contradictory evidence (Lertzman 2008; Beck 1992). The result is a classic case of what Eric Fromm famously termed an "escape from freedom." Granted a historically unprecedented amount of individual "negative" freedom but given very little in the way of "positive" freedom to change or steer giant modern institutions, including the state and corporations, modern individuals are faced with intense feelings of powerlessness, anxiety, loneliness, isolation, and alienation. In response, people escape from freedom, seeking submission to powerful fantasies that offer simple solutions to complex problems, while repressing the often highly irrational dimensions of the fantasy. Indeed, carbon offsetting, as will be shown in subsequent sections of this chapter, represents one such fantasy. To Fromm, modern capitalism, far from creating the rational economic man of economic textbooks, instead led to individuals who repressed a great deal of rational knowledge (such as, in the context of today's world, alarming scientific knowledge about climate change) as a psychological escape from its social and ecologically destructive nature (Fromm 1941).

Kean suggests that it is little surprising that an emergent risk society and its myriad crises brings with it a veritable explosion in the prescription and use of psychotropic drugs to treat depression, anxiety, and various other "mental" disorders (Kean 2006). As one study notes, the number of Americans on disability as a result of mental illness has ballooned from 1.25 million people in 1987 to over 4 million in 2010. The number of Americans taking some form of psychotropic drug has now reached one in eight (Whitaker 2010). As our faith in modern society wavers and manufactured risks proliferate, the individual, rather than behaving proactively, harnesses those tools – internal and external – at his or her disposal which "suture" the rupture to one's comfortable world view (Smith 1998).

From the vantage point of what Gramsci (1971, 12) defined as the historic bloc, the dominant class coalition at a specific point in history that is able to exercise hegemony throughout society as a result of its status within relations of production, this identity crisis threatens much more than one's personal sense of security and faith in progress. Should such insecurities radiate beyond the individual to infect the collective societal body, as has historically been the case within environmental movements, then the seeds of counter-hegemony might be sown. Indeed, a growing environmental consciousness in Western society has historically represented one of the most potent counter-hegemonic challenges to capitalist growth and development (Newell 2008; McCarthy and Prudham 2004; Paterson, Humphreys, and Pettiford 2003). Faced thus with its own existential crisis, the contemporary historic bloc has worked hard to engage the critiques, but as Newell notes, only in such a way that distances "global capitalism from the sources of environmental problems, accommodating some mild criticism of consumerism and globalization without allowing the 'fatal connection' between the capitalist mode of production and the ecological crisis to be addressed" (Newell 2008). It is through this "sustainable development" historic bloc that market environmentalism – carbon markets, payments for ecological services, ecotourism, and green consumerism – has subsumed the counter-hegemonic critique, rapidly becoming *the* predominant approach to solving our ecological ills in Western society and globally (Liverman 2004; McAfee 1999; Saurin 2001).

Perhaps market environmentalism's greatest achievement, when assessed from the perspective of the capitalist elite, has been its ability to neutralize opposition to the present mode of production under the contention that capitalism, and much more of it, is now required to solve our ecological ills. This bears resemblance to the process described by Slavoj Žižek in his book *Violence*, whereby liberal humanitarians such as George Soros amass outrageous wealth through predatory speculation and in the process destroy untold lives and economies, and then funnel a portion of that wealth into philanthropic endeavours as vehicle for "development" – taking with one hand to then give with the other (Žižek 2008, 21–2). Market environmentalism's bitter irony, as such, is the extent to which it harnesses that which destroys to mediate its worst impacts. In addition, however, market environmentalism transforms nature into an "accumulation strategy," commodifying species, genes, and bodies that heretofore have remained outside accumulation networks, and this precisely at a historical moment of intense global crises of overaccumulation (Smith 2007; Harvey 2003; Castree and Braun 1998). The profit opportunity embedded within market environmentalism fits well with the rationale that underpins an emerging body of work on "philanthrocapitalism." Its proponents suggest that doing good for the world, including its ecological support system, will come from a new breed of philanthropists who recognize the economic potential in saving the environment. Indeed, it is that potential, it is argued, that will provide the incentive for forward-looking philanthrocapitalists – Al Gore, Bono, George Soros, Richard Branson, and so forth (Bishop and Green 2009). The fact that so many of their business ventures are often enormous contributors to ecological crises – Richard Branson owns Virgin Airlines, a major carbon emitter, while dubbing himself a carbon crusader – is hardly relevant within this narrative.

Finally, market environmentalism's impact on the citizen is to further solidify a neoliberal subjectivity that posits the individual, rather than institutions and structures, as both cause of and solution to the problem (Maniates 2002; Bryant and Goodman 2004). What this process illuminates overall is the intense dialectical interplay between the fears and discontents of individuals, ever-searching for reassurances that our foundational narratives continue to hold true, and the much broader needs of our current political-economic system that risks collapse should the masses reject capitalism's necessary illusions. It is within this context that the popularity of Al Gore, as cultural icon and carbon warrior, has, no doubt, been so fantastical.

Al Gore as Carbon Warrior

For a number of years now I have been teaching courses in both "world politics" and "environmental politics," and every year I devote a number of classes in each to the politics and policy of global-warming governance. I have always found it fitting to begin our discussion with a critical consideration of Al Gore and his global-warming message, and every year I can expect, invariably, that upon the introduction of our subject at least a handful of students will begin to dismissively roll their eyes, while whispering to their closest neighbour. These students are not Gore critics – far from it. Rather, they count themselves as among a group of devout followers who have granted Gore a saintly status, worshipping a prophet who will, they hope, deliver us from the coming apocalypse. In this sense, for some, it borders on blasphemy to question Gore's message – you're either with Gore or you're with the sceptics – even if the goal is to improve our collective ability to address the global-warming crisis. I would argue that this stems from the extent to which Gore's message has succeeded in reconciling modernity's obvious contradictions, thereby allaying our deep discontents.

Prior to his explosion on the global-warming stage, most were familiar with *Vice President* Al Gore, or *Senator* Al Gore from Tennessee. His political career began in 1977 after his election to the U.S. House of Representatives, and that career lasted until 2001, at which point he ran an unsuccessful campaign for the U.S. presidency. Throughout his political tenure, critics consistently painted Gore as a lacklustre individual, devoid of those characteristics which would lead to widespread popular appeal. Such claims reached a fever pitch during his candidacy for the presidency with his critics claiming he was too robotic and distant to inspire the average American voter (Turque 2000). While it's possible to contest the accuracy of such claims, it nevertheless came as a surprise to many that Gore's image was transformed almost overnight into one of a mega rock-star carbon warrior. Indeed, Gore has been far more popular and far more adored as carbon warrior than he ever was as a U.S. politician.

Gore himself can boast an impressive list of eco-credentials. In 1992, just prior to his election as vice president of the United States, he published his phenomenally popular *Earth in the Balance: Ecology and the Human Spirit*, with new editions appearing in 2000 and 2006. In 2006 Gore's bestseller, *An Inconvenient Truth: The Planetary Crisis of Global Warming and What We Can Do about It*, appeared on bookstands, accompanying the release of his documentary of the same name, which premiered at the Sundance Film Festival and grossed $49 million worldwide. Since then Gore has published *Our Choice: A Plan to Solve the Climate Crisis* (2009) and has penned countless op-ed pieces for major U.S. newspapers on the same subject. Based on a slide-show presentation on global warming that Gore had been delivering across the United States following his electoral defeat for the U.S. presidency in 2000, the documentary *An Inconvenient Truth* went on to win an Academy Award for Best Documentary Film in 2007, and in that same year Gore won the Nobel Peace Prize, which he shared with the Intergovernmental Panel on Climate Change, for his work on publicizing the global-warming crisis.

In 2006 Gore founded The Alliance for Climate Progress, a non-profit organization that undertakes education campaigns on the causes of, and solutions to, global warming, and which claims more than 5 million members worldwide (The Alliance for Climate Protection 2011). Further capitalizing on his Oscar and Nobel success, in 2007 Gore partnered with producer Kevin Wall in the founding of Live Earth, a for-profit company that "seeks to leverage the power of entertainment through integrated events, media, and the live experience to ignite a global movement aimed at solving the most critical environmental issues of our time" (Live Earth 2011). On 7 July 2007, Live Earth produced a series of global concerts to "combat the climate crisis," which included a mix of "legendary" acts and current headliners, including Madonna, The Police, Metallica, Bon Jovi, Alicia Keys, John Mayer, Kanye West, and The Black Eyed Peas. Presenters included Al Gore himself, Leonardo DiCaprio, Cameron Diaz, Naomi Campbell, Kevin Bacon, and Robert Kennedy Jr, amongst others. With viewers across the world tuning in to watch the concerts, which took place on seven continents, organizers have since contended that the event was responsible for inspiring "2 billion people worldwide to engage with the issues and the solutions surrounding the global warming crisis" (Live Earth 2011). Currently Gore sits as chairman and co-founder, with David Blood, former CEO of Goldman Sachs Asset Management, of Generation Investment Management (GIM) LLP, a global investment firm dedicated to incorporating "sustainability factors" into its investment portfolio. Presently GIM is the largest shareholder in Camco, which holds one of the largest international carbon asset portfolios worldwide (Lohmann 2010, 236). In December 2010 GIM was commanding funds valued at US$3.3 billion (Stockpickr 2011).

There can be little doubt that Al Gore has done more than any other person to publicize the global-warming crisis, and as a result, he has achieved nothing less than iconic status within the mainstream global-warming movement and, more importantly, for the average citizen who, while eschewing direct activism, nevertheless counts her/himself as among the concerned masses. However, what is especially worthy of analysis in relation to Gore's global-warming work is, as mentioned in the introduction to this chapter, the absence of a critical self-reflexivity on the part of Gore's followers and admirers that might interrogate the content of his message, and thus its implications for effectively addressing global warming. This is far from insignificant given the vast contradictions between that message on the one hand and its ability to inspire meaningful change on the other.

Following immediately on the heels of Gore's Oscar success, a little-known free-market think tank out of Tennessee released a report detailing what it labelled as Al Gore's "Inconvenient Truth." The Tennessee Center for Policy Research, using publicly obtained records from the Nashville Energy Service, noted that Gore's Nashville mansion, which includes twenty rooms, eight bathrooms, and a pool house, consumed 221,000 kilowatt-hours of electricity in 2006, compared to an average American household consumption of 10,656 kilowatt-hours. The figures revealed that Gore's mansion alone consumed 20 times more electricity than the average American household, carrying a price tag of almost US$30,000 for the year. Over and above this figure, Gore paid an average of $1,080 per month in natural-gas bills (Tennessee Center for Policy Research 2007). Following these revelations, the Internet was abuzz with talk of Gore's other home in Virginia, his family farm in Tennessee, and his private jet, which he used to travel to various locations throughout the United States to deliver his Inconvenient Truth slideshow presentation. While the source, a right-wing think tank presumably hostile to the climate change agenda, indeed raised the ire of many global-warming activists, the fact that the information was a matter of public record and thus fully verifiable could not help but raise some uncomfortable questions. This was compounded by Gore's purchase in May 2010 of an $8.8-million luxury mansion in Montecito, California. The residence, located in an exclusive gated community where the likes of Oprah Winfrey and Michael Douglas also own properties, includes, among other amenities, five bedrooms, nine bathrooms, and six fireplaces (Koch 2010).

Once again critics were quick to highlight the perceived contradiction between Gore's global-warming message in contrast to his everyday behaviour. In response to the 2007 Tennessee Center for Policy Research report, a former Gore advisor responded by saying: "I think what you're seeing here is the last gasp of the global warming skeptics. They've completely lost the debate on the issue so now they're just attacking their most effective opponent" (Tapper 2007). Yet for many observers, such lavish levels of consumption, far over and above that required by any one individual and his or her family to meet their needs, would seem to suggest an intense disjuncture between rhetoric and reality. Responding to this, a Gore spokesperson noted that for Gore's Tennessee mansion, the Gore family purchased their power through Green Power Switch, a program of the Tennessee Valley Authority (TVA) that includes renewable energy sources – wind, solar, and methane gas – in its traditional mix of energy sources derived from fossil fuels (Tennessee Valley Authority 2011). In addition, the Gore's installed solar panels on their home, used compact fluorescent light bulbs, and purchased "offsets for their carbon emissions to bring their carbon footprint down to zero" (Tapper 2007).

The idea that one's carbon footprint can be reduced to zero is best known through the concept of "carbon neutrality," with "carbon neutral" becoming the *New Oxford American Dictionary*'s Word of the Year in 2006. It is defined as: "making or resulting in no net release of carbon dioxide into the atmosphere, especially as a result of carbon offsetting" (Oxford Dictionaries 2011). Given that Gore's overall consumption levels are grossly disproportionate to those of the average American or Canadian consumer, who already qualifies as a super-consumer based on comparative global data (Global Footprint Network 2011),[2] and since the purchase and use of green energy, solar panels, and fluorescent light bulbs can make but a small dent in such exorbitantly high levels of greenhouse gas (GHG) emissions, carbon offsetting serves as the vehicle through which Gore ultimately is able to claim carbon neutrality.[3]

Interrogating the Message: Carbon Offsetting's Politics of Inaction

Modern society is in the midst of a transition, away from what Beck et al. have termed "first modernity" towards a new "second modernity." It is the transitional state which they refer to as "reflexive modernity," whereby the unintended consequences of modernity's handmaidens – capitalism and techno-science – produce, among other things, new natures and new subjectivities (Beck, Bonss, and Lau 2003). Reflexive modernity, rather than denoting a heightened level of consciousness for citizens in the West, indicates recognition of the fact that "mastery is impossible" (Latour 2003). As discussed in the first section of this paper, phenomena such as global warming challenge the belief that we can ultimately master nature, yet it would be a mistake to assume that reflexive modernity will necessarily inspire the necessary corrections. Instead, we may seek out reassurances that our existence remains stable and that all is well, or at least easily corrected. Is this not what Al Gore provides us with, the reassurance that those very same structures of an emerging dystopia, with minor tinkering, can be harnessed to fix our most trenchant societal and ecological problems?

Carbon offsetting lies at the heart of contemporary international governance efforts to deal with global warming. With the creation of the United Nations Framework Convention on Climate Change (UNFCCC) in 1992 at the Rio Earth Summit, state signatories quickly began negotiations for a global greenhouse gas emissions reduction treaty, culminating with the creation of the Kyoto Protocol whose first commitment period began in 2008. During negotiations, the United States, represented by Al Gore as vice president, successfully pushed to have the protocol transformed into a global pollution trading instrument (Lohmann 2010, 236). Specifically, the United States made its participation in the Protocol contingent upon the adoption of a market-based framework through which countries with greenhouse gas reduction commitments could meet their targets. Carbon trading and carbon offsetting serve as the two essential pillars of this market-based approach, conceptually understood as "flexible mechanisms." Each permits the purchase of emission reductions, at least on paper, through non-source activities. In the case of carbon offsetting, the Kyoto Protocol uses its Clean Development Mechanism (CDM), Joint Implementation (JI), and Carbon Sinks to facilitate the purchase of carbon credits achieved through emission-reduction projects in the Global South, European economies in transition, or in relation to the sale of excess credits allotted according to a country's forest cover, respectively (Lohmann 2010; Bumpus and Liverman 2008). It is estimated that in 2010 a number of European countries, having failed to meet their Kyoto Protocol targets, budgeted $3.9 billion to buy offset credits worth 550-million tonnes of CO_2 (Spash 2010, 184). Proponents of flexible mechanisms suggest that it is faster and costs significantly less to reduce carbon emissions in developing and transitional countries than in developed countries, while they further neutralize domestic political opposition to the global-warming agenda (Bumpus and Liverman 2008; World Bank 2007; Taiyab 2006). In the case of the CDM in particular, proponents argue that it represents a powerful vehicle for generating domestic sustainable development in the South given the carbon finance and technology that CDM projects will potentially attract (Boyd, Boykoff, and Newell 2011).

Parallel to the emergence of the Kyoto Protocol's internationally regulated carbon market within which offsets are bought and sold by states, a voluntary market has emerged to take advantage of the opportunity to profit from the increasing popularity of offsetting among private businesses and individuals. It is within this context that the international voluntary market has burgeoned over the past few years;

the market grew by 200 per cent between 2005 and 2006, with a record 24 million tonnes of carbon traded in 2006, worth US$91 million
(Lovell, Bulkeley, and Liverman 2009). In 2007 it was reported in the
Financial Times that the global voluntary offset market was expected
to be worth $4 billion by 2010 (Harvey and Fidler 2007). Consumers of
voluntary carbon offsets pay retailers to offset their GHG emissions on
anything from air travel and business events, to weddings and baby
showers, with comprehensive packages available to cover one's entire
carbon footprint in a year. Retailers then invest in emission-reducing
projects such as tree planting, renewable energy, methane capture,
lighting, ocean fertilization, fly-ash reprocessing, and biofuels, with the
understanding that a commensurate trade-off has been achieved (Bumpus and Liverman 2008; Lohmann 2010).

In reality, such trade-offs are fraught with uncertainly and are no-
toriously hard to verify. As various observers have noted, embedded
within the offset market are a set of perverse incentives which entice
offset producers to over-inflate or misrepresent the capacity of the offset project to deliver quantifiable emissions reductions (Spash 2010;
Lohmann 2010, 2006). In particular, offset producers are required to
develop a hypothetical "business-as-usual" scenario within which
baseline emissions are calculated in the absence of the offset project.
From this, producers are expected to demonstrate the additionality of
their proposed project in terms of its contribution to reducing greenhouse gases, which then qualifies them for carbon finance. In reality,
such projects may require no real reduction in GHGs since the estimate
is to withhold future emissions. The result is that producers have an
incentive to produce baseline scenarios that are as high as possible so
that their proposed project appears to be reducing far more of a particular greenhouse gas than would in fact be the case, qualifying the
project to earn more carbon credits to be sold on the market for a profit
(Lohmann 2010, 245). A 2007 review of hundreds of approved Chinese
hydro-power offset projects in the Kyoto offset pipeline showed that
none should have qualified to produce offset credits based on the Clean
Development Mechanism's criteria (Lohmann 2010, 245).

In 2010, firms in China, India, and Central America were found to
have "gamed" Kyoto's carbon offset market. This opportunity emerged
from a process whereby greenhouse gases are assigned a "global warming potential" equivalency which measures their equivalency in comparison to carbon dioxide. HCFC-22, an ozone-destroying refrigerant
still in use throughout much of the Global South until its scheduled

phase-out in 2030 under the Montreal Protocol, produces as a by-product the greenhouse gas HFC-23, estimated to be 14,800 times more potent than CO_2 at trapping heat (*The Economist* 2010). Producers that destroy rather than emit HFC-23 are thus eligible to earn a significant amount of carbon offset credits for sale in Kyoto's official market, with one observer noting that "destroying a tonne of HFC-23 is a lot cheaper than avoiding the emission of more than 10,000 tonnes of carbon dioxide" (*The Economist* 2010). The result has been that various firms, aware of the potential for super-profits, have been gaming the market by intentionally increasing their production of HFC-23 in order to earn more carbon credits for sale in Kyoto's offset market, controlled by the CDM. So lucrative is the opportunity that HFC-23 reduction projects have now become the CDM's primary source of emissions credits, accounting for 59 per cent of the offset credits sold in the EU ETS in 2009, worth $695 million (*The Economist* 2010).

While such perverse incentives represent a potential Achilles' heel within international offset markets, a related problem has to do with the uncertainty of calculating "global warming potential" equivalencies. As Lohmann notes, the UN's Intergovernmental Panel on Climate Change in 2007 recalculated HFC-23's global-warming potential, increasing it over a 100-year horizon by 23 per cent (Lohmann 2010, 244). Indeed, baseline estimates are calculated over 100 years "to correspond with the approximate residence time of carbon dioxide in the atmosphere" (Lohmann 2010, 244). When offset projects displaying an extremely high degree of variability are proposed, as is the case with forestry projects, for example, given the natural and anthropogenic risks posed to forests within such a time frame (fires, decay, infestations, cutting, etc.) and given the vast diversity between tree species, it becomes nearly impossible to calculate and guarantee the actual carbon dioxide reductions to be achieved through offsetting (FERN 2000).

In 2002 the UK mega-band Coldplay released the album *Rush of Blood to the Head*, announcing that emissions associated with the album would be offset through the planting of 10,000 mango trees in Karnataka, India. Dubbed "The Coldplay Forest," fans were given the opportunity to participate in the scheme; the British-based Carbon Neutral Company allowed fans to purchase a $25 certificate verifying that they had "dedicated trees in 'The Coldplay Forest'" (Ma'anit 2006). By 2006 reports emerged revealing that only a few hundred of the 10,000 saplings that had been distributed to small farmers for planting remained alive. The Carbon Neutral Company blamed Indian participants for the project's failure, suggesting they did not meet their "contractual obligations," while members of Coldplay claimed no responsibility for the outcome. In fact, a project evaluation concluded that local drought played a significant role in the project's failure, with local participants unable to access the necessary water to sustain the trees once planted; between 1995 and 2004 the monsoon failed to arrive each year. Participants also complained of not receiving the promised financial compensation for planting and upkeep (Dhillon and Harnden 2006; Ma'anit 2006). This experience, hardly isolated, demonstrates the significant uncertainty inherent to many offsetting schemes, which prove unable to deliver on their promise of an overall reduction in the level of greenhouse gases in the atmosphere (Lohmann 2006). Nevertheless, the participation in such initiatives of rock superstars such as Coldplay, with the Rolling Stones and others later undertaking their own forest offset projects, lends a certain "cool quotient" (Richey and Ponte 2011) to offsetting, whereby the fan, by replicating the behaviour, useful or not, can affirm his or her own self-worth – no need for scrutiny.

The above example highlights an additional significant problem associated with the voluntary offset market: there remains as of yet no standard regulatory system to ensure the quality of voluntary offsets, or their overall compliance with their stated goals (Lovell and Liverman 2010; Lovell, Bulkeley, and Liverman 2009). Offsets within the voluntary market are typically sold, especially in the case of forest projects, prior to the achievement of emissions reductions, opening the door to unfulfilled commitments and thereby further undermining the credibility of the market and its ability to deliver tangible greenhouse gas reductions.

Overall, critics note that in addition to the problems outlined above, offsets, at the most basic level, encourage the continued and even expanded dependence on fossil fuel use in the North, since we've now found an alternative, however questionable it may be, to reducing our own emissions at the source (Lohmann 2010, 243). Offsets function as a disincentive to structural transformation within the current fossil fuel economy as they suppress the need for identifying real alternatives, thereby delaying our eventual day of reckoning.

Offsetting and the Individual: Denial Dons the Mask of Action

While ample empirical evidence now exists to refute the claim that carbon offsetting represents a reasonable tool in the fight against global warming, Al Gore's message of carbon neutrality through offsetting remains highly seductive. In fact, it is by way of its politics of inaction that the message has helped to cement Gore's iconic status as carbon warrior, for it ultimately reaffirms *who we are* within the logic of our own civilizational narratives. Indeed, Gore tells us that capitalism and techno-science, the very tools of our manufactured dystopia, are just as important and legitimate as ever. We are thus able to placate our deep discontent through the simple purchase of the offset – all is well. In this sense, as Spash suggests, offsets, by offering us "a painless way to avoid human-induced climate change," should be likened to Aldous Huxley's fictitious drug "soma" in his *Brave New World*. Soma, he states, "offered inhabitants of a future Earth the means to distract themselves from addressing life's problems while supporting the established social and economic order in the promotion of happiness through hedonistic pleasures" (Spash 2010, 192). Similar to the myriad antidepressants in use today in North America – Prozac, Zoloft, Cymbalta, Lexapro, Effexor – offsets numb the painful and threatening reality facing our civilization, attesting thus to their stunning popularity.

Yet as the above quote suggests, offsets should not simply be read as a psycho-social device through which denial is realized, and whereby the "established social and economic order" is maintained, however important this might be. Indeed, the offset provides the individual with much more than that, fulfilling some of our deepest yearnings which may be entirely disconnected from the fear and uncertainty so prevalent in modern society today. At its most basic level, Gore's message – that there is no need for personal self-sacrifice and austerity to solve the global-warming challenge – sanctions self-indulgent and pleasure-seeking behaviours that are now recast as ecologically acceptable. That flight to and vacation in the Caribbean, continued conspicuous consumption, the choice to drive rather than take public transit all can continue apace in the world of the offset. Lohmann (2006) recalls the British executive who, upon discovering that her carbon footprint was 24 tonnes of CO_2 per year according to the Carbon Neutral Company's carbon calculator, compared to the 10-tonne average per person per year in the UK, referred to herself as "a monster." It was with great relief that she discovered she could offset her emissions for a mere £156 per year through tree-planting and energy projects, leading her to assert: "A cost of £156 is nothing ... think of the money you spend on lipstick and magazines" (Lohmann 2006, 191–2; Spash 2010; Climate Change Wales 2011). Offset retailers typically highlight the painless, indeed inconsequential, impact of offsetting on one's personal life. As Ma'anit notes, the offset retailer Climate Friendly out of Australia claims that "in five minutes and for the cost of a cappuccino a week you can go climate neutral," while Drive Neutral out of the United States suggests that "for about the cost of a single tank of gas, you can neutralize your CO_2 emissions for an entire year" (Ma'anit 2006). Given the entirely voluntary nature of offsetting, offset retailers are acutely aware of the need to pitch their product in a way that showcases its benign attributes, while connecting it to those things we find most pleasurable – driving, drinking cappuccino, conspicuous consumption, and so forth. The message suggests that we can now undertake such activities free of guilt; however, should this not suffice, retailers frequently invoke in relation to the offset particular "consumer subjectivities" or "ethical dispositions" in order to advance the idea that consumers are participating in a much bigger project. This is especially the case given the absence of a tangible product – the offset is produced through a distant and abstract action bearing no material deliverable (Lovell, Bulkeley, and Liverman 2009).

In this way, analysis of the offset in relation to subject formation must necessarily consider how the offset not only provides, though inadvertently, self-gratification through material consumption, but how it simultaneously becomes a signifier for *who it is we want to be*, even if its track record is largely contestable. Indeed, the offset is frequently framed in a way that suggests that, in addition to its primary function of reducing the overall stock of greenhouse gases in the atmosphere, it offers both ecological and development dividends – "sustainable side-benefits," if you will (Lovell, Bulkeley, and Liverman 2009). With the vast majority of offset projects occurring in the Global South, retailers consistently emphasize the symbiotic relationship between the offset and tangibles such as poverty reduction, community development, and biodiversity conservation. The U.S.-based ClearSky Climate Solutions Company, for example, notes:[4] "ClearSky projects offer everyone a chance to benefit: local communities, native ecosystems, our partner organizations, and concerned individuals. Purchasing offsets through ClearSky allows you to balance your greenhouse gas emissions, contribute to community and economic development in our project areas, improve native ecosystems, and promote sustainable, progressive solutions to the problem of global climate change" (ClearSky Climate Solutions 2011). The act of offsetting can be, therefore, highly symbolic and affirming and project a particular identity to those around you. It is an identity that in addition to establishing one's eco-credentials simultaneously suggests altruism, benevolence, compassion, and solidarity. In a related way, those personal acts that once qualified as ecologically destructive are re-signified as not only green, but as necessary for alleviating the suffering of others in distant lands.

Of course, what each individual ultimately derives from the act of offsetting will vary according to that individual's specific motivations, wants, and desires. Pleasure, self-gratification, existential reassurance, meaningful environmental action are all possible motivations, none necessarily entirely exclusive of the others. It would be a mistake, however, to minimize the extent to which Al Gore's personal sanctioning of consumptive promiscuity as the path to green deliverance has been the key to offsetting's stunning popularity. By taking the road most travelled, Gore ultimately reaffirms our civilizational narratives, while assuaging our guilt.

So What Does It All Mean?

Al Gore alone is not responsible for the popularity of carbon neutrality, he didn't invent the offset, even if he profits handsomely from it, and he didn't single-handedly usher in the era of market environmentalism as a counter to more traditional and austere eco-agendas. No, Al Gore isn't that powerful. Nevertheless, as eco-icon and carbon warrior, Al Gore represents the crystallization of a set of sometimes divergent, at other times mutually dependent, human impulses that require affirmation and validation in the face of increasingly uncertain times. In this sense, is it any wonder that Gore's message has been so phenomenally well accepted? Sadly, the far-reaching implications and consequences of his message, and of the more general societal move to market environmentalism, means we are fully unprepared to deal effectively with contemporary environmental problems such as global warming.

In the first instance, and as already suggested above, offsetting ultimately stalls the identification of meaningful solutions by leaving the present fossil fuel economy in place; we are told that no lifestyle and/or systemic changes are necessary, allowing the world's oil giants to continue to feed and profit from the insatiable machine that is present-day consumer capitalism. As a result, the existential challenges to capitalism itself are held at bay by inverting the logic of traditional environmentalism to suggest that more markets and more consumption, not less, are necessary. Within this logic, the actions of the individual are identified as singularly responsible for both creating and solving contemporary ecological problems, representing the triumph of a neoliberalized individualism that, in typical "common sense" fashion, tells us that we can, and should, consume our way out of any problems we might encounter. Gore's iconic status as carbon warrior is especially significant in this respect. As eco-entrepreneur and capitalist, mega-consumer, and carbon offsetter, Gore enables the seemingly conflict-free marriage of a set of highly contradictory actions and messages; such contradictions melt away in the body of Gore. His rock-star fame, singularly achieved through his global warming work, only strengthens the allure of his message, thereby mystifying further its obvious paradox.

This process becomes further troubling when we consider the evidence that suggests that the intrinsically motivated environmental activist – the person who voluntarily engages in environmental activism since he/she values it as "inherently worthwhile" – may find his/her environmental motivations "crowded out" by the introduction of market-based schemes such as offsetting (Spash 2010, 189). Indeed, recent research has shown that the introduction of extrinsic (i.e., market-based) incentives may crowd out voluntary intrinsic activities by rewarding only those actions that occur within the market logic. This is doubly problematic when the market "solution" itself is highly suspect in its ability to deliver actual results, as is the case with offsetting. Spash notes that what we may see is an overall decrease in desired behaviours, rather than the reverse, as economists tend to argue (Spash 2010, 189).

In addition and relation to the problems outlined above, carbon offsetting ultimately represents the spatial displacement of responsibility for global warming mitigation from North to South. While even Northern leaders recognize that global warming originated as a result of Northern industrial development patterns and the extensive and intensive exploitation of the world's resources that accompanied such patterns, offsetting disavows this reality by sanctioning continued Northern profligacy of the mass consumerism of Northern citizens, whereby Southerners are now charged with cleaning up our mess. The result is to fortify the historic unequal relations of power between North and South, leading many to liken offsetting to "carbon colonialism" whereby the South's resources and peoples remain locked in a neocolonial pattern with the North (FERN 2000). In addition, a well-documented body of evidence is now emerging to reveal the extensive human rights abuses associated with various offsetting projects in the South. The most frequently cited examples have been the cases of poor and indigenous communities being forcibly removed from their lands to make way for tree plantations

(FERN 2000). It is also often the case that the benefits from offsetting projects are highly unevenly distributed among community members in the South, with participation in project-related decision-making monopolized by elite actors (Corbera, Kosoy, and Martínez Tuna 2007; Corbera, Brown, and Adger 2007; Lovell, Bulkeley, and Liverman 2009; Ervine 2010). Such examples contest the idea of a straightforward development dividend in relation to the offset, whether delivered through the voluntary market in carbon offsets or formal mechanisms such as the Kyoto Protocol's Clean Development Mechanism. Nevertheless, it is an idea that remains powerfully embedded within a post-colonial imaginary that today, as in the past, continues to cast the Northerner in the role of benevolent saviour, saving the South through his or her superior knowledge and altruistic intent.

In the last instance, any genuine attempt to address the global warming crisis will require meaningful action rooted not in displacement and loopholes but in a fundamental redefinition of modernity that accepts that "mastery is impossible" (Latour 2003). With the tools of modernity – capitalism and techno-science – thus destabilized, it might then be possible to identify our dystopian present as in part a product of our structural past. More than this, we may be prompted to confront the painful reality that maybe we're just duping ourselves, that offsetting represents nothing more than fool's gold – flashy and shiny but ultimately worthless. Nevertheless, this chapter has also demonstrated that the myriad impulses wrapped up in our collective denial – fear, self-gratification, pleasure – are sufficiently powerful that we may very well continue to repress the cognitive dissonance produced by the offset. So long as eco-icons such as Al Gore persist in peddling the fantasy that modernity's failings are but minor aberrations to an otherwise desirable and stable system, we will continue to evoke his image as a substitute for avowal. In this case, we may be left polishing our gold until its veneer fades away, and with it the time required to make the necessary changes. Time will tell.

NOTES

1 A Malthusian understanding of environmental crises identifies human population growth as primarily responsible for resource depletion and ecological degradation. In contrast, more critically oriented perspectives foreground the unequal distribution of power (economic, political, etc.),

globally and within nation states, as the primary factor responsible for environmental decline (See Peluso and Watts 2001).

2 The Global Footprint Network provides comparative global data on the ecological footprint of various nations. According to its website, an ecological footprint represents a measurement of "how much land and water area a human population requires to produce the resources it consumes and to absorb its carbon dioxide emissions, using prevailing technology." Based on this measurement, in 2007 the average American citizen required 8 hectares per person, the average Canadian citizen 7 hectares per person, while citizens in China and India needed only 2.2 and 0.9 hectares respectively (Global Footprint Network 2007).

3 According to the TVA website: "Once electricity from renewable sources enters the grid, it mixes with, and is indistinguishable from, electricity from conventional resources. Because electricity is all the same, it is impossible to know if the electricity you are using comes from 'green' electricity sources or 'brown' electricity sources." The site goes on to suggest that the increased use and thus supply of green sources will, however, allow for the displacement of brown sources out of the power grid (Tennessee Valley Authority 2011). The argument certainly can be made that the adoption of modest lifestyles could do more to displace brown sources from the energy grid than after-the-fact solutions.

4 Lovell, Bulkeley, and Liverman (2009) provide a detailed analysis of offset narratives, including that of "global-local connections" which is described here. This chapter borrows from the analysis developed by these authors in their piece.

5

(Product) RED: Glam Aid, Consumer Citizens, and the Colonization of Governance

COLLEEN O'MANIQUE AND MOMIN RAHMAN

(RED) was created by Bono and Bobby Shriver to help eliminate AIDS in Africa by teaming up with the world's most iconic brands to produce (PRODUCT) RED branded products. Each time someone buys a (PRODUCT) RED product, up to 50% of the profit goes to the Global Fund, which provides funding to specific African AIDS programs in a handful of countries based on proven results. Since its launch in March 2006, (RED) partners have generated more than any other cause-related marketing campaign: $110 million for the Global Fund. Over twenty brands now participate in this initiative including Motorola, American Express, Gap, Emporio Armani, Converse, Apple, Hallmark, Dell, Microsoft Windows, and Girl Skateboard Company.

www.bobbyshriver.com

Launched at the 2006 World Economic Forum, the (Product) RED campaign encourages corporations to brand specific goods as AIDS charity commodities.[1] Participating companies purchase a license to produce (RED) branded goods and a portion of the profits from their sale are channelled to the Global Fund to Fight AIDS, Tuberculosis, and Malaria (Global Fund). The initiative was conceived and promoted as both a tremendous marketing opportunity for the companies involved and as a simple mechanism through which Western consumers can help resolve one of the worst humanitarian crises in human history.[2]

Most analyses frame the (RED) campaign as a strategy of broadening corporate social responsibility (CSR) (Richey and Ponte 2011) that departs from the direct emphasis on purchasing specific ethically produced products such as green and fair trade goods.[3] This broadening out of the strategy – its decoupling from specific products – is seen as a significant shift, and we concur with such analyses. In this chapter, however, we adopt a wider lens than previous commentaries by arguing that we must understand this shift in corporate strategy as reflective of the broader sociological formation of neoliberal societies. We pay specific attention to the ways in which (RED) constructs the AIDS crisis and how the identified shift in corporate social responsibility strategies – including the increasing use of celebrity icons – derives from and contributes to neoliberal social formation. We argue that campaigns such as (RED) can do more harm than good by their individualization of social justice activities, which in turn legitimizes the contemporary socio-political order that renders invisible both the inequalities of advanced capitalism and the need for collective and democratically agreed-upon responses.

In developing our argument, we begin with a brief description of the justification of the irritatingly parenthesized (RED) business model – the brackets symbolize an embrace of suffering Africans. The common framework justifying (RED) tends to acknowledge some of the shortcomings while at the same time defending it for having the potential to raise political awareness and provide extra funds for antiretroviral drugs (ARVs) that would otherwise not have materialized. (RED) emerges as a "pragmatic" solution that is saving lives, superior in many ways to traditional bureaucratic political realms where politicians merely blow hot air while accomplishing very little (Youde 2009). The role of celebrity icons has been an important factor in promoting this alternative solution as pragmatic, meaningful, simple, and above all, effective; previous critiques illustrate the ways in which particular "aid celebrities" garner attention for the campaign and thus legitimize the premise of (RED) (Littler 2008; Richey and Ponte 2011; Goodman and Barnes 2011).

Challenging this approach in the following sections, we suggest that a critical understanding of (RED) is furthered by a wider appreciation of how celebrity culture serves the current capitalist order. Celebrity endorsement of (RED) is first and foremost a conventional method of enhancing celebrity power and particularly their power to model consumption. This overriding function produces tensions in how celebrity-commodity culture operates in the service of such cause-related branding, suggesting both a lack of durability to (RED) as a brand and a lack of potential for serious political awareness and engagement in consumers. We consider the broader social formation that has made consumption into the dominant form of citizenship in neoliberal societies, reflecting a shift in governance away from social citizenship, secured and supported by the state, to market citizenship, where citizens become responsible for helping themselves in a more privatized social order (Bakker and Gill 2003). It is this foundation of individualized consumerist participation in the social order that explains the successful resonance of campaigns like (RED). In the final section, we conclude that (RED) is not simply about the branding of international aid, specific products, or particular celebrity icons. Rather, it contributes to the colonization of democratic governance by business by both privileging consumer identity and rendering collective politics inefficient in comparison to the market. Even if we do not see much (RED) in the future, the work of depoliticization will have been significantly furthered by its existence; consumers will have moved onto the next trendy philanthropic business campaign addressing the next global emergency, while the democratic space available in the social will have shrunk even further.

The Business Model of Philanthropy as "Pragmatic"

When U.S. Treasury Secretary Bob Rubin told us we "had to be like Nike" to really tell our story, I got a little depressed. Through DATA, we had been doing well working the policy ideas in DC and getting the occasional mention in the *New York Times*, but millions of Americans would not be convinced to help Africa without a story-telling offensive, similar to the one Nike waged via their 365-day-a-year advertising.

There just seemed to be no way we could become as experienced as Nike or have its marketing budget. Then someone suggested we get Nike to "be like us" – a little arrogant, but the right idea! (RED) came from this idea. It shows that a simple challenge can make big things happen. We owe Mr. Rubin for challenging us.

http://www.bobbyshriver.com/red.php

CEO Bobby Shriver thus explains the inspiration behind (RED) on his website, both the narrative requirements of branding their cause and the idea to license charitable donations as commodity products. (RED) has received extensive media coverage and endorsement from an "A" list of celebrities that includes Oprah Winfrey, Elle Macpherson, Scarlett Johansson, and Penelope Cruz, and it was featured in the rebranding of Africa in the July 2007 special "Africa Issue" of *Vanity Fair*, guest edited by Bono. The intent of the issue was to raise the profile of Africa in the eyes of the Western public and to demonstrate values of justice, freedom, and equality "through pharmacology, agro-ecology and technological help for those in extreme circumstances, in their hour of need" (Bono 2007, 32). A number of politicians, super-philanthropists, and celebrities all "passionate about Africa" adorn 20 historic cover photographs.[4] The business model that was being launched is indeed new and simple. Corporations pay a licensing fee to label one or more of their products (RED), marketing specifically to consumers with a social conscience. (RED) advertises that up to 50 per cent of gross profits from a (RED) branded product go to the Global Fund, although for some products the contribution is as low as 5 per cent, and (RED) does not disclose the total contributions of all participating corporations or products. As of May 2011, (RED) has channelled $170 million to the Global Fund out of a total of $13 billion, for projects in Rwanda, Swaziland, Ghana, Lesotho, Zambia, and South Africa.[5]

(RED) is not the first business response to HIV and AIDS in Africa. Corporations with business interests in Southern Africa including Anglo American, De Beers, and Coca-Cola began providing ARVs to certain employees as early as the late 1990s (Daly 2000), while pharmaceutical companies have been involved in drug donations and have supported various projects to strengthen community responses as part of their corporate philanthropy (O'Manique 2004). (RED), however, brings together corporations without a direct stake in the pandemic, whose bottom lines, workforces, or corporate images are not necessarily "at risk," signifying what Richey and Ponte describe as a new, disengaged form of corporate social responsibility (2011).

Thus, corporations benefit from being branded as socially conscious, which should increase overall profitability (Alcañiz et al. 2010; Wymer 2006), while Western consumers get products that construct them as compassionate global citizens, and Africans get the medicines that they need to stay alive. According to *New York Times* columnist Ron Nixon (2008), (RED) "has become one of the largest consumer-based income generating initiatives by the private sector for an international humanitarian cause." The many proponents of (RED) view the innovative business model as effective and sustainable, and (RED)'s critics have been accused of missing the point: it saves lives, measured by the number of African people who are the recipients of ARVs via the (RED) campaign (Olatunbosun-Alakija 2008; O'Manique and Labonte 2008a, 2008b; Youde 2009). Dr Richard Feachem, executive director of the Global Fund, endorses the business strategy on the (RED) website as a means of making "socially responsible consumption" appealing to both consumers and profitable to companies, and hence "pioneering a sustainable model for the involvement of the private sector in the fight against disease and poverty." In these welcoming views, it becomes irrelevant, for example, that in the first year of its roll-out, (RED) raised $18 million for the Global Fund, while estimated spending on advertising (RED) was approximately $100 million.[6] The idea behind (RED) is that both the corporations *and* the Global Fund benefit through the marketing of (RED) products.

The distinctiveness of the campaign is that the sustainability of the philanthropic model is predicated on higher profits for the participating corporations that result from everyday, "normal" purchasing, with (RED) promotional discourses explicitly framing it as *not* charity (Richey and Ponte 2011; Youde 2009) and privileging the relationships with its merchant partners (Wirgau et al. 2010). The motive is profit first and charity as a by-product of profit, rather than a traditional understanding of charity as a moral choice outside considerations of profit. The criticisms of the model have been widespread in both public and academic discourse and are manifested in three main arguments: (RED) renders invisible the current global economic and trade regime that has produced many of the structural conditions for both the divisions between North and South and the unfolding of the current HIV/AIDS pandemic; this complexity is replaced by a simplistic consumer strategy and an equally simple (and racist) imaginary of "African AIDS" and the HIV/AIDS pandemic; this strategy ultimately privileges private, corporate actors and solutions as opposed to democratically accountable political organizations.[7] In his assessment, Youde acknowledges the validity of such arguments, but he remains positive on (RED), arguing that it should be understood as a "pragmatic" response that also has the potential for politicization of consumers, citing previous examples of consumer boycotts (also a "market strategy") and their consciousness-raising effects (Youde 2009).

We are sceptical that there may be potential for such consequences. There is as yet little evidence from marketing or political research to support such claims on (RED),[8] and there is some evidence on cause-related marketing that suggests a cynicism in consumers (Samman et al. 2009). But more significantly, the supporters of (RED) implicitly downplay the importance of its negative effects with regard to its role in the discursive and political struggle of neoliberal globalization. While almost one-half of the world's inhabitants – over three billion people – live on less than US$2.50 a day and the world's richest one-fifth consume almost 80 per cent of the world's resources (Shah 2010), (RED) serves to obscure the connection between global capitalism and the West's over-consumption and the huge disparities in health and life chances that (RED) claims to be helping to resolve.

It is this level of the cultural and ideological that is critical, precisely because (RED) both is a reflection of social structures and actively contributes to sustaining and transforming them. If (RED) is a new form of philanthropy, then it tells us something about the neoliberal social formation that makes it possible. (RED) provides an exemplar of how contemporary neoliberal political discourses of the limited state and the expansive business sector are legitimized through the sociological culture of the times. The decline of public and state provision and private charitable actions for their own sake are the result of changes in the social, ideological, and political shape of late capitalist societies that have provided for the emergence of particular "aid celebrities" working in conjunction with new CSR strategies and a climate of "socially engaged" consumers. It may be that (RED) is indeed the latest manifestation of CSR strategies (Littler 2008; Richey and Ponte 2011), but this would not be possible unless put forward in a culture that already emphasizes consumption as the major form of identity formation and has produced a governance crisis which is far broader than the delegitimization of international aid. We turn to a critical assessment of celebrity within such campaigns with a focus on its role in commodity and consumer culture.

From Glam Aid to Consumer Identities

The celebrity-philanthropist-political alliance has been a central feature of the (RED) campaign. (RED) deploys celebrities in full measure, as in the initial wave of promotion such as the July 2007 edition of *Vanity Fair*, published with 20 different versions of the cover, shot by celebrity photographer Annie Leibovitz. Each shows a celebrity and a politician "having a 'conversation' about Africa. 'It's a visual chain letter,' says Leibovitz, 'spreading the message from person to person to person.'"[9] The politicians were shown with many popular celebrities from the entertainment world, from actors to rap stars, and also well-known business billionaire philanthropists Bill Gates and Warren Buffet. While the mix plays to (RED)'s originality in combining business with charity and politics, we should not forget that the inclusion of entertainment celebrities is important as a way of gaining attention (celebrities sell magazines after all) and of converting that attention into action – in this case, consumption of products. The various corporations producing these branded goods have used actors and supermodels in their individual advertising campaigns, as well as in videos promoting the business model itself. And why not? If this modelling of lifestyle provokes a compassionate form of consumption, then perhaps we are bending capitalism towards social justice in some small measure as part of the expanding business strategy of corporate philanthropy, as Youde suggests (2009).

We must remember, however, that celebrity philanthropy primarily serves the needs of celebrities' cultural standing because creating and maintaining these reputations is central to their success as celebrities (Turner 2004; Littler 2008). Moreover, it is the reach and integrity of these cultural meanings that provokes consumption, both of the celebrities as media commodities and of the range of lifestyle products that they endorse, such as those branded in the (RED) campaign. Furthermore, celebrity endorsement of the campaign and the products, in alliance with important political figures, may help to gain attention but it also helps to legitimize this equation of consumer activity with action to achieve social justice. Indeed, it may be that the shift effects a combination of the pleasure of consumerism with social activism, so that social justice becomes both "simple" and "pleasurable." It is of course important to understand the role of particular celebrity icons in raising the profile of charity campaigns as previous analyses have done (Littler 2008; Magubane 2008; Richey and Ponte 2008, 2011), but when that campaign is predicated on commodity culture, it is also critical to understand the role of celebrity in general within that culture over and above the legitimizing role of particular celebrity icons such as Bono.[10]

As many social theorists have pointed out, in late capitalist modernity, consumption has replaced other anchors to social identity and strategies for defining our selves (Bauman 2001, 2007; Giddens 1991). Lifestyle consumption becomes the major form of self-definition in late capitalism and the expansion of celebrity culture in the mass media age has converged and concurred with the expansion of the consumer society (Marshall 1997; Rojek 2001). Celebrity functions as a "pedagogical tool": "Celebrity taught generations how to engage and use consumer culture to 'make' oneself" (Marshall 2010, 36). Given that the very discourse of celebrity branding that the mass audience is immersed within clearly serves commodity culture, we are deeply sceptical whether the emphasis on (RED) can really become activism over consumption. The rising tide of cause-related and ethical consumption is more likely to reinforce the principle of consumption over and above ethics or social justice. Richey and Ponte describe (RED) as an example of "Brand Aid" and identify the duality in this new strategy – help for corporate brands and the rebranding international aid (2011, 10). Campaigns like (RED) are fundamentally dependent on the central role of consumption in the "making of the self" and hence they must be understood as privileging the icon of the consumer: "glam aid" to the self as well as "brand aid" to corporations and development policies.

We also suggest that the dynamic force of consumer and celebrity culture further undermines the potential for a cause to be privileged over the consumer. The momentum of consumption and celebrity is fundamentally about *novelty* rather than sustained focus or attention. There has been an acceleration of mediatization, driven by changes in information technologies, which have transformed commodities (including the celebrity-commodity) into cultural symbols or signs for particular styles of life and identities (Bauman 2007; Rojek 2001), most thoroughly theorized by Baudrillard's work on the consumer society and its dependence on media technologies of promotion (Poster 2001). An inevitable consequence is therefore that novelty trumps durability: "Baudrillard depicts the contemporary capitalist body politics as hyper kinetic. Everything tingles, radiates, reverberates. All is in flux, everything is reflected or refracted through various media, speed is hypnotic, there is a carnival of hyperreal appearances, an appetite for excitement" (Porter 1993, 5). As Bono says: "Product (RED) piggybacks the excitement and energy of the commercial world to buy lifesaving AIDS drugs for Africans who cannot afford them" (Bono 2007, 32), but this "excitement and energy" comes from the mediatized "hyperkinetic" circulation of commodities as lifestyle images. And, commodities – like celebrity – are often short-lived. Most of the production systems behind celebrities are attempts to first create novelty that garners attention, and then to switch strategies to transform novelty into a durable celebrity-commodity (Turner 2004, 33). Similarly, with successful brands there are constant attempts to produce new and exciting iterations of both the brand and specific new products in order to sustain their attraction to consumers. In this culture, can (RED) really sustain any focus on its individual commodities, or its overall message and brand? Of course, new celebrities can be used to endorse products, and new product lines can be added, providing some novelty or excitement, but can the excitement of the brand as a new form of social activism really survive its normalization? Can (RED) remain "cool" enough to sustain its contributions over the long term? Recent research supports this scepticism. A survey by Samman et al. demonstrates that while respondents could easily identify celebrities associated with international development work (with (RED)'s progenitor Bono named most frequently), their ability to connect them to a specific cause was much more limited and often imprecise (2009). Moreover, the audience/consumers in this survey demonstrated some cynicism about celebrity endorsement of charity, with Bono in particular being singled out as primarily motivated by self-promotion, regardless of the fact that he was also (rather mistakenly, in many critics' minds) taken to be knowledgeable about international development. We need more evidence on how consumers respond to such cause-related branding but we question whether the sociocultural contexts that structure celebrity and consumption are in fact dialectically opposed to attempts to incorporate effective charity into capitalism. It may be that, after all, campaigns like (RED) may not have staying power precisely because of their business and promotional model.

The Individual Consumer Citizen as Neoliberal Icon

In promoting (RED) through the individualized discourse of celebrity/commodity pedagogy, we are reinforcing the fact that "the individual continues to represent the ideological center of capitalist culture" (Marshall 1997, 17). Of course, in all forms of consumption, a mass response is the most desired, but in fact, promotional techniques focus on interpellating individuality. This apparent tension is actually central to the consumption relationship; we are both individuals and part of a collective. In this vein, it may be that the individual consumers of (RED) products experience their consumption as political engagement, both as individuals and as part of a broader humanitarian project as Youde suggests they will (2009). Nonetheless, there is yet little evidence to convince us that this would also provoke a desire to become overtly politically engaged as opposed to participating in other forms of individual action, apart, perhaps, from further "compassionate" purchasing.

The individual effects of purchasing (RED) goods are, cumulatively, to create profits for corporations as a primary outcome. The happy consequence of providing money for the Global Fund is also a direct result, but it is a secondary outcome of the act of consumption and not only does this privilege consumption over charity but, moreover, in doing so it actually subsumes the latter under the former. Historically, charitable "good works" have been part and parcel of the secularized work ethic that provided the impetus to the development of modern rational capitalism (Weber 2002). Celebrity culture has also mirrored this relationship and in this mode, two related outcomes are achieved through celebrity philanthropy: a cause will receive extra publicity and the celebrity will add another positive dimension to their symbolic capital, enhancing their own value as a commodity (Littler 2008, 241). Thus, celebrity *noblesse oblige* modelled the ethical idea that we, as individuals, should reinvest in the social rather than simply indulge ourselves. The rise of cause-related marketing by corporations and charity campaigns such as (RED) essentially merges this supra-market charitable aspect of the traditional work ethic with the function of celebrity commodity branding. When these are merged, the separation between work and charity ethic of the capitalist spirit is transformed with the previous moral obligation of charity now brought into the accumulation ethos, indeed legitimizing the hedonistic potential of consumer power over and above charitable impulses. (RED) therefore assists in the larger project of colonization of the individual by neoliberalism by reinforcing the constitution of the self as a consumer citizen, devoid of charitable actions conceived *outside* our market existence.

Moreover, the individualist interpellation that is central to "narcissistic" commodity culture makes more extended forms of collective political action difficult to envisage as a consequence of (RED). While acknowledging that the ideology of neoliberalism has been embraced unevenly, and even resisted in some spaces, one cannot discount the profound effect that it has had on, in Harvey's words, "capturing the ideals of individual freedom and turning them against the interventionist and the regulatory practices of the state ... Neoliberalism required both politically and economically the construction of a neo-liberal market-based culture of differentiated consumerism and individual libertarianism" and essentially the promotion of the narcissistic exploration of the self as central to culture (2005, 42–6). The socio-economic system is legitimized through cause-related marketing, and our engagement with it is framed in the language of individualism, and hence, our "compassionate" consumption is also reduced to individual consumer actions, as opposed to collective political activities. Today, our purchase of *Campbell's V8* will contribute to fighting heart disease in women; a *Wacoal* bra will help end breast cancer; and the "simple act of kindness" of a *McDonald's* Happy Meal will support Ronald McDonald House. What need, then, is there for "old style" political engagement? It is not simply a question of whether shopping becomes the alternative to collective strategies for an increased aid budget, or for a more just and transparent global financial and trade system, or for mandatory and enforceable codes of corporate conduct; rather, the consumption model renders more direct forms of politics illegitimate and ineffective. Many Western governments have already adopted consumer models for public services since the 1980s as part of the neoliberal project, and while these were framed as attempts to provide efficiency in service delivery and choice, they have also had the consequence of delegitimizing state and collective provision and encouraging the notion of citizenship as a market relationship (Hugman 1994; Walsh 1994).

The common-sense regulatory role of government is increasingly the creation and maintenance of the conditions for the accumulation of capital, as the previous domains of the state that worked to guarantee basic human security and the citizenship rights of people are weakened, are privatized, or disappear altogether. Four years since the global financial meltdown, banks and corporations are back to making mega-profits, while the costs of the crisis, and burden of debt, falls on ordinary people. An estimated $5 trillion was used to bail out the financial sector, and the crisis today is used as the justification to slash investments in health, education, employment, infrastructure, and social and environmental protections (George 2010). The multiple converging crises of wealth polarization, growing food insecurity, human-induced climate change, the enclosure of the commons, and the erosion of democracy are seen as separate and distinct from 'The Economy,' which is understood in the popular vernacular as apolitical. Private economic interests shape the rules and roles of national and global governance through the increasingly powerful influence of capital and the convergence of economic norms and state practices such as the privatization of state services and the redefining of the nature of citizenship (Brysk 2005, 18–19). Susan George states: "The ordinary person, once, but no longer considered a 'citizen' – how quaint! – is simultaneously reduced to the status of consumer" (George 2010, 21). More and more, ordinary people feel powerless, with little democratic control over the conditions of their lives. (RED) both privatizes while creating an illusory democratization of development practice. Where the state has failed, *you* can make a difference! (RED) serves as a palliative to the circulating anxiety and sense of powerlessness that accompanies the rising democratic deficit within mainstream political institutions. The "just consumer" supplants the "just citizen," and social justice itself is a commodity (O'Manique and Labonte 2008a, 2008b).

Within the trend towards the increased power and authority of individuals and private foundations to shape governance structures, (RED), then, can be viewed as a spoke in the wheel. As Christopher Caldwell writes in the *Financial Times*: "philanthropy is the route through which celebrity can be laundered into political power. It is also one means by which the responsibility for important tasks is being reassigned from democratic structures to less democratic ones" (Caldwell 2007). The point is therefore not just about seeing (RED) as just a pragmatic business model in the context of an imperfect world, but seeing it as a wider system of colonizing governance that contributes to shaping the nature of citizenship.

(Not Seeing) RED: Colonizing Governance

The overriding discourse of campaigns such as (RED), then, makes it less likely that other forms of political engagement will be conceived outside of a consumerist/capitalist model, fundamentally colonizing the space of governance as a democratic space that is, on principle, outside the market. Not only is this achieved by promoting the neoliberal idea of the citizen consumer, as argued above, but we are also seeing the symbiotic delegitimization of collective political institutions. The influence of foundations, philanthropists, and the super rich in shaping global public-health priorities and perspectives has been rising gradually, in line with the movement away from collective and state responsibility for the protection of social rights and the provision of social goods (People's Health Movement et al. 2008). The increasing influence of private actors has also been secured within UN decision-making circles through private-public partnerships (O'Manique 2004, 54–5) and the growing power of philanthrocapitalists (as discussed in Fridell and Koning's introduction to this book). The Bill and Melinda Gates Foundation, with an annual budget exceeding that of the WHO, is perhaps the most powerful of a growing number of private actors shaping the global health-policy agenda, who offer technocratic solutions and a particular form of neoliberal rationality – a firm belief in market solutions to global health problems, top-down, vertical approaches to specific diseases, and magic bullets (People's Health Movement et al. 2008, 256), a process that began in the early 1990s with IMF/World Bank Structural Adjustment Programs. The World Bank's health

strategy was a key instrument in aligning health policy in African countries to the neoliberal canon, ascribing health mainly to the private domain, through the introduction of market forces into the health sector,
and the allocation of resources based principally on technical efficiency
and cost effectiveness criteria (O'Manique 2004, 58).

(RED) can be seen as a further extension of this neoliberal rationality in its promotion of a technocratic and rationalistic understanding
of problems and solutions to HIV and AIDS, and in shaping priorities
for investments in health. While AIDS treatment has become one of
the most popular agendas for international donors, programs are often
skewed by the priorities of Western donors, who are attracted to technological quick-fixes with results that can be easily measured in quantifiable terms and are easy to market to their national constituencies.
In many places in Southern Africa, ARV provision is being scaled up
in the context of structural unemployment, increased privatization of or
the absence of broader public-health systems and social supports, and
the prevalence of a whole range of other chronic and infectious diseases
(Barnett and Whiteside 2002; Poku 2004; Fassin 2007; Garrett 2007).
(RED), however, is silent on the question as to why African's cannot afford ARVs or why the highest levels of HIV infection are found in sub-
Saharan Africa, constructing a very specific and simple representation
of HIV/AIDS in Africa to external audiences. The business model has
been legitimized through its endorsement by The United Nations Joint
Programme on HIV and AIDS (UNAIDS), the World Health Organization (WHO), other multilateral organizations, and *The Lancet* – the most
prestigious medical journal in the world – which, in its 5 August 2006
edition, branded itself (RED). In addition to donating $30,000 to the
cause, the issue advertised the new (RED) product line and encouraged
other businesses to join. The editor of *The Independent* makes the claim
that the constant exposure to the (RED) message that "6,500 Africans
died needlessly yesterday of a preventable and treatable disease" has
been instrumental to increasing the pressure on the U.S. government to
ramp up its HIV/AIDS strategy (Valelly 2007). Many of (RED)'s critics
do not dispute that ARV scale up is a critically important component
of the institutional response to the pandemic; their concern is with this
particular telling of the story of AIDS in Africa, in which HIV is ravag-
ing Africa *because* of a lack of medicines. As Barnes explains: "the HI
virus spreads and proliferates and AIDS kills because of the diseased
relationships of the social body," while ARVs only address the narrow
biomedical aspects of the virus (2008, 78).

If one begins to entertain the notion that the current plight of the people who are dying of AIDS in Africa (and elsewhere) is due to a very long chain of complex historical processes, the RED claim for easy change becomes more far fetched. On a planet drowning in waste and pollution, for instance, will weaning Americans from their gas guzzlers, fast food and the frenzied pursuit of fad/fashion/fetish in all things be easy? No. Will putting the voices, bodies and needs of their poorest citizens – rural women and children – at the top of the agenda of African governments be easy? No. Will reversing the tides of centuries of economic and social marginalization be easy? No. (Barnes 2008, 75)

The current aid regime addressing the HIV/AIDS pandemic is disconnected from the socio-economic, geopolitical, and environmental conditions that shape huge disparities in health and life chances, risk, and resilience. Ponte and Richey describe (RED) as a form of disengaged corporate social responsibility "completely separated, with some exceptions, from the operations in which these corporations are involved" (Richey and Ponte 2011, 147). So, for example, while the purchase of a (RED) iPod might channel $10 to the Global Fund, the indirect human and environmental costs of that same iPod – both the upstream and downstream environmental and human costs (the coltan mining,[11] the exploitation of low-wage labour embodied in its production and distribution) – might in fact negate any net benefit to human life. Indeed, the profitability that is central to the (RED) model is dependent on a global political economy hospitable to neoliberal rules, regulations, and standards. Corporations are a significant political force within the global governance regime with its lax labour, human rights, and environmental standards. Rowley states: "Philanthropic models such as (RED) are so deeply imbricated in neoliberal assumptions that consumption and poor health are rendered as discrete properties, rather than as phenomena that hold an obverse and occasionally parasitic relationship with each other (2011, 91).

(RED) is both symptom of and participant in the naturalization of neoliberal reforms and the normalization of the idea that they are, in fact, the only real options and solutions available today to the world's various crises. The legitimacy of neoliberal globalism is dependent upon the interpellation of subjects who buy (in the case of (RED), quite literally) into the market model, who see themselves as market citizens and assume that individual freedom is generated through the freedom of the market. In her discursive critique of (RED) Sarna-Wojcicki demonstrates how (RED) is marketed as a method of dissent through the "subversive, anti-establishment tone" of the brand, the depiction of shoppers as "agents of change" and as part of a community of first-world consumers – a community that does not include the African AIDS patient (2008, 28). (RED) redeploys the relationship between global capitalism, consumer identity, and charitable giving in ways that are deeply political in their normalization of unequal relations of power, through the deliberate erasure of the relationships between and among corporate power and profitability, Western (over)consumption, and the concrete, daily, lived realities of those living in poverty, with or without HIV infection.

Conclusion

We have argued for a broader analytical frame than has been evident in previous accounts of the (RED) phenomenon. Whilst we agree that the (RED) campaign is significant as a new form of corporate social re-sponsibility, we suggest that it is part and parcel of the entrenchment of a neoliberal momentum, and hence, not a "pragmatic" solution to the HIV/AIDS crisis in Africa. What little evidence there is on consumer responses indicates a reflexive cynicism about both CSR more gener-ally and aid-related celebrity more specifically. (RED) may therefore signify only a temporary and/or minor expansion of corporate social responsibility, while contributing to the widespread shift away from perceptions of the state as the guarantor of citizenship rights (including the rights to the basic constituents of health) towards the legitimacy of corporate power and market citizenship. (RED)'s incorporation of the charity ethic into accumulation strategies effects a rehabilitation of hedonism within the capitalist spirit, while simultaneously giving the illusion of the transformation of development practices into more ef-ficient modes through the involvement of corporations and business strategies. As Rowley states:

> Unless we connect the worlds of production and consumption, it be-comes too easy to individualize and commercialize responses to global inequity. Such policy solutions focus on the importance of individual "behavioural adjustments," whether on the part of the consumer to buy more "responsibly" or on the part of labouring bodies to work harder. This individualist logic masks the ways in which underdevelopment is historically and structurally determined; and, it further masks the ways in

which individual consumers in the North are implicated in the construction of the very inequity that their consumption is supposedly designed
to change. (2011, 95)

Marchand and Sisson Runyan remind us, however, that the current direction in which global governance is heading is not a forgone conclusion but
"an open ended process that creates myriad (re)interpretations and contradictions and counter-discourses and practices as activists and scholars continually expose the politics of globalization-cum-imperialism
and propose alternatives to it" (2011, 21). Resistance to the deeper
movement towards market citizenship and the celebrity-philanthropy-
state alliance in the governance of the life economy involves exposing
the collateral damage of business strategies like (RED). The parentheses
around RED symbolize an embrace, but it is not the claimed embrace
of our African brothers and sisters. The real embrace is of the Western
consumer, that necessary icon of contemporary neoliberal capitalism.

NOTES

1 (Product) RED was launched at the 2006 World Economic Forum in Davos,
   Switzerland, by Bono, the U2 rock-star celebrity and American politician
   Bobby Shriver, a member of the Kennedy family and established political
   activist, philanthropist, and businessman. Bono has long been identified
   with charity causes focused on Africa, co-founding with Shriver the organization DATA (Debt, AIDS, Trade in Africa) in 2002, which aims to raise
   awareness on these issues. (RED) is distinct because it is conceived of and
   explicitly marketed as a *business model* of charity, one that is "enlisting the
   private sector to eliminate AIDS in Africa" according to the website
   www.bobbyshriver.com.
2 Corporate philanthropy is an increasing part of business strategies in the
   twenty-first century and an increasing expectation on the part of consumers
   (Alcañiz et al. 2010). Wymer notes the billions donated by Fortune 100 companies in 2004: "Corporations that support popular social causes receive
   favourable publicity and favourable consumer responses ... Three general
   categories are: (a) corporate giving, (b) sponsorships, and (c) cause-related
   marketing" (Wymer 2006, 1). The last category is most relevant to our discussion of (RED) since it directly links donations to product sales, but (RED)
   is more expansive than most campaigns, involving a large range of corporations and products. Within this category, researchers in marketing identify

"fit" between the brand and the cause as important to consumers (Trimble and Rifon 2006; Zdravkovic et al. 2010), and again, this makes (RED) distinctive in its scale.

3 There is an emergent critical literature on the (RED) campaign (Littler 2008; O'Manique and Labonte 2008a, 2008b; Richey and Ponte 2008; Ponte et al. 2009; Wirgau et al. 2010; Youde 2009), including a special issue on (RED) published by *The Journal of Pan African Studies* (Vol. 2, 2008) that included many different initial critiques. Littler also focuses more broadly on the contradictions of ethical consumption (2009), something that Richey and Ponte take up in their study of the (RED) campaign, providing a thorough breakdown of its history, the role of "aid celebrities," and the rebranding of African AIDS as a distant problem (2011).

4 See Richey and Ponte (2011, 69) for their analysis of how the African victims are represented in this issue.

5 http://www.joinred.com/aboutred

6 See Nixon 2008.

7 See, for example, the critiques of (RED) from the 2008 Special Issue of the *Journal of Pan African Studies*, in addition to Hintzen 2008; Wirgau et al. 2010; Richey and Ponte 2011; and Rowley 2011.

8 It is simply too early to tell or nobody is interested in asking yet. We have found no comprehensive analysis on how consumers are actually reacting to the campaign.

9 For the covers and text, see http://www.vanityfair.com/politics/features/2007/07/onthecover_slideshow200707#intro. The notables gracing the covers were a mix of the political, business, and entertainment worlds: the then Senator Barack Obama; President Bush and Secretary of State Condoleezza Rice; Archbishop Desmond Tutu; Queen Rania of Jordan; Muhammad Ali; Maya Angelou; actors Don Cheadle, Brad Pitt, George Clooney, and Djimon Hounsou; pop-music stars Madonna, Jay-Z, Alicia Keys, and Bono; comedian Chris Rock; financier Warren Buffett; Bill and Melinda Gates (as heads of their charitable foundation); Oprah Winfrey; and former model Iman.

10 Richey and Ponte (2011) emphasize in their study the "aid celebrity" and how aid celebrities provide certain meanings that legitimize "Brand Aid." While they discuss consumer society in chapter 5 of their book, there is only brief mention of the role of celebrities rather than an integration of the role of celebrity culture within consumer culture (see pp. 156–9). They focus on "causumerism" or the rise of consumption related to causes.

11 According to Global Witness, for over a decade Western consumer demand for electronics – iPods, cell phones, computers – has spurred on warring

parties who have been plundering the mineral resources of the region, including soldiers from the Congolese National Army, who "have carried out the most horrific human rights abuses, including widespread killings of unarmed civilians, rape, torture and looting, recruitment of child soldiers in their ranks, and forced displacement of hundreds and thousands of people" (Global Witness 2009).

6

Cosmopolitanism Reinvented: Neoliberal Globalization and Thomas Friedman

FEYZI BABAN

Best known for his journalism, Thomas Friedman writes an influential foreign-affairs column for the *New York Times*. Although he lacks the fame and glamour of some of the contemporary icons such as Bono or Oprah, Friedman's "expertise" on globalization has elevated him to the status of an intellectual celebrity. His two books, *Lexus and The Olive Tree* and *The World Is Flat*, became instant successes in the popular-book universe, now overcrowded with books explaining globalization to ordinary readers. His account of globalization, which provides as enthusiastic endorsement of liberal, free-market capitalism and its penetration into every corner of the world, extends far beyond that of journalistic observation of this important phenomenon. More importantly, while not the most comprehensive of books nor certainly among the most well written or well researched on globalization, Friedman's books gained an iconic status as "must read" works on globalization. Friedman's intellectual fame is not limited to his books on globalization or his column in the *New York Times* but spans from his close relationship to influential business leaders to his close relationship to politicians. In fact, what makes his writing so influential is his close proximity to the centres of power. He ranks 32 in *Harvard Business Review*'s list of "The 50 Most Influential Management Gurus," plays golf with Obama, and advises him on the Arab Spring. He is a regular participant of the World Economic Forum where he communicates his ideas to the wealthy and powerful. He reportedly presented sections of his book *The World Is Flat* to IBM's strategic planning unit and spends time with high-powered CEOs of major corporations to explain his theory of globalization. As a result, his ideas find a hospitable place in the mainstream media and speaker's circuit and have played an important role in shaping globalization debates. Perhaps, the extent of his celebrity status with respect to debates on globalization can be seen by the fact that a simple search on Google of the phrase "Friedman and globalization" brings up over six million hits.

In this chapter I argue that the significance and success of Friedman's account of globalization cannot be attributed to its intellectual quality but rather to its overzealous and skilful defence of neoliberal globalization. Žižek describes Friedman as a court philosopher, whose role is to make a case for the new world of global capitalism, a world that is dominated by "liberal communists" such as Bill Gates, George Soros, and CEOs of digital companies (Žižek 2008, 15). While these "liberal communists" give capitalism a new "human face," iconic figures like Friedman provide the ideological groundwork for representing global capitalism as the most humane economic system. As Fernandez argues in a recent book, Friedman's work plays a crucial role in articulating the ideological contours of global capital and masking its inherent power structures (Fernandez 2011). He does an excellent job, in fact, of painting this new world of capitalism as one which is anti-hierarchical, tearing down existing barriers in order to further human freedom. Forget about the capitalism of the past, in which big bloated companies stifled creation and innovation, and forget about the state that chains people everywhere with its overgrown and oppressive bureaucracy. This new world of globalization, according to Friedman, is all about empowering ordinary people everywhere, irrespective of race, nationality, and religion. As Žižek points out, it is no longer possible to differentiate between the slogans of the left and this new form of global capitalism, as it seems that this newly emerging global capitalism is more revolutionary than the left revolutionaries ever were. Friedman occupies a special place in this world of revolutionary capitalism, as he is certainly one of the most skilful popular writers to represent this deeply ideological world view as simply a matter of factual reality and to construct this narrative of contemporary capitalism as one that is friendly to ordinary people.

Friedman's account of globalization is a comforting experience in that, in a rather accessible style, he unravels the complexities of globalization, outlines its underlying forces, explains its contradictory developments, and of course, tells us what we need to do to survive in this world. It does not matter whether you live in New York, Bombay, Lima, Berlin, or Istanbul. What Friedman tells us is applicable regardless of where you live; it is all about integration. Well, perhaps it is not so applicable if you live in Chiapas, sub-Saharan Africa, or Gaza, but

Friedman will be quick to remind you that you are going against the tide of unstoppable change. So, it is your fault that you are not enjoying the benefits of globalization. It is unfortunate that the recent financial crisis cast a doubt on his rather optimistic account of global forces, especially "the electronic herd" shaping our lives for the better. Friedman's rendition of globalization is a powerful attempt to reincarnate an old fashion liberal cosmopolitanism that, in the seventeenth century, sought to unite humanity around a single cultural framework. Discredited in the wake of decolonization after the Second World War, the rise of globalization has provided a new impetus to this form of cosmopolitanism. In this chapter I also argue that Friedman's work presents a picture of a new form of liberal cosmopolitanism that elevates the very particular world view of neoliberal capitalism to a universal moment that unites and benefits humanity irrespective of the individuals' location within the overall hierarchy of capitalism. Furthermore, similar to the previous version of liberal cosmopolitanism, Friedman's account of globalization poses a false dichotomy between the universal and the particular in which the particular must either be absorbed by the universal moment of global capitalism or erased by it. In the following section I provide a quick overview of this particular cosmopolitan outlook. The article then concentrates on Friedman's account of globalization as a specific articulation of this cosmopolitanism. The final section focuses on the significance of Friedman's work in attempting to establish a hegemonic representation of globalization as the representative of a specific liberal world view.

Cosmopolitanism Revisited

Ever since stoics in ancient Greece contemplated the idea of uniting humanity by moving away from one's own particular attachment to culture, cosmopolitanism has become a powerful ideal with the potential to facilitate greater understanding and solidarity among human beings (Fine 2007, 105). However, cosmopolitanism also always generates a strong reaction as it poses a hard to resolve dilemma: how does one give his/her first allegiance to humanity and be loyal to his/her immediate cultural community? Cultural attachment provides individuals with a sense of anchoring and belonging that enables them to make sense of a complex set of meanings. Abandoning such a sense of anchoring can be a deeply discomforting thought for many who believe that making sense of this world, and feeling secure in it, requires being embedded in a certain cultural framework (Walzer 1996). This is why many approach cosmopolitanism with scepticism. Worse, cosmopolitanism has a history of being associated with imperialism and colonial thought that has, historically, attempted to create "civilized" subjects out of "savages" (Young 2001). This association is not accidental but coincides with the re-emergence of specific form of liberal cosmopolitan thinking during enlightenment. Like stoics, enlightenment thinkers were interested in establishing a universal reference around which humanity could converge (Hill 2000). Again, in similar fashion, while searching for a universal medium, enlightenment thinkers concluded that particularity, in the form of cultural attachment, was what prevented human beings from uniting around a common reference point. For instance, while devoting a significant portion of his theorizing towards developing a cosmopolitanism that would promote peace and stability around the world, Immanuel Kant's own assessments of other cultures were full of prejudices (Harvey 2000). How can we explain such contradiction in a thought, which manifests itself as cosmopolitan while at the same time displays blatant ignorance towards other cultures?

Perhaps this is not so much of a contradiction but an inherent failure in cosmopolitanism, which sees cultural attachment and particularity as an impediment to the greater unification of humanity. Traditional liberal cosmopolitan thinking assumes that we can overcome our differences, conflicts, and misunderstandings if we can only shed our attachment to our cultural belongings, ethnic affiliations, religious beliefs, or national identities. The enlightenment version of this cosmopolitanism invested heavily in the teleology of reason as the engine of human progress, which would deliver human societies from the clutches of tradition and other particular cultural attachments. Some cultures, sooner, and others, later, would evolve towards the civilizing mission of reason as the universal reference point for humanity. However, the universality of reason was nothing but a false assumption as the logic of reason formulated by enlightenment thinkers was a culturally specific manifestation of reason as materialized in seventeenth-century Europe. What is evident in the teleological understanding of reason illustrated within enlightenment thinking is the elevation of one particularity to the status of universal as a way of uniting all other cultures (Laclau 1995).

The privileged and ahistorical representation of reason as the main carrier of human progress in modern liberal cosmopolitan thinking had a devastating impact on the understanding of difference and marginality. This rather problematic understanding of reason created a false dichotomy between the universal and particular, one in which the relationship between the two can only be understood in conflictual terms (MacIntyre 1988). As a result, colonialism identified its main missions as a need to bring a civilizing voice of reason to those who had failed to develop it by themselves and a need to control and govern these people until they had adopted to the universal logic of reason. It may sound somewhat unreasonable to link cosmopolitanism with colonialism, but unfortunately the road from a colonial attitude to uncritical cosmopolitan thinking is a rather short one if one does not pay attention to the underlying assumptions informing traditional cosmopolitan thinking: a teleological understanding of history, a belief in the existence of a hierarchical relationship between the universal and the particular, and the false choice between cultural attachment and human solidarity.

Decolonization, which gained impetus after the Second World War, further contributed to the demise of this particular cosmopolitan thinking as colonized people around the world quickly realized the false universality informing the civilizing mission of colonialism. The problematic history of cosmopolitanism and its association with universalization convinced many that it was time to dispense with this idea, which was believed to be beyond rehabilitation. I have argued elsewhere that while cosmopolitanism has a problematic history, the cosmopolitan ideal itself has a critical value as a way of thinking about solidarity among human beings (Baban 2006). As Nussbaum (1996) has argued, as a form of allegiance to humanity, cosmopolitanism is a noble cause and reminds us that there are some fundamental values and qualities that connect us together despite our visible differences (Nussbaum 1996). While it may be a worthy cause to rethink the cosmopolitan ideal in a global world, in which cultural difference and multiplicity are fundamental conditions of human existence, such an endeavour has a twofold challenge: first, the challenge of formulating a cosmopolitan ideal that does not require giving up cultural differences to show solidarity with the rest of humanity and, second, avoiding the reproduction of new forms of cosmopolitanism that repeat the problematic logic of early modern cosmopolitan thinking. To discuss the first challenge is beyond the scope of this chapter, and there is, in fact, a growing body of literature that addresses this challenge by attempting to rethink cosmopolitanism from below as a lived experience rather than as a purely theoretical enterprise (Appiah 2006; Diouf 2000;

Hiebert 2002; Szerszynski and Urry 2002; Zubaida 2002). Unfortunately, in recent years there has been a strong urge to reproduce traditional liberal cosmopolitan thinking in a new format. Thomas Friedman's work on globalization is a perfect example of such an attempt. The next section will present a detailed discussion of how Friedman constructs this rather problematic form of liberalism cosmopolitanism in his work.

Globalization, Cosmopolitanism, and Designed Destiny

Friedman argues that with the end of cold war, which sharply divided the world among ideologically competing camps and erected walls between nations, we are now entering a new era of integration with a greater consolidation of human cultures (Friedman 2000, 8). The driving engine of this new world is globalization, whose logic of integration unleashes social and economic powers, changing the face of human societies and the way they interact with each other. As opposed to the old world marked by state sovereignty, power politics, and regulated economic activity, the new world of globalization is identified with a sense of greater international cooperation and diminished state sovereignty, unregulated markets, and technological advances that connect human societies faster than ever before. First and foremost, globalization is powered by free-market capitalism, which has its own particular culture and set of economic rules (Friedman 2000, 9). This free-market capitalism of globalization creates a "flat world" through an intricate set of processes and forces that create an integrated web whose span encompasses an ever-increasing number of countries (Friedman 2007, 51). If free-market capitalism defines the character and culture of this new world, technological advances constitute the infrastructure of the international system. The Internet, new media, computer-assisted production techniques, and cyber-optic infrastructure not only initiate a faster and more efficient interaction among human societies but also democratize access to information, enabling everybody to potentially become a player in the global world. As a result, as opposed to the slow, divided, and conflict-ridden processes of the old-world system, we are now witnessing an emergence of a new-world system in which speedy integration is quickly removing barriers among human societies, forcing them to become part of the same world culture.

At the centre of Friedman's argument is the belief that globalization, driven by free-market capitalism, is ultimately a democratizing force which operates at three levels: a democratization of technology, a democratization of finance, and a democratization of information. These three levels of democratization are made possible by the requirements of free-market capitalism, which Friedman calls the "Golden Straitjacket," which includes privatization, deregulation, low tariffs, and private-sector-driven economic growth; these requirements tie the hands of national governments to implement irrational policies and forces them to adopt and coordinate their policies with market forces (Friedman 2000, 105). Furthermore, global financial forces, which Friedman calls the "Electronic Herd," discipline governments who violate the rules of free market (Friedman 2000, 112). Finally, the U.S. government effectively promotes the implementation of these three democratizations and uses its army to protect their viability, just as the British government once supervised the global system in the nineteenth century (Friedman 2000, 381). According to Friedman, free-market capitalism is inherently democratizing because, through these three levels of democratization, people around the world do not have to be held hostage to their national governments. They can be players in the global system if they so choose. The cheap and abundant availability of information, together with the spread of finance and technology around the world, is, according to Friedman, breaking barriers by enabling formerly excluded groups and communities to participate in economic activity. This, in turn, encourages nations and governments to cooperate and become integrated.

Similar to many other accounts of globalization, Friedman's account is an enthusiastic one of free-market-driven globalization. His argument about globalization's positive impact on human societies reproduces the usual narratives about the inherent quality of the free market in "promoting freedom" around the world. While he does not use the word cosmopolitanism very often, his theory of globalization is in fact a theory of liberal cosmopolitanism where all humanity converges around similar values defined by the same logic. His overly enthusiastic endorsement of globalization and his optimistic expectations of its outcome as a way of improving the lives of human beings is an echo of earlier voices:

> The time will therefore come when the sun will shine only on free men who know no other master but their reason; when tyrants and slaves, priests and their stupid or hypocritical instruments will exists only in the works of history and on the stage; and when we shall think of them only to pity their victims and their dupes; to maintain ourselves in a state of

vigilance by thinking on their excesses; and to learn how to recognize and so to destroy, by force of reason, the first seeds of tyranny and superstition should they ever dare to reappear amongst us. (Condorcet quoted in Bernstein 1992, 35)

The paragraph above is written by the enlightenment thinker Condorcet and expresses his unconditional belief in the coming of the age of reason. Philosophers from Condorcet to Immanuel Kant expressed the belief in the promise of modernity to deliver human beings from darkness into a new world of change and progress, which would become the common destiny of humanity. While not intending to elevate Friedman's theorization to those of Condorcet and Kant, I argue that his presentation of a coming age of globalization is influenced by the same underlying assumptions about change and progress. Just as Kant's commitment to reason as a universal force to unite human beings constituted the core of his cosmopolitanism, Friedman's belief in free-market capitalism as a universalizing force also constitutes the core of his cosmopolitanism. Unfortunately this is the worst kind of cosmopolitanism and needs to be avoided in the global world, where manifestations of difference in the form of cultural practices, religious beliefs, and national identities are here with us to stay. Early modern thinkers believed that erasing such differences through the universal application of reason would be the way to achieve a more peaceful and stable world (Hall and Gieben 1992). The outcome was far from what they predicted. Not only have differences remained as strong as ever in an increasingly modernized world, but persistent loyalty of human beings to cultural and other differences has convinced many that the time of cosmopolitanism has passed and that there is no longer a need for common reference points to promote solidarity among human societies. In a similar way, Friedman's account of globalization reproduces the logic of eighteenth-century cosmopolitanism by adopting two of its rather problematic assumptions: the teleological understanding of human progress and the hierarchical relationship between universality and particularity.

Teleology of Globalization

Modernity introduced a vision of the world evolving towards a predetermined destiny that needed to be realized by the progression of humanity from one stage to another (Hall 1996). Differences among human societies were believed to exist as a result of their differing levels of progress in this long march towards an end point. Obviously, societies that discover and adapt to the liberating logic of modern rationality are also the ones that progress faster towards this preordained end. This teleological understanding of time and progress, with definite start and end points, assigns a common purpose to human history. This new idea of time fostered the belief that while human societies differ in their orientation and culture, they will end up in the same place if they follow the guidance of reason as the universal point (Eisenstadt 1987). Modernization theory is a good example of such a narrative, which prescribed that non-Western societies will reach the same level of development if they followed the path taken by Western societies (Eisenstadt 1973). From early formulations of colonialism to post–Second World War modernization theory, the traditional liberal cosmopolitanism derived its universalizing logic from this teleological understanding of time, constantly moving towards a predetermined end by the force of reason.

Friedman's account of globalization is influenced by this same teleological understanding of time. Instead of abstract reason, it is free-market capitalism that drives the engine of progress towards its preordained destiny. Friedman's characterization of the new, that is the new international order generated by globalization, is juxtaposed against the old order of the nation-state-based international system. The new order according to Friedman starts with the fall of the Berlin Wall and sharply differs from the old order of the post–Second World War. While "the cold war" represents the old system with characteristics such as conflict between super powers, primacy of national economies, regulated trade, restricted movement of people, and nuclear annihilation, the new system of globalization brings out a new era, which is characterized by the fast movement of people, goods and services, the breakdown of barriers between nations, privatization, and unregulated trade (Friedman 2000, 9). The difference between the old and the new order is as stark as day and night. The old system is about restriction, stagnation, division, conflict, and lack of movement. In contrast to this dark image of the old system, the new world of globalization is about integration, movement, speed, cooperation, and progress. While the old system erected walls between people and created serious obstacles to human progress, the new system removes those walls, enabling people to use their creative energy to achieve further human development. It is not accidental that Friedman chooses the collapse of the Berlin Wall as the starting point of this new era, as its symbolism is extremely significant in terms of imagining a world without barriers.

Modernity always differentiated itself from previous eras by emphasizing the sharp dichotomy between the new and the old. The concept of time in modernity is simultaneously continuous and disrupted, in that modernity marks a movement from the old to the new, while at the same time this movement represents a complete break from the old (Bauman 1991). The promise of modernity lies in its ability to initiate this transformation towards a better world in which individuals free themselves from the old traditions, irrational beliefs, and outdated communal ties (Martinelli 2005). This is why the concept of time in modernity does not progress in circles or reversals but, instead, moves in a linear line from one stage to another until it reaches its final destination where difference disappears as a source of conflict. This particular understanding of time, with a preordained end, constitutes one of the pillars of liberal cosmopolitanism (Vertovec and Cohen 2002). The promise of reaching an end point as the common destiny of humanity provides cosmopolitan thinking with its necessary assumption that it is desirable for humanity to move forward together from the darkness of the old into the light of the new. Of course, the promise of the new era lies not only in its difference from the old, but also in the positive leap it represents towards a common destiny.

This teleological understanding of history as successive progressions towards a predetermined end, where humanity reaches the ultimate point of unification, influences Friedman's interpretation of change. Globalization modernizes as it allows innovation to replace tradition. History moves on as a new stage of development just as the new economic forces that are unleashed by globalization replace the restrictive world of the cold war (Friedman 2000, 45). As a result, Friedman believes that there is only one possible way to proceed in this new world: "So, ideologically speaking there is no more mint chocolate chip, there is no more strawberry swirl and there is no more lemon-lime. Today there is only free-market vanilla and North Korea. There can be different brands of free-market vanilla and you can adjust your society to it by going faster or slower. But, in the end, if you want higher standards of living in a world without walls, the free market is the only ideological alternative left. One road. Different speeds. But one road" (Friedman 2000, 104). While Friedman employs colourful language in order to express his observations, they are nevertheless brutally ideological. The paragraph quoted above states his understanding of time and change: the only way to move forward is to adapt to the logic of the free market as there is no alternative to facilitate a better human existence. Of course, he is not the first one who has placed a free-market economy at the centre of human progress. Immediately after the collapse of the Berlin Wall, Francis Fukuyama also declared "the end of history" by arguing that with the disappearance of the central conflict between capitalism and communism, there is no alternative to free-market capitalism and liberal democracy (Fukuyama 1992). That there is no alternative to free-market capitalism and liberal democracy also means an end of history. Since history moves forward through conflicts and clash of opposites, the end of conflict also marks the end of history. Therefore, in the absence of politics, all that remains is the choice of the pace of adopting the logic of the market economy and liberal democracy. While never fully acknowledging his debt to Hegel, Fukuyama was influenced by his argument about "the end of history" where conflict among human beings ceases to exist, therefore making history an obsolete phenomenon (Grumley 1989). There is, however, a significant difference between Fukuyama and Friedman in that while Fukuyama placed both free-market capitalism and liberal democracy at the driving seat of human progress, Friedman gives the priority to the free-market economy and assumes that the implementation of a free-market economy may eventually lead to the implementation of liberal democracy.

Two world wars, the Holocaust, imperialism, colonialism, and slavery are all a testimony to the fact that modern history does not evolve along such a linear line of teleological progress. In fact, it is full of reversals, zigzags, and full circles. Despite strong evidence against such a linear understanding of history, there is still such a strong ideological commitment to seeing every stage of modernity as an improvement to the previous one. This ideological commitment is one of the strong impetuses behind traditional cosmopolitanism's desire to identify a common destiny for humanity. Fukuyama was quick to declare the end of history. Yet, the brutal Balkan wars and successive ethnic conflicts around the world, not to mention the Iraq War, have proven him wrong. Friedman was also very quick to declare the triumph of the free-market economy as the engine of globalization and the United States as its hegemonic leader. Similarly, the recent financial crisis and greatly slowed pace of global integration has also proved him wrong.

The Universal and the Particular in the Global World

Earlier I mentioned that modern liberal cosmopolitan thinking has a problematic approach towards the expression of difference. Since it aims to achieve an eventual solidification of human experience under a universal reference point, it views difference as something that needs to be controlled and eventually erased. Whether it is in the form of culture, religion, nationality, or ethnicity, modern cosmopolitan thinking sees any manifestation of difference as antagonistic to its core promise of establishing solidarity among human beings through their common experience. Liberal cosmopolitans believe that individuals' loyalty to their cultural particularities prevent them from expressing their identity as part of a larger humanity. Furthermore, as there is no end to how individuals may experience their cultural particularity, establishing common references through which to develop a shared culture of humanity becomes an impossible task. As a result, modern cosmopolitan thinking establishes a hierarchical relationship between universality and particularity in that the universal and the particular cannot coexist together. The linear and teleological understanding of history, which I discussed in the previous section, is largely responsible for this peculiar interpretation of universality. Since it is assumed that humanity moves towards a common and predetermined end, it is inconceivable to imagine a situation where the interaction between the universal and the particular can lead to multiple experiences in which one may express his/her cultural difference but also feel solidarity towards other human beings (McCarthy 2002). Instead, the linear understanding of time requires that the universal dissolves particularity into its framework. Therefore, the cosmopolitan future depends on the erasure of particular forms of life. The tension between the universal and the particular is also understood to be the engine of history in which human societies evolve towards their common destiny.

This antagonistic and hierarchical relationship between the universal and the particular is particularly visible in Friedman's interpretation of globalization. The title of his first book, *The Lexus and the Olive Tree*, explains the tension in the form of a dichotomy between the universal movement of globalization and the resistance of particular cultures to it. The Lexus represents the global system while the Olive Tree represents rootedness, belonging, and identity. The Lexus is identified with the drive for sustenance, improvement, prosperity, and modernization.

The Olive Tree, on the other hand, is identified with past memories and irrational urges to protect identity and belonging (Friedman 2000, 34). Friedman sees the Lexus in the Toyota plant in Japan, in the "Electronic Herd" of international financial markets and credit rating agencies, and in production patterns of multinational corporations. The Olive Tree, on the other hand, manifests itself in irrational ethnic fights such as between Palestinians and Israelis, Serbs and Muslims, and Armenians and Azeris, or in reactions against globalizations, such as 100 per cent tax on bottles of Coca-Cola in south France (Friedman 2000, 35). The Lexus constantly struggles with the Olive Tree as the Olive Tree reacts to the rational urges of the Lexus to create prosperity, material well-being, and further integration. These rational urges are threatening to the Olive Tree as they require the Olive Tree to give up on its irrational attachment to identity and belonging. While Friedman acknowledges that the Olive Tree is important for our well-being, it has to stay as a tapestry and colourful relic without interfering in the logic of globalization. However, he quickly remarks that the Olive Tree is one of the significant obstacles standing in the way of the Lexus. Interestingly enough, he traces this fundamental conflict between the universal and the particular back to Genesis and the story of Abel and Cain, which is an age-old quest for "material betterment and individual and communal identity" (Friedman 2000, 34).

Friedman's solution to this age-old tension between universality and particularity is no different from the ones proposed by traditional cosmopolitans: this tension between the universal and the particular can only be solved once the universal establishes itself as the common reference point and tames the particular's irrational urges to cling to the past and tradition. Since the universal represents the new and modern, and since the spirit of human history entails movement towards the new, the irrational urges of the particular cultural affiliations slow down this movement towards the shared end of history. Furthermore, in this antagonistic and hierarchical relationship, the universal is given the positive role of progress while the particular represents a negative and obstructionist role of progress.

Although Friedman's account is equally strong in its commitment to the primacy of the universal, the capitalist free-market economy is, in his explanation, the new universal which will carry human progress to its next stage. Friedman believes that the forces of the free-market economy will be the new universal in the global system to discipline the irrational urges of the particular cultural attachments. By applying the "Golden Straitjacket," which is the primacy of the private sector, balanced budgets, privatization, and deregulation, globalization unifies the economic decision-making project in different countries, forcing them to readjust their cultural assumptions about how an economy should be run. If politics manifest itself through variations, alternatives, and resistance to the "Golden Straitjacket," Friedman argues that the "victory of the Cold War was a victory for market forces above politics" (Friedman 2000, 107). Whether it is the Moody's Investor Services downgrading of India's credit as a result of nuclear testing or a young Palestinian businessman, whose father was Abu Jihad, one of the founder's of the Palestine Liberation Organization, Friedman's book presents many examples in which the universal force of free-market capitalism disciplines and transforms irrational tendencies of particular cultures. The "Golden Straitjacket" and the "Electronic Herd" are two important elements of globalization, which ensure the disciplining powers of universal free-market capitalism. Friedman tells us that according to the "Golden Straitjacket" and the rules of the free market, one size fits all. Every country may try to do some very minor modifications and implement small policy changes here and there, but, in the end, the general framework of the free market will reign and render political debates about policy alternatives irrelevant.

What is particularly interesting in Friedman's reformulation of the universal is both the unconditional belief in the ability of the market to carry humanity forward towards the next stage in history and the equal disdain for politics. Politics, according to Friedman, belongs to the realm of the Olive Tree in which differences manifest themselves in an irrational fashion and slow down human progress towards a better future. Illustrated by images of shiny new office buildings, a growing number of information technology companies employing highly qualified engineers, golf courses, and Pizza Hut billboards in India's Silicon Valley (Bangalore), in the new flat world, the life of an engineer in Bangalore is no different from that of an engineer in Kansas. In this new flat world, geographical or cultural differences do not matter as long as you adapt to the requirements of the "Golden Straitjacket" and cooperate with others around the world in real time "on an equal footing" (Friedman 2007, 8). From India to Mexico, a new and similar trend is visible, in which countries and peoples who learn to live by the rules of free-market capitalism quickly catch up with the rest of the world and lift themselves out of the condition of poverty. In this "flat world" the differences between the Third and First Worlds do not matter anymore.

Similarly, differences between being Indian, Mexican, American, or French also do not matter anymore. After all, places resemble each other, people dress and talk the same way, and even if they do not talk the same language, they can understand each other very easily. What matters now is whether any given country or individual has the ability and capacity to accept the wisdom of the free market. Friedman warns us that while "we are connecting all the knowledge centers of the world together in a single network," which will result in an era of "prosperity, innovation and collaboration," politics and terrorism can get in the way of this process (Friedman 2007, 8). It is interesting that he equates politics with terrorism as a destructive force. However, this is not entirely surprising since politics not only emphasizes differences but also contains an element of uncertainty that refuses to accept predetermined outcomes. Put differently, political engagement brings out variable forms of negotiations in which differences over matters can be settled sometimes peacefully and other times more violently. Furthermore, political engagement by definition is a contingent act that may challenge established orders and redefine hierarchies (Rancière 2006, 2010). As a result, politics poses a threat to traditional cosmopolitan thinking and its strong urge to universalize.

From Hegel to Kant, enlightenment philosophers have been preoccupied with the contingency of politics. Hegel's end of history thesis, based on the assumption that history will no longer move forward once the conflict between human beings ceases to exist is, in part, also the end of politics, where there is no longer a need to negotiate differences as differences disappear eventually (R. Fine 2001). Similarly, Kant identified particularity, which fosters differences among human beings, as an important obstacle to achieving emancipation. Reason was a powerful force to deal with the contingency of particularity. As more and more people accept the enlightening force of reason, irrational urges that are fostered by particular attachments and belongings will be eliminated (Honneth 1997). This is precisely why Friedman approaches politics with scepticism – it has the potential to disrupt the universal moment of free-market capitalism. According to Friedman, there is no possibility of achieving prosperity and stability, since the persistence of politics can only be a disruptive force, which delays and prevents human progress towards a better life.

Immanuel Kant in his *Perpetual Peace* asserts that a cosmopolitan world order can only be realized by liberal states as they do not go to war with each other (Kant 1903). According to Kant, liberal states do not go to war with one another as they are ruled according to the principles of reason. As opposed to illiberal states that are susceptible to irrational urges of their leaders or of traditional beliefs, liberal states use the universal voice of reason to deal with their internal matters as well as with their dealings with each other. According to Kant, there is, however, another reason why liberal states do not go to war with each other: international free trade, which effectively encourages cooperation and integration. As states trade with one another, their relationships and interest are further interwoven. As a result, conflict between states ceases to be a zero-sum game and ends up damaging all parties involved. Since conflict becomes costly and highly destructive, states naturally avoid getting into wars with one another. Kant believes that avoidance of conflict by liberal states is a natural outcome of the universal reason guiding the decision-making process and governance policies. While states that are ruled by illiberal regimes may not refrain from going to war against their own interests, liberal states will always act in a rational manner which prevents them from acting against their own interest.

While never acknowledging Kant's theory of why liberal states do not go to war against one another, Friedman develops a very similar theory, which he calls "the Golden Arches of Conflict Prevention." His theory is based on his observation that no two countries with a McDonald's have fought a war against each other. Friedman argues that when a country develops a middle class that is big enough to support a McDonald's network, citizens in that country lose their appetite to fight wars and prefer to "wait in line for burgers" (Friedman 2000, 249). Perhaps Friedman does not mention Kant, because Kant placed liberal democratic regimes at the centre of his conflict prevention theory. Friedman, on the other hand, does not see liberal democracy as one of the conditions of conflict prevention. Instead, market economy with a big enough middle class, according to his theory, would be sufficient enough to achieve the same result. I have no way of knowing whether Friedman was aware of Kant's famous essay *Perpetual Peace*, in which Kant developed his theory of a cosmopolitan world order. Given that Friedman mentions Montesquieu's explanation about the ability of free trade to unite nations around the world, it is possible that he was also aware of Kant's argument about liberal democracy promoting peace and stability around the world. Even if he was not aware of Kant's famous essay, Friedman follows the same logic: the spread of free-market capitalism around the world increases rational behaviour, which eliminates irrational policies that lead to wars and other conflicts. As people become richer, investing in the system and interacting with similar minded people around the world, the reasons for wars and conflicts disappear, leading to a prosperous and peaceful world order.

The spread of universal reason around the world did not result in the further integration of different societies as anticipated by cosmopolitan thinkers of eighteenth century Europe. Instead, it generated a strong reaction by non-Western societies, who correctly identified this particular manifestation of reason as an assault on their particular forms of life. With the spread of colonialism and imperialism, it quickly became clear that there was nothing universal about enlightenment reason. When Gandhi asked why the wonderful qualities of British liberalism such as freedom, equality, and human autonomy did not apply to Indians, he was forcefully questioning the contradiction at the heart of modern cosmopolitanism. It was clear to many in the colonized world that history, guided by reason, did not produce the same results for the colonized as the colonizers. Similarly, Friedman wants us to believe that free-market capitalism as a universal force will flatten the world and increase prosperity for all around the world. Free-market capitalism, however, is not an abstract universal force but is, in fact, a concrete and particular set of relationships and institutions that place individuals and societies in different locations in its structure of hierarchy. The way free-market capitalism develops and establishes itself in different parts of the world is not an abstract and neutral process but is a process that is controlled and framed by concrete actors with very specific interests. Friedman correctly identifies that the "Electronic Herd," which is populated by financial companies, is one of the dominant forces of globalization, not the workers employed in thousands of subcontracting companies producing goods for multinational companies. The interests of financial institutions and multinational corporations do not coincide with those of workers and farmers. The recent financial crisis brutally revealed the fact that there is nothing universal about free-market capitalism's ability to produce prosperity for all.

Globalization and False Cosmopolitanism

Edward Said in his *Orientalism* explained very well that without the intellectual power of writers and scholars, it would not have been possible to establish colonialism as a legitimate form of control (Said 1978). The power of orientalism emanated from the fact that it was able to establish a certain regime of truth, which justified defining, explaining, controlling, and eventually ruling other people. Every epoch needs its own intellectuals to create its own narrative to mask embedded power sources in its hierarchies. The period of late globalization is no exception. Microsoft, Shell, McDonald's, and Dell can sell their goods and services around the world, but they cannot sell globalization as an idea. They can convince governments to give them preferential treatments to relocate to their territories, but they cannot convince people that what they do benefits everybody equally. People who lose their houses in the United States as a result of risky practices of financial institutions, people in Cochabamba revolting against water privatization, female workers who are locked up in sweatshops in many developing countries, and Indian farmers who lose their ability to control their seed production as a result of agricultural giant Monsanto's penetration into the Indian market all know very well that globalization does not benefit them as it does the "Electronic Herd." The stark realities of experiencing the impact of globalization daily make many people aware that some have more power in the global world than others. As Žižek argued, this deeply unequal nature of the globalization process in fact requires court philosophers such as Friedman to present another image which focuses on a positive story of liberal market economy at the service of human masses all around the world. This is why Friedman's narrative is important: because, as Fernandez aptly argued, it does an excellent job of selling neoliberal globalization (Fernandez 2011). Friedman's carefully crafted cosmopolitanism is the narrative of Lexus. It tells a sophisticated story of globalization as the new universal engine of human history, levelling the field for everybody around the world. It is full of small stories and anecdotes, which display how ordinary people better their lives within this new world. However, inconvenient stories do not make it into his narrative. Although he claims that he simply describes what he observes, his is, in fact, a deeply ideological account of globalization, where examples are carefully selected to confirm the linear narrative of globalization. Both books are full of stories that are carefully selected to make the case for the particular interpretation of neoliberal globalization that Friedman presents in his books. They are vivid, persuasively argued, accessible to a general reader, and present a world in which we have no choice but to accept the inevitable force of the Lexus.

The stories he uses to make his case, however, are gross generalizations that simplify complex interactions of social, economic, and political forces within the global world. He tells the story of a Syrian man who watches Israeli television and is bothered by the fact that yogurt is sold in fruit-coloured containers in Israel while in Syria they are just black and white. It was not the occupation of the Golan Heights but the yogurt containers that bothered him about Israel. He tells Friedman, "it is not fair that we are a hundred years behind the Israelis and they just got here" (Friedman 2000, 71). From this example Friedman deduces that the prosperity and wealth that comes with accepting the logic of globalization can transform the Syrian man's hostility towards Israel into feelings of jealousy and admiration. Of course, this particular story does not mean much as one can find hundreds of other examples of Syrians bothered by and angry about Israel's occupation of the Golan Heights. Conveniently enough, in Friedman's stories ordinary people around the world either tell him how they benefit from globalization or admit that their failure is due to their inability to adapt to the logic of globalization. For example, a Thai real-estate dealer who lost everything in the real-estate market crash and was selling sandwiches admits to Friedman that "Thailand had messed up." He tells Friedman that even though he lost everything, he is not angry because capitalism is the only way to move forward (Friedman 2000, 102). Friedman was taken aback by the fact that not only was the vendor not angry despite the fact that he lost everything but he was also able to understand that global capitalism was good for him. Speculative activities of international investors who also greatly contributed to the crash did not make it into Friedman's story, and obviously, he has not met a single person in Thailand who was angry about unregulated global forces and elites using people's lives as a tool to become rich. Similarly, he speaks to a Malaysian human rights activist who vigorously refuses to accept that globalization amounts to a new form of colonization and tells him that curry is currently the national food in Britain (Friedman 2000, 357). Even though the overwhelming majority of human rights activists and organizations around the world do an excellent job of documenting the adverse effects of globalization on people's lives, Friedman never ends up meeting even one such person or member of such an organization.

He talks to a Kuwaiti Sunni woman whose brother married a Shia woman whom he met through an Internet chat room (Friedman 2000, 264). Palestinians living under brutal occupation in Gaza and the West Bank do not make it into any of Friedman's stories about the wonders of globalization. Almost every single story and example in his books validates his account of globalization. Given that there are so many accounts of people who have been adversely affected by globalization, it is curious that, somehow, none make it into the collection of Friedman's anecdotes. This selected presentation of stories, in fact, is not accidental. They intend to convince us that what Friedman tells in his books is not just simply his subjective account of globalization; they represent lived experience of everyday globalization. Finally, in chapter 15, Friedman talks about some of the adverse effects of globalization. He mentions that as globalization disturbs old structures and introduces new ways of doing things, it is only natural that there will be some negative consequences. However, he is quick to remind us that globalization is not to be blamed for these negative outcomes. Some will lose their jobs, some communities will become obsolete, and the ones that adopt the logic of new times will be winners. People will fall behind in this new world of globalization not because there is anything systemically wrong but because they are slow movers (he calls them "turtles") (Friedman 2000, 334). Because failure in this new world is an individual outcome and not a systemic one, the only way to deal with negative outcomes of globalization is to change individuals. Naturally Friedman denounces protests against globalization as reactionary movements and points out that there is nothing in common between these protests and the ordinary men and women who are wise enough to understand what globalization offers to them to improve their lives. After all, globalization emerges from below, "from street level, from people's very souls and from their deepest desires" (Friedman 2000, 348).

Just as colonialism justified its civilizing mission with the false universality of bringing others to the level of advanced civilization, Friedman's narrative of globalization seeks its legitimacy in a false universality of free-market capitalism. Behind the universal civilizing mission of colonialism lies a huge looting of foreign lands, an extermination of other cultures, and a forceful adoption of hegemonic cultures. Behind the universal, progressive mission of free-market capitalism, there is the "Electronic Herd" and other global economic forces, who benefit greatly, while millions of others become victims of the same process. The UN Development Report documents that "the three richest people have assets that exceed the combined GDP of the 48 least developed countries; the 15 richest have assets that exceed the total GDP of Sub-Saharan Africa; the wealth of the 32 richest people exceeds the total GDP of South Asia" (United Nations 1998, Box 1.3). Similarly, when Friedman describes in great detail India's success in adopting the logic of globalization, he fails to mention that since the liberal reforms, there has not been a significant change for the 75 per cent of the population living on less than $2 per day or for the more than half of all women and three-quarters of all children below the age of three in India who are anaemic (Kampfner 2010, 143). If growing disparity between the rich and the poor on a global level is not enough to reveal the true logic of globalization, the recent financial crises made it clear that, unlike Friedman's assertion that globalization is a universal force which benefits everybody, the system is working for the benefit of the very few whose ability to control unregulated global financial markets results in further poverty and misery for millions around the world. It is ironic that nearly $11 billion worth of bonuses was distributed to wealthy city-of-London financial speculators in 2010, while most other segments of society are subject to the most savage spending cuts in the British history since Margaret Thatcher's government (*The Economist* 2011a).

While the financial sector was mainly responsible for the crisis, somehow ordinary people ended up paying the price. It would be interesting to know if Friedman would still subscribe to the deeply ideological account of globalization he provided in his books since the true extent of the global crises is now well known. My suspicion is that he would. As I mentioned earlier, Friedman's main preoccupation is not to provide a thoughtful analysis of globalization with all of its complexities. Such an analysis would require an understanding of history that does not evolve linearly but in fact one that has many circles and parallel stories written by opposing forces. Friedman tells us that globalization marks an end of politics since economic forces instil a single logic of governance and render politics irrelevant. If politics is about emphasizing differences, negotiating them, and finding a way to resolve conflicts emerging from differences in a just way, democratic regimes cannot survive without political engagement. Given the pivotal role politics plays in a democratic environment, it is not surprising that Friedman adopts a rather peculiar understanding of democracy where democracy is reduced to only the making of economic choices. A short glance around the world reveals an emerging trend where authoritarian regimes work quite well with free-market economies. Some of the emerging economic powers of the new global systems such as Russia and China show no signs of democratizing but work very well with free-market capitalism. Similarly, smaller players such as Singapore, United Arab Emirates, or Malaysia do not have serious trouble adapting to free-market capitalism without changing the nature of their political systems. It seems that influential economic forces, such as international financial markets and multinational companies, are not too concerned about the lack of democracy in these countries as long as profits are secure and a low-wage labour force is readily available. But, then, there is also no indication that Friedman himself is concerned about this comfortable coexistence between authoritarianism and free-market capitalism. As long as individuals and companies have the freedom to consume and make economic choices without restrictions, that is democratic enough for Friedman. Kant's cosmopolitanism had a higher standard for liberal democracy. Friedman's version of democratic freedom is a far cry from that of traditional cosmopolitans.

Conclusion

Since globalization emerged as a powerful force in international politics within the last two decades, there has emerged a powerful group of icons whose main objective is to sell this new development as the new phase in human progress. Their views and arguments find a much greater reception in the mainstream media, and overall, they enjoy an intellectual hegemony in shaping public opinion. Friedman is one of those intellectual icons who has done a very skilful job of presenting a deeply ideological account of neoliberal globalization as factual reality. The power of his narrative comes from the fact that he presents globalization as the universal reference point for human progress. In contrast to the old systems, where human societies were divided along narrow cultural and political narratives, globalization, according to him, ushers us into a new era in which we can all surpass our differences and unite around the same logic if we can manage to adapt to the requirements of free-market capitalism. His narrative is a compelling one because it promises that anybody can become a winner in this new progressive era. The punditry of Friedman rests on his ability to rejuvenate a discredited version of cosmopolitanism in which a certain particular culture or world view is represented as the universal meeting point of humanity. The Enlightenment thinkers hoped that a certain articulation of modern rationality would provide humanity with a universal meeting point. Friedman knows that the time for such a culturally charged universal is over. Instead, the neutral tone of the free-market capitalism emerges as the new universal that can eliminate pesky differences and conflicts among human beings. While Friedman does not coin his narrative as one of cosmopolitanism, it is, in fact, a reformulation of the traditional cosmopolitan narrative. It shares the central assumptions of traditional cosmopolitanism in that it rests on a linear and teleological understanding of history, coupled with an assertion that the end of human conflict requires giving up cultural particularities. Just as traditional cosmopolitanism rested on the false universality of a culturally specific form of Western modernity, Friedman's cosmopolitan narrative finds its claim to universality in the logic of free-market capitalism.

This is rather unfortunate as we need more than ever before a cosmopolitanism in the form of human solidarity and common understanding in order to respond to common problems of humanity in the increasingly globalized world in which we live. However, the cosmopolitanism we need is not the one that is presented by Friedman. Friedman portrays a cosmopolitan vision in which U.S. interests are taken to be representative of the interests of humanity, and the overall framework of the entire global system is determined by the priorities of a few powerful economic actors. Instead, as I have argued elsewhere, the type of cosmopolitanism we need in the global world is one that is not founded on a false universality of hegemonic powers but one that reaches universal reference points through a negotiation of differences (Baban 2006). Rather than reducing cultural and other differences that are unique to human experience to an abstract set of universal values, a critical cosmopolitanism would establish a non-hierarchical form of universality which is embedded within the lived experiences of individuals. Fortunately, there is a growing literature which is aware of shortcomings of traditional cosmopolitan thinking and is emerging from the margins of the global power relations (Connolly 2000; Ikas and Wagner 2009; Mignolo 2000; Pieterse 2004; Vertovec and Cohen 2002; Zubaida 2002). Of course, this literature does not receive the same attention in the mainstream media outlets as Friedman's work. However, works such as these play a key role in inspiring new thinking and will eventually challenge the hegemonic representation of Friedman's narrative.

Governance Fantasies: Joseph Stiglitz and the Citizen-Bureaucrat

GAVIN FRIDELL

The past three decades have witnessed the unprecedented extension of global capital. Yet, as is frequently noted, this development has not been accompanied by the emergence of global regulatory institutions that are both effective and democratic. The result has been an oft proclaimed global governance "gap" (Cooper 2007; Held and McGrew 2000). This chapter argues that this governance gap – even as it continues to widen – has increasingly been filled at a symbolic and ideological level through a "governance fantasy." Prestigious iconic figures have stepped up to act as celebrity diplomats and special advisors (Kinsley 2008; Bishop and Green 2009; Cooper 2007) holding out the promise that the existing transnational networks of public and civic institutions offer spaces for the democratic regulation of global capital and the amelioration of its most oppressive effects. Among these figures are well-known "citizen-bureaucrats" (to quote "rock-star economist" Joseph Stiglitz (2002a)), who are key to the functioning of the governance fantasy, playing on our hope that global institutions offer substantial space for independent thinkers to act on behalf of global public interest. They generally serve as "advisors" or "policymakers" and possess significant stature within policy, leadership, academic, and media circles. Their ranks include celebrated intellectuals such as Stiglitz, Jeffrey Sachs, Jagdish Bagwati, Martin Wolf, Paul Collier, William Easterly, and Lawrence Summers.[1]

Among these iconic intellectuals, the specific image of Stiglitz perhaps reveals the most about the overall nature of the citizen-bureaucrat, as he is renowned for having acted *particularly* independently and autonomously, encapsulating the truest example of the spirit of the citizen-bureaucrat. In 2000, Stiglitz was forced to resign as Chief Economist of the World Bank after having publicly criticized the neoliberal policies of the bank's sister organization, the International Monetary Fund (IMF). After a prestigious career working for prominent economics departments, several years as an economic policy advisor to U.S. President Bill Clinton, and three years at the upper echelons of the World Bank, Stiglitz swiftly became a celebrity among globalization critics and was proclaimed "the Rebel Within" (Press 2002; Chang 2001). Much of this popularity was derived not solely from his economic policy ideas, which diverse commentators have pointed out are not particularly radical or new and remain largely within the framework of neoclassical economics (Fine and Van Waeyenberge 2005; Hart-Landsberg and Burkett 2004; Kennedy 2003; Freund 2003; Mandel 2002; Chang 2001). Rather, Stigltiz's appeal has stemmed to a large extent from his willingness to jeopardize his high-ranking position in the corridors of power in order to defend his neo-Keynesian ideas. This has won him admirers for his political determination and has buffered up his iconic, citizen-bureaucrat status. In a world in which giant government and corporate bureaucracies increasingly dominate political life, squeezing out alternative visions and narrowing available options, the citizen-bureaucrat offers the fantasy of the independent thinker who still finds space *within* these unwieldy bureaucracies to put forward a *rebellious* agenda.

The core premise of this chapter is that Stiglitz must be understood not solely as an economist and policymaker, but also as a contemporary icon whose status is derived from efforts to promote his image in a manner similar to celebrities, including interviews in a range of mass media, book signings, feature articles in major newspapers, keynote addresses, public lectures, and central involvement in major international events organized by non-governmental organizations (NGOs) and formal international institutions, like the United Nations (UN). In the contemporary era, celebrity culture has become increasingly pervasive in all aspects of our daily lives, a core location for the elaboration of cultural identity, and a key node in the legitimation of neoliberal capitalism, instilling power in those able to turn their image "into a commodity to be marketed and traded" (Turner 2010; Marshall 2010, 2006; Turner 2004, 13, 18). Stiglitz's image is one of a dissenting citizen-bureaucrat who both devotedly climbed to the top of the world's powerful institutions and dissented from them, giving hope that one can be both a rebel *and* an insider, appearing to reconcile the disparate desires to be both submissive to powerful institutions and free from them, and offering a template for aspiring "policymakers."

Yet, a sober assessment of Stiglitz's actual career reveals the weakness of this reconciliation. For a renowned "policymaker," Stiglitz has had surprisingly little influence on "making" policy and his dissenting opinions have been either ignored or strictly narrowed to remain within legitimate neoliberal boundaries. As a result, Stiglitz's greatest political impact may lie not in his ability to construct and defend a space for a pragmatic, alternative policy framework to neoliberalism, as he would have it, but in helping to construct and reinforce the "ideological fantasy" of the citizen-bureaucrat which "sustains at the level of fantasy what it seeks to avoid at the level of reality" (J. Dean 2009, 56; Žižek 1989). Applying Jodi Dean's insightful Žižekian analysis of the "free trade fantasy," I argue that Stiglitz is one exemplary component of a broader "governance fantasy." Reproduced with significant financial backing from economic and political elites, yet more than a "trick or illusion duping the poor, gullible masses," the governance fantasy is embedded in our everyday practices and seeks to answer "who we are" (J. Dean 2009, 55–6). The governance fantasy has the power to "link together a set of often conflicting and contradictory promises for enjoyment and explanations for its lack (for people's failure to enjoy despite all of the promises that they would)" (J. Dean 2009, 50). It tells us how to satisfy our desires (through transparent, scientific, democratic global governance), but also explains why our desires have not yet been fulfilled. In the case of Stiglitz, the lack of space for genuinely independent citizen-bureaucrats in our world today is obscured by the practices of Stiglitz himself, who partially acknowledges the limits of his position while insisting they stem from oversights around how things *should* function in the governance fantasy – fulfilling what Dean (2009, 58) refers to as the "'excuses, excuses' role of fantasy." In what follows, this chapter will contrast Stiglitz's iconic image as a "good" citizen-bureaucrat with the impact of his policy career, demonstrating the ways in which the governance fantasy fills in for the lack of actually existing democratic global governance.

The Good Bureaucrat

Despite the oft-proclaimed assertion among mainstream media, politicians, and economists that capitalism is directly at odds with bureaucracy, social scientists and historians have long pointed out that the opposite is the case: modern capitalism has in fact given birth to the largest bureaucracies in the history of humankind, required to codify, police, and regulate the "unregulated" market. Critical thinkers from a variety of traditions have criticized the emergence of these bureaucracies, both corporate and state, for the intense feelings of isolation, powerlessness, alienation, and anxiety they can cause and the manifold techniques in which they administer and discipline human behaviour with unprecedented range and depth (Konings 2010; Olsen 2005; Scott 1999; Wood 1999; Foucault 1990; Deutscher 1969; Marx 1963; Polanyi 1944; Fromm 1941). Yet, while this negative conception of the state is undeniably persuasive, it does runs the risk of downplaying the extent to which people *also* see the state bureaucracy in a more positive light, as a force for instrumental ends to enhance their control over their social environment (Konings 2010). This view is equally pervasive in modern society and, in particular, among bureaucrats themselves, some of whom see bureaucracy as a tool through which they can attain the role of the "good bureaucrat."

Perhaps the most influential Western conception of the good bureaucrat comes from Max Weber's work on the modern state, which he depicted as a relatively efficient and rationale bureaucratic structure that claimed the monopoly of the legitimate use of force within a given territory. At the top, the state was run by an executive of political leaders who lived primarily "for" politics, having a personal passion for the exercise of power, and below were thousands of bureaucrats who lived primarily "off" politics, seeking steady income and employment and socialized into the passive role of obedient, impartial, civil servant (Olsen 2005; Weber 1970, 84–6, 95). Weber's analysis of capitalism and bureaucracy provides fruitful ground for an understanding of one major vision of the good bureaucrat – one who is efficient at and devoted to the act of being a professional bureaucrat and climbing the administrative ladder. Yet, Weber's relatively positive portrayal of the modern bureaucracy significantly downplays the alienating aspects of bureaucracy and naturalized competitive and acquisitive behaviour that is historically specific to capitalism (Wood 1995, 146–80; Deutscher 1969). Weber assumed bureaucrats desired mostly individual gain and minimized the extent to which bureaucrats, who as workers *must* live "off" politics to meet their material needs (food, shelter, etc.), also aspire to live "for" politics at the same time – to gain a bit of "positive freedom" to influence the world around them (Fromm 1941).

An exploration of the complex social objectives, desires, and fantasies of particular bureaucrats and how they relate to bureaucratic institutions offers a route towards a second understanding of the good bureaucrat – one who seeks to "do good" for society within the confines of the bureaucracy, not because of the bureaucracy's purported merits but despite its many shortcomings. This type of good bureaucrat has long been a topic of Western literature, in particular in the great works of nineteenth-century historical realism, such as the novels of Honoré de Balzac and Leo Tolstoy. Writing about a period when industrial capitalism and the modern state were only beginning to emerge and develop, the major works of historical realism are replete with characters that seek to come to terms with this contradictory process, one which both celebrates individuals and frees them from the bondages of the past while simultaneously alienating them from each other, from the products they produce, and from the institutions which rule over society. The major characters are invariably "honest representatives" from the elite or middle class who seek to remedy society's social ills by upholding the values of capitalist ideals. In terms of the state bureaucracy, many turn to it in hopes of encountering something akin to the efficient, impartial, and rational institution envisioned by Weber, only to discover instead corruption, tyranny, and "a world in which decent people can no longer find any opportunity for action" (Lukács 1964, 166).

The disillusioned, alienated bureaucrat is captured in historical realist novels through stories of particular characters that represent broader social types and demonstrate "the organic, indissoluble connection between [a person] as a private individual and [a person] as a social being, as a member of a community" (Lukács 1964, 8; 1962). In Tolstoy's *War and Peace*, set in the context of the years leading up to and including the War of 1812, Prince Andrew is one such character who can be taken, among other things, as a representative of the good bureaucrat. As a high-ranking adjutant for the Russian army, Prince Andrew begins the novel with a keen desire to make an impact on the world and please those above him, and he expresses his willingness to give anything "for a moment of glory, of triumph over men, of love from men I don't know and never shall." After having tasted the bitterness of defeat in battle, and after meeting his hero, the French Emperor Napoleon Bonaparte, who displayed "paltry vanity and joy in victory," Prince Andrew comes to recognize the "insignificance of greatness, the unimportance of life which no one could understand, and the still greater unimportance of death." Disillusioned with both the Tsarist and Napoleonic states, Prince Andrew loses all interest in the reformist ideals that had previously enticed him and grows more bitter and irritated with politics, finding personal salvation only on his deathbed through his belief in "divine love" (Tolstoy [1869] 1993, 209, 231, 746). Prince Andrew's particular story is echoed by the experiences of countless others throughout the novel, even the most powerful leaders, including Napoleon himself, whom Tolstoy argued was merely the "involuntary tool" and "slave" of historical forces beyond his or any individual's actual control (Tolstoy [1869] 1993, 492–3, 553).

The Tolstoyan perspective offers a vision of the good bureaucrat that is distinctly different from the Weberian one. While the Weberian good bureaucrat is *good at being* a bureaucrat, the Tolstoyan good bureaucrat seeks *to do good* through the bureaucracy. While the Weberian bureaucrat climbs the social ladder of the bureaucracy, loyally and faithfully believing in its socially beneficial role, the Tolstoyan bureaucrat gradually becomes disillusioned with the bureaucracy, determining it to be the primary obstacle to aiding society, and often breaks completely with it in despair. There is a fundamental tension between the two bureaucrats: it would appear that one cannot be both a successful career bureaucrat within the bureaucratic hierarchy and, at the same time, a disillusioned dissident bureaucrat that escapes from the bureaucracy's chains. This tension is no doubt the cause of much contemporary angst about bureaucracies, especially among bureaucrats themselves who, if they accept this dichotomy, would appear to be stuck between the rather depressing and disempowering choice of "cog in the machine" or disillusioned outsider. Here is where the governance fantasy and Joseph Stiglitz as citizen-bureaucrat come to the rescue; like the cop in the Hollywood movie who follows his heart while ignoring the stifling rules of his superiors, Stiglitz allows us to believe that the seeds of dissent exist within the very institutions of power themselves. The image of Stiglitz reconciles the disparate visions of the two good bureaucrats, giving hope that one can be both a rebel *and* an insider.

Stiglitz: "The Rebel Within"[2]

As is often the case with high-ranking officials that dissent from the powerful institutions they had worked for, there was little indication of a rebel in Stiglitz's career prior to his struggle with the World Bank. "To be sure, he was on the 'liberal' side of the American political spectrum," states Chang (2001, 1), "but no one can claim to have foreseen the controversies that he was to create during his tenure at the World

Bank." Stiglitz was born in Gary, Indiana, in 1943, the son of middle-class "New Deal" Democrats. He received his PhD in economics at MIT in 1967 before moving on to hold a number of highly prestigious university positions and to study under and work with some of the most renowned economists in the Western world (Stiglitz 2002a).

Far from probing the works of radical thinkers, Stigltiz's research has centred around the typical fare of mainstream neoclassical economics: economic modelling based on abstract mathematical formulas. These models are derived from highly deductive reasoning based on an array of speculative assumptions around human nature (assumed to be universally self-interested, hedonistic, competitive, and accumulative), methodological individualism (atomized individuals are taken to be the foundation of society as opposed to social and collective wholes, such as institutions, classes, and the national economy), and equilibrium (economy and society are assumed to be moving towards a relatively static balance between supply and demand as opposed to being dynamic and constantly changing). While social scientists have long criticized these assumptions for being ahistorical and asocial, and for neglecting key issues around historical specificity, power, conflict, social change, and the nature of modern institutions, mainstream economists have typically viewed economic modelling as superior to research in the "subjective" social sciences, which they have mostly ignored (Milonakis and Fine 2009; Fine and Van Waeyenberge 2005). To Stiglitz, a passionate defender of rigorous modelling, the mathematical and formulaic orientation of economics allows for it to be value-free, objective, and more akin to the natural sciences, where the "law of supply and demand" can no more be repealed than "the law of gravity" (Stiglitz and Walsh 2006, 91; Stiglitz 2002a).

Where Stiglitz has diverged from neoclassical orthodoxy has been in his scepticism about the scientific precision of the dominant economic models, which he argues have neglected key social realities, such as assuming perfect employment when such a situation never occurs (Stiglitz and Charlton 2006, 1–56; Stiglitz 2002a; Roemer 1995). From this vantage, Stiglitz has produced a variety of neo-Keynesian works (void of Keynes's own objections to methodological individualism and mathematical modelling (Milonakis and Fine 2009, 268–308)) that have challenged some of the assumptions of conventional neoclassical economics, including research on how distribution of income effects economic growth, on the instability and inefficiency in markets caused by

imperfect information, technological change, and the existence of monopoly corporations, and on the relative merits of public institutions in
insuring capitalist markets run efficiently.

His most significant contribution to the field of economics has been
his central role in developing the "information-theoretic" approach,
which challenges the neoclassical assumption that markets are efficient
aside from limited and occasional failures. In contrast, Stiglitz has argued that markets generally work imperfectly due primarily to "information asymmetries" between different market agents, and that those
who have greater access to information (richer companies in richer
countries) are able to exploit this imbalance to their own advantage.
Stiglitz's proposed solution is to treat information as a "public good,"
with the state playing a role to ensure that information is universally
distributed and that the proper institutional infrastructure exists to
limit the negative impacts of information asymmetries (such as regu-
lating the banking and financial sector or breaking up monopolies and
enforcing competition policies) (Stiglitz and Charlton 2006, 1–56; Fine
and Van Waeyenberge 2005; Roemer 1995; Stiglitz 1994).

Stiglitz's information-theoretic approach provides an important
challenge to one of the pillars of neoclassical economics (perfect markets) but remains firmly embedded within its overarching framework,
rooted in the same assumptions around self-interested and optimizing
human nature, methodological individualism, and the superiority of
highly deductive mathematical models. All "non-market" issues (the
social and political) are relegated to the sidelines, either as benign institutions responding to market failure (like the state) or as aberrations or
externalities to the existing capitalist system, as opposed to outcomes
of its everyday operation (such as violence, domination, poverty, and
inequality) (Milonakis and Fine 2009, 295–308; Žižek 2008, 2; Lebowitz 2006; Fine and Van Waeyenberge 2005; Taylor 2005; Hart-Landsberg
and Burkett 2004; Chang 2001, 1–15). Stiglitz's work thus challenges the
status quo of neoclassical economics while at the same time remaining
entrenched within it.

A telling example of the complex and contradictory nature of Stiglitz's work is his book *Whither Socialism?*, developed in the early 1990s
as the Stalinist states of Eastern Europe were collapsing. The dominant
paradigm that emerged out of the West and was adopted in Eastern Europe was that of "shock therapy," which involved market liberalization
and wholesale, rapid privatization of state assets, resulting in a social
and economic disaster in the region.[3] In his book, Stiglitz rejects shock

therapy in favour of a more gradual approach that recognizes that markets have to be "made" through limited state involvement, not just to protect private property rights (as neoclassical economists would have it) but also to ensure competition and address information asymmetries. At the same time, he dismisses the prospects of market socialism as an alternative, claiming it suffers from the same conceptual weaknesses of neoclassical economics: neglecting information asymmetries. Yet, while his reflections on neoclassical orthodoxy are rooted in the core literature in economics, his comments on socialism are based almost entirely on a handful of neoclassical models of market socialism from the 1930s, ignoring the great bulk of political economic, social, philosophical, and historical thought on socialism over the past 200 years (Fine and Van Waeyenberge 2005; Roemer 1995). While situating his ideas as a "third way" between neoclassical economics and market socialism, Stiglitz reveals scant knowledge of the latter, and his work is firmly situated in the former, arguing for the necessity of developing a society driven by market logic and competition. When Stiglitz does diverge from the neoclassical paradigm, he does so in a limited manner; at one point, he argues, contra neoclassical economics, that public institutions can be made to run more efficiently if they pay higher salaries to top employees ("$500,000 a year") to compete with private industry – society, he asserts, needs to develop a "greater tolerance of inequities" (Stiglitz 1994, 242).

Stiglitz's relatively slim divergence from neoclassical orthodoxy is not unique to him but, rather, reflects the gradual narrowing of the entire field of economics since the late nineteenth century (and, more rapidly, since the 1970s), which has seen economics expunge its social and historical content along with the insights of classical and Marxist political economy (such as methodological holism and an awareness of the limits of excessive abstract mathematical formalism) (Milonakis and Fine 2009). This narrowing has occurred not solely as an academic affair but as part of the professionalization of economics and a requirement for career success, especially as economists, far more than any other social scientist, are frequently employed outside of academia as highly paid, private consultants for capital and government (Lowrey 2011). As Dimitris Milonakis and Ben Fine (2009, 49) state in their extensive survey of the history of economic thought, those practitioners who continue to draw on classical and Marxist political economy "must pay a heavy price for their intellectual integrity – one that they are not always willing and able to bear." In Stiglitz's case, the nature of his critique allowed him to position himself as a *critic within* the dominant paradigm, with enough legitimacy to attain a high-ranking position as a citizen-bureaucrat in the Council of Economic Advisors under U.S. President Bill Clinton, serving first as a member from 1993 to 1995 and then as Chair from 1995 to 1997.

As a member of the Clinton Cabinet, Stiglitz revelled in his new role, which allowed him to apply his economics background to drafting "policies in almost every sphere." Stiglitz was involved in far more policy decisions than can be discussed here, but the most significant to him was his overall contribution in helping to "define a new economic philosophy, a 'third way,' which recognized the important, but limited, role of government" (Stiglitz 2002a). Critics have correctly observed that the "third way" – much like Stiglitz's critique of shock therapy – does not part from the overall logic of the neoclassical economics and "continue[s] to be rooted in existing patterns of ownership, in the dominating principle of self-interest, and in the belief that (outside of a few exceptions) the market knows best" (Lebowitz 2006, 41). Indeed, Clinton's "third way" politics were little different from the conservative "Reaganomics" that preceded it – it has the same emphasis on free markets, free enterprise, global market integration, economic growth, government downsizing, and the abandonment of redistributionist policies, only with the addition of a "values" discourse based on opportunity, individual responsibility, and community (Peck 2008, 103–74; Henwood 1996). To Stiglitz, however, in the wake of his four years with the Clinton administration, the "third way" represented a major shift in economic philosophy, and he stated that "America's economic policy had been successfully redefined" (Stiglitz 2002a).

Stiglitz's success as an economic advisor opened further doors to him as a citizen-bureaucrat, and in 1997 he was offered, and accepted, the position as Chief Economist and Senior Vice President at the World Bank. Throughout the 1990s the World Bank had been suffering from a crisis of legitimacy in the wake of failed neoliberal policies, seen most vividly in the crisis-stricken economies of the former Soviet Union, and the appointment of Stiglitz allowed the bank to appear open to criticism and willing to make changes to adjust to the poor results of their pro-market prescriptions. For his first year at the bank, Stiglitz kept a relatively low profile, supporting policies and positions that he would later critique, but became increasingly more disenchanted with "market fundamentalism" and more vocal about his opposition to the direction of policy in his second and third year (Fine and Van Waeyenberge 2005;

Chang 2001). As someone who prides himself on independent thought (one of the benefits of being a citizen-bureaucrat), Stiglitz encountered a stifling intellectual environment at the bank, where sound "economic principles" were often sacrificed by "politics" imposed by the U.S. Treasury (Stiglitz 2002a). As many critics have pointed out, rather than being a mere technocratic institution producing value-neutral knowledge, the bank operates in a highly political manner, spending tens of millions of dollars each year to produce policy reports, data analyses, journals, and seminars designed to promote a particular kind of "knowledge": one which defines the needs of capital as the needs of everyone and pro-market policies as the only road to combating poverty, regardless of empirical outcomes or evidence to the contrary (Goldman 2006; Taylor 2005; Cammack 2002).

Within this context, Stiglitz's aspirations for change at the bank were quickly frustrated and his loyalty tested in response to the East Asian economic crisis in 1997/8, initiated when speculative hedge funds attacked the currencies in the region, sparking a massive outflow of "hot money" and plunging the entire region into crisis. Stiglitz spoke out publicly against the IMF's role in the crisis, both for pressuring the region to adopt "excessively rapid financial and capital market liberalization," which helped spark the crisis in the first place, and for imposing strict monetary and fiscal restraints on the region in exchange for bailout loans that further exacerbated the crisis after it began (Hart-Landsberg and Burkett 2004; Stiglitz 2002a; 2002b, 89; Wade 2001; Gowan 1999, 60–127). Stiglitz was not alone in his critique of the IMF's handling of the crisis but, states Chang (2001, 1), "it was a great shock for many people, especially those in the IMF, to find such public chastisement coming from its sister organization's intellectual leader." Stiglitz reportedly received a "gag order" from World Bank President James Wolfensohn in 1998, but he remained undeterred in his public criticism. Eventually, he was compelled to resign from the bank in 2000, with the U.S. Treasury played a key role in pressuring for his removal (Fine and Van Waeyenberge 2005; Stiglitz 2002a; Press 2002; Chang 2001; Wade 2001).

The Weberian good bureaucrat was ever-present in Stiglitz's rise to his high-ranking advisory positions, which ultimately necessitated playing within the rules of acceptable political and economic discourse, steering a prestigious and careful career within the bounds of legitimate academic pursuits, building contacts with powerful public and private sources, and, at least initially, demonstrating himself to be a loyal and faithful adherent. Stiglitz was not unaware of these sorts of submissive and competitive pressures and the role they play in determining the careers of bureaucrats. As a "citizen-bureaucrat," however, Stiglitz believed he was in a unique position to avoid many of the pressures faced by "political hacks" and instead "work for the adoption of economic policies that were consistent with economic principles." When the limitations of his position became clearer to him, Stiglitz donned the garb of the dissenting Tolstoyan bureaucrat, having "had [his] fill of bureaucracy" (Stiglitz 2002a). Within months of his departure from the bank, Stiglitz (2000) wrote an infamous and scathing critique of the IMF and U.S. Treasury in the *New Republic*, condemning them for "not using smart economics" in their prescriptions for Eastern Europe and East Asia, and accusing IMF economists of being "third-rank students from first-rate universities."

Yet, while the Tolstoyan bureaucrat of fiction generally meets with despair or disgrace upon breaking with powerful institutions, Stiglitz's dissent marked new heights for his popularity and public renown. In 2001, he was awarded the Nobel Prize in Economics, the same year that he was proclaimed "the Rebel Within" (Chang 2001). The following year, he published his most famous book, *Globalization and Its Discontents* (2002b), which became an international bestseller and was translated into 28 languages. In the book, Stiglitz summarizes and expands on his overall critique of neoliberal economic policies, with particular focus on a biting critique of the IMF. Drawing on cases from around the world, but paying particular attention to Eastern Europe and East Asia, Stiglitz criticizes policies of rapid, wholesale privatization, market liberalization, and fiscal austerity, which had become "ends in themselves" and "were pushed too far, too fast, and to the exclusion of other policies that were needed" (Stiglitz 2002b, 53–4). The reason for this, argues Stiglitz, was primarily the "ideological fervor" and "market fundamentalism" of IMF economic advisors who blindly imposed their agenda without regard for the sort of policies required to "make globalization work": stronger regulations on capital flows and the financial sector, social safety nets, environmental regulations, and debt forgiveness, along with more democratic global governance and fairer international trade policies to assist poorer countries in better "managing" and "sequencing" liberalization (Stiglitz 2007b; Stiglitz and Charlton 2006; Edwards 2003; Stiglitz 2002b, 12, 214–52; Eichengreen 2002).

Stiglitz's powerful and passionate critique of failed global economic policies required political courage and personal integrity and certainly made him enemies at the IMF and the institutions he had previously worked for and their apologists (see Kennedy 2003; *The Economist* 2002). At the same time, the nature of his rebellion allowed him to preserve, and in some circles enhance, his own prestige as one of the world's top global policy advisors and "rock-star economists," a regular participant of both the World Social Forum and the World Economic Forum (Mishkin 2010; Stiglitz 2007b, 1–7). Since leaving the World Bank, Stiglitz has worked as a professor at Columbia University; published extensively in top-rated newspapers, magazines, and journals; given countless media interviews; authored and co-authored bestselling books expanding on his ideas about globalization (Stiglitz 2007b; Stiglitz and Charlton 2006; Stiglitz 2003), the war in Iraq (Stiglitz and Bilmes 2008), and the recent global economic crisis (Stiglitz 2010); and participated in a 2008 French documentary, *Around the World with Joseph Stiglitz*.[4] While barred from the most powerful international advisory positions, Stiglitz has maintained a high profile as a top-ranked citizen-bureaucrat, advising a variety of policymaking bodies and meeting "with prime ministers, presidents, and parliamentarians on every continent" (Stiglitz 2007b, x; Press 2002). Most notably, since the onset of the global economic recession in 2007, Stiglitz has lead two international commissions with particular "Stiglitizian" orientations. In 2008, he was asked by conservative French President Nicolas Sarkozy to chair the Commission on the Measurement of Economic Performance and Social Progress, which is devoted to promoting "better metrics" to statistically quantify all economic and non-economic aspects of human well-being and sustainability (Stiglitz, Sen, and Fitoussi 2009). In 2009 he was appointed by the president of the UN General Assembly as Chair of the Commission of Experts on Reforms of the International Monetary and Financial System (also known as the "Stiglitz Commission"), whose report called for countries to avoid protectionism while at the same time restoring the "balance between market and government" through tighter financial regulations and counter-cyclical policies, including social security measures, infrastructure development, and credit guarantees (United Nations 2009, 18).

There are several factors that help explain how Stiglitz has been able to publicly rebel from powerful institutions while still remaining within the parameters of legitimate dissent. First, Stiglitz's well-articulated and engagingly written criticisms of the Washington Consensus, as pointed out by Fine and Van Waeyenberge (2005, 149), "are, and always have been, standard criticisms, and had been made by progressive scholars, albeit from different perspectives, for a decade or more before being adopted, pretty much without acknowledgement, by Stiglitz himself." What made these criticisms unique was that they had been embraced by a high-ranking citizen-bureaucrat at a time when neoliberal institutions were already facing a crisis of legitimacy. Stiglitz's public denouncement took place only months after the Seattle protests in 1999, which involved massive street protests outside the WTO Ministerial Conference, ushering in a chain of global justice protests that continue to disrupt meetings of the WTO, World Bank, IMF, G8, and G20 to this day (Goldman 2006; Fine and Van Waeyenberge 2005; Taylor 2005; McNally 2002; Press 2002; Mandel 2002; Chang 2001; Wade 2001). This timing situated him to become a popular rallying point for a reform movement that was already well under way: now, *even* a former chief economist and senior vice president at the World Bank agreed with the overarching critique of globalization.

To those on the radical or anti-capitalist left, Stiglitz's actions reflected the growing force of the globalization critique, which had managed to reach the upper echelons of global power. His Tolstoyan dissent gave him reasonable legitimacy among diverse sectors of the left, who celebrated Stiglitz's (2002b, 6, 9) acknowledgment that "the critics are right," and that "until the protestors came along there was little hope for change and no outlets for complaint." Writing for the left-wing magazine *The Nation*, Eyal Press (2002) extolled the virtue of Stiglitz's "fiercely independent" and "potentially radical" thought, proclaiming that "Only a few years ago, it was possible for pundits to claim that no mainstream economist, certainly nobody of Stiglitz's stature, took the criticism of free trade and globalization seriously. Such claims are no longer credible." With perhaps greater sobriety and self-admitted scepticism, Marxian academic Bill Freund (2003, 102) expressed the view of many on the radical left that one of the greatest values of Stiglitz's work was that it allowed one to point to an eminent economist and policymaker and offer the same critiques "frequently associated ... as views of a 'looney' or 'extreme' left."

To those further into the reformist camp or the centre, or even the right, Stiglitz's dissent also represented the voice of protest coming to halls of power, but in a manner translated into something more palatable and less threatening to the current order, wrapped as it was in the cloak of Stiglitz's previous Weberian loyalty and relatively acceptable policy discourse. Stiglitz (2002b, 5, 248) assured them that "globalization has helped hundreds of millions of people attain higher standards of living, beyond what they, or most economists, thought imaginable but a short while ago" and that those "who vilify globalization too often overlook its benefits." These statements reflect the somewhat vague and at times contradictory nature of Stiglitz, who has been able to speak to multiple audiences, often with extremely divergent perspectives, while riding the tide of a broad reform movement that often has had little clear direction of its own. Siddharth Mohandas (2002), writing for the centrist *Washington Monthly*, noted the undeniable power of Stiglitz's critique, coming as it was from "a venerated insider," making it "no longer merely a matter of protesters in the street." Even the fiercely neoliberal magazine *The Economist*, which published a dismissive, almost hysterical, review of Stiglitz's *Globalization and Its Discontents*, had to acknowledge that Stiglitz is "an author superbly qualified to write the definitive account of globalization" and "a brilliant economist – and he cares, he cares" (*The Economist* 2002).

Second, while being scathingly critical of the IMF and the U.S. Treasury, Stiglitz has been careful to tread softly – if not apologetically – with the institutions that he directly worked with: the World Bank and the Clinton administration. Despite the World Bank being a long-time promoter of neoliberal reforms, with a reputation for "not necessarily welcom[ing] public dissent," Stiglitz focused his earlier fire on the IMF, insisting that the World Bank's opinions were consistently ignored and overruled by the IMF, even in instances where the Bank was "contributing literally billions of dollars to the rescue packages" (Eichengreen 2002; Stiglitz 2000). In recent years, Stiglitz has begun to tack on "… and the World Bank" to his critique, while still saving most of his fire for the IMF (Stiglitz 2007b, 15, 300–3; Stiglitz and Charlton 2006, 20).

Similarly, despite the fact that Clinton was in office from 1993 to 2001, during the Asian economic crisis and Stiglitz's dismissal from the World Bank, Stiglitz has attributed blame specifically to the U.S. Treasury while absolving Clinton of any responsibility, believing that Clinton "supported both [his] stances and the values that underlay them, but … the US Treasury often did not adequately inform [Clinton] about the policies they were advocating, let alone ask for his approval" (Stiglitz 2002a; Kahn 2002). These comments present somewhat shockingly lacklustre and anaemic portrayals of the U.S. president and World Bank officials, and it is difficult to ascertain the extent to which they are strategic or reflect Stiglitz's genuine views. They certainly would have assisted Stiglitz in preserving good relations with powerful backers. They also have had the effect of downplaying his own complicity in some of the actions he now publicly criticizes; Stiglitz, after all, was a member of the Clinton administration during the implementation of both the North American Free Trade Agreement (NAFTA) in 1994 and the World Trade Organization (WTO) in 1995, both of which he today deems to be "unfair" to developing countries (Stiglitz 2007a; Stiglitz and Charlton 2006). He was also in Clinton's cabinet during the lead up to the Asian crisis, during which time the U.S. government put intense pressure on Asian economies to weaken capital restrictions which played a significant role in causing the economic crisis – Stiglitz asserts that his own views on a more gradual and selective liberalization were trumped by the Treasury Department, which drafted policy in tandem with the IMF, without consulting the president, and with "a virtual absence of theory and evidence" (Stiglitz 2002b, 100–3; Gowan 1999).

A third factor explaining the preservation of Stiglitz's legitimacy in the wake of his dissent has been the political nature of his intellectual work, in particular his understanding of the modern state. Steeped in neoclassical economics and neglecting most research in the social sciences exploring questions of power, class, conflict, and historical specificity, Stiglitz's work reveals a weak understanding of the state "as essentially benevolent, a special institution ... for the correction of market failures and undesirable social outcomes" (Milonakis and Fine 2009; Fine and Van Waeyenberge 2005, 159). The result is a relatively superficial understanding of politics, where bad economic policies emerge as a result of misguided "ideology" or "special interests"; everything from his own dismissal at the World Bank to the policies that devastated the economies of Eastern Europe and East Asia can be attributed to this unfortunate combination (Stiglitz 2007a, 2007b; Stiglitz and Charlton 2006; Kennedy 2003; Stiglitz 2002b). This perspective assumes that U.S. foreign policy is, or at least should be in the absence of "political" distortions, driven by a relatively benign "national" and "global" interest, as opposed to the "special interests" of elite American classes. These elite interests, however, far from being merely "special," are in fact central to the objectives of state policy. Significant sectors of U.S. capital have in fact benefited significantly from the crises Stiglitz decries as irrational, with U.S. corporations gaining enhanced access to foreign markets, buying foreign assets at rock-bottom prices, and making profits off highly speculative financial activities (Klein 2007; Fine and Van Waeyenberge 2005; Taylor 2005; Harvey 2003; Cammack 2002; Gowan 1999). Stiglitz agrees that sectors of U.S. capital, in particular the financial sector, have benefited from the crises but dismisses as "conspiracy theory" any suggestion that these outcomes are the result of deliberate U.S. statecraft as opposed to "interests and ideology" (Stiglitz 2002b, 129–30).

While a great deal more can be said about Stiglitz's understanding of the state than can be delved into here, from the perspective of his iconic status as a citizen-bureaucrat, his relatively benign conception of the state has allowed him to separate "bad economic policy" from the institutions that make them. This applies not only to the White House and the World Bank but, in a round-about way, even to the IMF and the U.S. Treasury; the culprit, for Stiglitz, is never the institutions themselves, nor the economic system that they work to reproduce, but rather the people *within* the institutions, duped by misguided ideologies and bullied by special interests into giving advice on the basis of "bad economics" (Stiglitz 2002b, 106, 119). States Stiglitz (2002b, 207): "We cannot talk meaningfully about the motivations and intentions of any institution, only of those who constitute and govern it." Open up the institutions, provide greater democratic accountability and transparency, and replace "third-rank" economists with those of Stiglitz's rigour, and the outcomes would be very different.

In this way, Stiglitz makes a key departure from the Tolstoyan bureaucrat who turns on modern institutions and the economic system they are intertwined with, seeing them as the root cause of bad politics; the modern state and the capitalist market compel good people to do bad things. To Stiglitz, it is the other way around: bad policymakers wreck essentially good institutions and a good economic system in need of reforms. Thus, while the Tolstoyan bureaucrat ends in despair, Stiglitz despairs over specific policies while remaining broadly loyal to the ideals and institutions themselves. This is not merely a philosophical difference, but a significantly political one, allowing Stiglitz to carefully manoeuvre between Tolstoyan dissent (from the policies) and Weberian loyalty (to the institutions), constructing an iconic image as a rebellious, tough-minded, independent citizen-bureaucrat – a governance fantasy that, in many ways, is more powerful than Stiglitz's actual policy prescriptions.

The Power of the Citizen-Bureaucrat

The iconic image of the citizen-bureaucrat offered by Stiglitz is premised on a seeming reconciliation between two very different understandings of the modern bureaucrat and a recasting of each of them into more empowering roles: a loyal Weberian bureaucrat who is also a fierce, independent thinker and a rebellious Tolstoyan bureaucrat who remains reasonably legitimate in the eyes of powerful institutions and world leaders. The extent to which this reconciliation and recasting goes beyond the iconic image itself, however, is highly questionable.

In order to recast the rebellious Tolstoyan bureaucrat within the boundaries of legitimate dissent, Stiglitz's rebellion has in many ways been highly "scripted"; while contesting World Bank power, the "choice of what will be contested" has already been scripted in advance (Mooney Nickel 2009, 386). Stiglitz has challenged the Washington Consensus while remaining within the overall framework of neoclassical economics. He has rebelled against the specific institution of the World Bank while remaining devoted to the broader political and ideological structures that the bank is situated in. Even while criticizing the policies of powerful institutions, questioning their openness and democratic accountability, Stiglitz has sought not to eliminate them but to persuade them to adopt a new policy direction, one which Stiglitz maintains would be in their own best interests, as well as "save the capitalist system" (Stiglitz 2007b, xvii; 2002b, 195–252). In doing so, rather than confront the historical and class nature of these powerful institutions, Stiglitz has affirmed their legitimacy: as Marx (1963, 88) has observed, "Whomever one seeks to persuade, one acknowledges as master of the situation."

Perhaps most significantly, his emphasis on objective, "good economics" as opposed to ideological, "market fundamentalism" has persistently denied the *textuality* of his own ideas – that they are contestable and subjective (Mooney Nickel 2009). Instead, Stiglitz's poses his own ideas as being beyond "ideological battles and toward fixing the problems of capitalism," through the expert management and administration of life based on value-free science (Žižek 2008; Stiglitz 2007b, xii; Stiglitz and Charlton 2006, 36). Yet, far from transcendence, Stiglitz's ideas are rooted in the same dominant ideological and political foundations as the sources of power he seeks to challenge. The superiority of objective economic science and mathematical modelling, the beliefs that human beings are individualistic, competitive, and accumulative by nature, and overarching assumptions about the benefits of the market and private property and about the benign nature of the state are never up for grabs or even discussion (Milonakis and Fine 2009; Fine and Van Waeyenberge 2005; Hart-Landsberg and Burkett 2004; Cammack 2002). Consequently, while Stiglitz's work represents a challenge to the dominant policy paradigm, it does so *within* the confines of a narrow divergence in a manner that also serves to depoliticize neoliberalism, reify its central assumptions, and disavow the primary social and political dynamics that shape global capitalism.

A similar situation emerges with Stiglitz's recasting of the Weberian bureaucrat as both loyal and fiercely independent. Even though Stiglitz has demonstrated political courage and independent spirit in breaking with the World Bank, there is little evidence that this independence had much of an impact on his efforts as a citizen-bureaucrat working within the institutions. While fiercely critical of the policies leading to the East Asian crisis, much of these policies were conducted while Stiglitz himself was a member of the Clinton administration. While having developed a reputation as a lead international promoter of a "fairer" world trading system, Stiglitz (2007a) has acknowledged that during his years with the Clinton administration "the global-trade agreements we pushed through were often unfair to developing countries" (see also Stiglitz and Charlton 2006).

All of this is not to say that Stiglitz's views have not been "heard." His impact on the policy world goes beyond his formal, direct involvement and entails his broader effect on policy discourse as he has engaged in complex dialogue within and between the "administrative sphere" and the "public sphere" to contest and determine the overall framing of policy issues (Torgerson 2010). Many of his concepts have become central to major policy debates today. Of key importance, however, is that the impact of Stiglitz's ideas has not been from the *nature* that he promotes or intends; his ideas have not been embraced by world leaders, heading relatively benign states, rationally calculating what is in the "national" or "global" interest on the basis of sound, scientific evidence. Rather, world leaders head distinctly capitalist nation-states and global institutions, developed by their very nature to defend and support the interests of elite classes who seek, as Paul Cammack (2002, 8) states, to "present a set of policies infused with the class demands of capital as if they were inspired by disinterested benevolence" (Goldman 2006; Taylor 2005; Harvey 2003; Gowan 1999).

Against these hegemonic institutions, Stiglitz's voice is one of countless others – albeit coming from a particularly active and celebrated personality – demanding reforms of vastly different degrees and kinds to the status quo. As hegemonic institutions resist and battle back, these voices are invariably distorted or shuttled aside. Thus, despite Stiglitz's willingness to constrain his policy proposals in a manner that reifies many of neoliberalism's central assumptions and contextualizes his ideas as pragmatic and scientific, his ideas that are most original and independent have been virtually ignored in the corridors of power (Edwards 2003). The image that Stiglitz has pursued as a pragmatic citizen-bureaucrat, capable of being granted access to the ears of the powerful because of the objective, non-ideological nature of his advice is thus an artificial one. The more that Stiglitz's ideas adhere to the dominant paradigm, the more they are embraced; the less that they adhere to these needs, the more they are resisted.

While Stiglitz's policy career may not have borne the "pragmatic" fruit that he has intended, one thing his career has accomplished has been to buffer up his image as a renowned citizen-bureaucrat. His tireless scholarly and diplomatic efforts have provided him with ample evidence of his symbolic "policy strength."[5] Despite bearing constant witness to "bad economic policy" winning the day, Stiglitz persists in acting *as if* the search for good policies is the goal of the world's powerful institutions; to paraphrase Slavoj Žižek (1989, 31–2), he knows very well how things really are, but still he is acting as if he did not know. The result is an ideological fantasy, reproduced through his writings, interviews, presentations, and advisory work. After having been cast out of the World Bank as punishment for voicing unapproved views, Stiglitz's own insistence on the relatively benign nature of his dismissal (driven by stubborn, ideological enemies in the IMF and U.S. Treasury), on the merits of his own position (derived from having worked at the World Bank and with the Clinton administration), and on the solution to the problem (convincing world leaders of the rational and scientific nature of his policy prescriptions) has served to obscure more than he has revealed about the limited room for genuine dissent in today's neoliberal era.

The political impact of Stiglitz, far beyond the place his work plays in alternative policy circles, has been to provide the iconic image of the citizen-bureaucrat: an image which conveys a governance fantasy of empowerment amid the preponderance of alienated bureaucracies and the pervasiveness of neoliberal ideology. The citizen-bureaucrat offers a symbolic antidote to a world in which giant government and corporate bureaucracies increasingly squeeze out alternative visions and narrow available options. To those both within and outside these bureaucracies, Stiglitz offers a hopeful alternative (a "third way"), between the disempowered good bureaucrats of the Weberian variety (loyal and obedient) and the Tolstoyan one (rebellious and outcast). Yet, as Balzac (2002, 202) observed: "Lies are often preferable to the truth." The iconic image of the citizen-bureaucrat works to deny that which a sober assessment of Stiglitz's actual career suggests: that the available options for the good bureaucrat in today's neoliberal era, far from expanding, are more narrow than ever before. The politics of the citizen-bureaucrat lies less in providing a space for genuine dissent within the institutions of global governance than in conveying a fantasy about the existence of such a space that fills in for its failings and contradictions in actual practice.

NOTES

1 For a reference to Stiglitz, along with Jeffrey Sachs and Paul Krugman, as "rock-star economists," see Mishkin (2010). For an argument about economist and liberal pundit Paul Krugman's "wilful optimism" that has informed this article, see Martijn Konings, "The Ups and Downs of a Liberal Consciousness, or, Why Paul Krugman Should Learn to Tarry with the Negative," *ephemera* 9 (4) (2009), http://www.ephemeraweb.org/journal/9-4/9-4konings.pdf (accessed 3 August 2010). For a critical appraisal of Sachs as a celebrity teacher, see Richey and Ponte (2011).

2 This expression was popularized at the time by Chang (2001).

3 Under "shock therapy" reforms, the percentage of those living in poverty in Russia increased from 2 per cent in 1989 to 23.8 per cent in 1998 (Klein 2007, 262–95; Stiglitz 2002b, 133–65; Gowan 1999, 187–247).

4 For more on Stiglitz's extensive publications and interviews, as well as the documentary *Around the World with Joseph Stiglitz*, see his website at http://www.josephstiglitz.com/ (accessed 8 June 2010).

5 The notion of "policy strength" is derived here from Thorstein Veblen's ([1899] 1953) broader conception of "pecuniary strength" – one's ability to demonstrate explicitly wasteful consumption as a symbol of honour and success in a capitalist society.

Bibliography

ABC News. 2005. "Angelina Jolie Inspires International Adoptions." October 1. http://abcnews.go.com/GMA/story?id=1175428&page=1.

Adler, Bill, ed. 1997. *The Uncommon Wisdom of Oprah Winfrey.* Secaucus, NJ: Birch Lane Press.

Adorno, Theodor W. 1991. *The Culture Industry.* London, New York: Routledge.

Albanese, Catherine L. 2007. *A Republic of Mind and Spirit: A Cultural History of American Metaphysical Religion.* New Haven: Yale University Press.

Albiniak, Paige. 2010. "The Real Post-Oprah Era Opportunity." *Broadcasting and Cable*, March 29. http://www.broadcastingcable.com/article/450830-The_Real_Post_Oprah_Era_Opportunity.php.

Alcañiz, Enrique B., Ruben B. Caceres, and Rafael C. Perez. 2010. "Alliances between Brands and Social Causes: The Influence of Company Credibility on Social Responsibility Image." *Journal of Business Ethics* 96 (2): 169–86. http://dx.doi.org/10.1007/s10551-010-0461-x.

The Alliance for Climate Protection. 2011. "The Alliance for Climate Protection." Accessed January 27. http://www.climateprotect.org/.

Alter, Jonathan. 2010. "Obama's Class Project." *Newsweek*, September 13. http://www.thedailybeast.com/newsweek/2010/09/13/how-obama-is-making-real-progress-on-education.print.html.

Anburajan, Aswini. 2007. "Breaking Down Oprah's Numbers." *MSNBC*, December 7. http://firstread.msnbc.msn.com/archive/2007/12/07/502240.aspx.

Antipode. 2010. "Special Issue on Capitalism and Conservation." 42 (3).

Appiah, Kwame Anthony. 2006. *Cosmopolitanism: Ethics in a World of Strangers.* New York: W.W. Norton.

Avins, Mimi. 2000. "Flocking to the Church of Oprah." *Los Angeles Times*, June 25. http://articles.latimes.com/2000/jun/25/news/cl-44508.

Baban, Feyzi. 2006. "Living with Difference: Cosmopolitanism, Modernity and Political Community." *Studies in Political Economy* 77: 107–29.

Bakker, Isabella, and Stephen Gill. 2003. "Ontology, Method and Hypotheses." In *Power, Production, and Social Reproduction*, ed. Isabella Bakker and Stephen Gill, 17–46. Basingstoke: Palgrave Macmillan.

Bakker, Karen. 2007. "The 'Commons' versus the 'Commodity': Alter-Globalization, Anti-Privatization and the Human Right to Water in the Global South." *Antipode* 39 (3): 430–55. http://dx.doi.org/10.1111/j.1467-8330.2007.00534.x.

Bakker, Karen. 2010. "The Limits of 'Neoliberal Natures': Debating Green Neoliberalism." *Progress in Human Geography* 34 (6): 715–35. http://dx.doi.org/10.1177/0309132510376849.

Balzac, Honoré de. 2002. *Cousin Bette*. New York: The Modern Library.

Barboza, Steven. 2010. "The Oprah Effect: The Industry behind Her Show's Guest List." *Atlanta Post*, July 13. http://www.bet.com/news/news/2010/07/14/businesstheindustrybehindoprahsguestlist.html.

Barnert, Deanna. 2011. "Oprah Talks OWN and Her Journey." *SheKnows.com*, January 7. http://www.sheknows.com/entertainment/articles/822088/oprah-talks-own-and-her-journey.

Barnes, Teresa. 2008. "Product RED: The Marketing of African Misery." *Journal of Pan African Studies* 2 (6): 71–6.

Barnett, Clive, Paul Choke, Nick Clarke, and Alice Malpass. 2010. *Globalizing Responsibility: The Political Rationalities of Ethical Consumption*. London: Blackwell.

Barnett, Tony, and Alan Whiteside. 2002. *AIDS in the Twenty-First Century*. Basingstoke: Palgrave Macmillan. http://dx.doi.org/10.1057/ 9780230599208.

Barron, Lee. 2009. "An Actress Compelled to Act: Angelina Jolie's *Notes from My Travels* as Celebrity Activist/Travel Narrative." *Postcolonial Studies* 12 (2): 211–28. http://dx.doi.org/10.1080/13688790902887189.

Barthes, Roland. 1972 [1957]. *Mythologies*. New York: Farrar, Strauss and Giroux.

Bauman, Zygmunt. 1991. *Modernity and Ambivalence*. Ithaca: Cornell University Press.

Bauman, Zygmunt. 2001. "Consuming Life." *Journal of Consumer Culture* 1 (1): 9–29. http://dx.doi.org/10.1177/146954050100100102.

Bauman, Zygmunt. 2007. *Consuming Life*. Cambridge: Polity Press.

BBC. 2005. "Donate Live 8 Profit Says Gilmour." July 5. http://news.bbc.co.uk/2/hi/entertainment/4651309.stm.

BBC. 2006. "Live Aid 1985: How It All Happened." Last modified July. http://www.bbc.co.uk/music/thelive8event/liveaid/history.shtml.

BBC. 2010a. "BBC Apologises Over Band Aid Money Reports." November 4. http://www.bbc.co.uk/news/entertainment-arts-11688535.

BBC. 2010b. "Geldof Challenges BBC Aid Claim." March 7. http://news.bbc.co.uk/2/hi/8554048.stm.

Beaumont, Peter. 2010. "Haiti Earthquake: Six Months On." *The Guardian*, July 10. http://www.guardian.co.uk/world/2010/jul/10/haiti-earthquake-aid-survivors.

Beck, Ulrich. 1992. *Risk Society: Towards a New Modernity*. London: Sage Publications.

Beck, Ulrich. 1999. *World Risk Society*. Malden, MA: Blackwell.

Beck, Ulrich, Wolfgang Bonss, and Christoph Lau. 2003. "The Theory of Reflexive Modernization: Problematic, Hypotheses and Research Program." *Theory, Culture & Society* 20 (2): 1–33. http://dx.doi.org/10.1177/026327640 3020002001.

Bell, Daniel. 1976. *The Cultural Contradictions of Capitalism*. New York: Basic Books.

Bello, Walden. 2004. *Deglobalization: Ideas for a New World Economy*. London: Zed Books.

Benjamin, Mark. 2010. "Clooney's 'Antigenocide Paparazzi': Watching Sudan." *Time*, December 28. http://www.time.com/time/world/article/0,8599,2039887,00.html.

Berlant, Lauren. 2006. "Cruel Optimism." *Differences: A Journal of Feminist Cultural Studies* 17 (3): 20–36. http://dx.doi.org/10.1215/10407391-2006-009.

Bernstein, Richard J. 1992. *The New Constellation: Ethical-Political Horizons of Modernity/Postmodernity*. Cambridge, MA: MIT Press.

Bhagwati, Jagdish. 2002. *Free Trade Today*. Princeton: Princeton University Press.

Bishop, Matthew. 2008. "To Capitalism's Defenders: Don't Be So Defensive." In Kinsley 2008, 120–3.

Bishop, Matthew, and Michael Green. 2009. *Philanthrocapitalism: How Giving Can Change the World*. New York: Bloomsbury Press.

Bobby Shriver Website. 2011. Accessed March 24. http://www.bobbyshriver.com/red.php.

Boggs, Carl. 2000. *The End of Politics*. New York: Guilford.

Bonilla-Silva, Eduardo. 2008. "The 2008 Elections and the Future of Anti-Racism in 21st Century Amerika or How We Got Drunk with Obama's Hope Liquor and Failed to See Reality (Lecture Delivered at the Association of Humanist Sociologists' Meeting in Boston, November 7, Posted to Blog)." *Black and Progressive Sociologists for Obama*, November 28.

http://sociologistsforobama.blogspot.ca/2008/11/eduardo-bonilla-silva-problem-with.html.

Bono. 2007. "Guest Editor's Introduction." *Vanity Fair*, July.

Bono. 2009. "Rebranding Africa." *New York Times*, July 9. http://www.nytimes.com/2009/07/10/opinion/10bono.html?_r=5&ref=opinion&pagewanted=all.

Bork, Robert H. 1997. *Slouching towards Gomorrah: Modern Liberalism and American Decline*. New York: Regan Books.

Boyd, Emily, Maxwell Boykoff, and Peter Newell. 2011. "The 'New' Carbon Economy: What's New?" *Antipode* 43 (3): 601–11. http://dx.doi.org/10.1111/j.1467-8330.2011.00882.x.

Boykoff, Max, and Michael Goodman. 2009. "Conspicuous Redemption? Reflections on the Promises and Perils of the 'Celebritization' of Climate Change." *Geoforum* 40 (3): 395–406. http://dx.doi.org/10.1016/j.geoforum.2008.04.006.

Boykoff, Max, Michael Goodman, and Jo Littler. 2010. "'Charismatic Mega-fauna': The Growing Power of Celebrities and Pop Culture in Climate Change Campaigns." *Environment, Politics and Development Working Paper Series, Working Paper #28, Department of Geography, King's College London.* http://www.kcl.ac.uk/sspp/departments/geography/research/epd/workingpapers.aspx.

Brenner, Robert. 2006. *The Economics of Global Turbulence*. London: Verso.

Brockington, Dan. 2008. "Powerful Environmentalisms: Conservation, Celebrity and Capitalism." *Media, Culture & Society* 30 (4): 551–68. http://dx.doi.org/10.1177/0163443708030040701.

Brockington, Dan. 2009. *Celebrity and the Environment: Fame, Wealth and Power in Conservation*. London: Zed Books.

Brown, Elaine. 2002. *The Condemnation of Little B*. Boston: Beacon Press.

Bryant, Raymond, and Michael Goodman. 2004. "Consuming Narratives: The Political Ecology of 'Alternative' Consumption." *Transactions of the Institute of British Geographers* 29 (3): 344–66. http://dx.doi.org/10.1111/j.0020-2754.2004.00333.x.

Bryman, Alan. 2004. *The Disneyization of Society*. London: Sage.

Brysk, Alison. 2005. *Human Rights and Private Wrongs: Constructing Civil Society*. New York: Routledge.

Buck-Morss, Susan. 2009. "Obama and the Image." *Culture, Theory and Critique* 50 (2–3): 145–64. http://dx.doi.org/10.1080/14735780903240109.

Buffett, Warren, and Bill Gates. 2008. "Bill Gates and Warren Buffett Discuss 'Creative Capitalism.'" In Kinsley 2008, 20–39.

Bumpus, Adam, and Diana Liverman. 2008. "Accumulation by Decarbonization and the Governance of Carbon Offsets." *Economic Geography* 84 (2): 127–55. http://dx.doi.org/10.1111/j.1944-8287.2008.tb00401.x.

Bunting, Madeleine. 2005. "A Day with Bono: 'We Have to Make Africa an Adventure.'" *The Guardian*, June 16.

Bunting, Madeleine. 2010. "The Issue of Celebrities and Aid Is Deceptively Complex." *The Guardian*, December 17. http://www.guardian.co.uk/global-development/poverty-matters/2010/dec/17/celebrity-aid-development-bono-brad-pitt.

Caldwell, Christopher. 2007. "Unaccountable Generosity." *Financial Times*, September 8. http://www.ft.com/intl/cms/s/0/7fe5cc9a-5d75-11dc-8d22-0000779fd2ac.html#axzz1NqhAE9vY.

Cameron, John, and Anna Haanstra. 2008. "Development Made Sexy: How It Happened and What It Means." *Third World Quarterly* 29 (8): 1475–89. http://dx.doi.org/10.1080/01436590802528564.

Cammack, Paul. 2002. "Attacking the Poor." *New Left Review* 13 (January– February): 125–34.

Carr, David. 2002. "O Magazine is Expanding to South Africa." *New York Times*, April 8. http://www.nytimes.com/2002/04/08/business/o-magazine-is-expanding-to-south-africa.html?scp=4&sq=david%20carr%20AND%20Oprah%202002&st=cse.

Carr, David. 2007. "Citizen Bono Brings Africa to the Idle Rich." *New York Times*, March 5.

Carr, David. 2009. "A Triumph of Avoiding the Traps." *New York Times*, November 22. http://www.nytimes.com/2009/11/23/business/media/23carr.html?_r=1&scp=1&sq=David%20Carr%20AND%20Oprah&st=cse.

Carroll, Rory. 2010. "John Travolta Flies Scientologists' Aid to Haiti." *The Guardian*, January 26. http://www.guardian.co.uk/world/2010/jan/26/john-travolta-scientology-aid-haiti.

Castree, Noel. 2003. "Commodifying What Nature?" *Progress in Human Geography* 27 (3): 273–97. http://dx.doi.org/10.1191/0309132503ph428oa.

Castree, Noel. 2005. "The Epistemology of Particulars: Human Geography, Case Studies and 'Context.'" *Geoforum* 36 (5): 541–4. http://dx.doi.org/10.1016/j.geoforum.2005.08.001.

Castree, Noel, and Bruce Braun. 1998. "The Construction of Nature and Nature of Construction: Analytical and Political Tools for Building Survivable Futures." In *Remaking Reality: Nature at the Millennium*, ed. Noel Castree and Bruce Braun, 3–42. New York: Routledge.

CBS News World. 2010. "John Travolta Pilots Haiti Relief Flight." January 26. http://www.cbsnews.com/stories/2010/01/26/world/main6142734. shtml.

Chancer, Lynn S. 1992. *Sadomasochism in Everyday Life: The Dynamics of Power and Powerlessness*. New Brunswick, NJ: Rutgers University Press.

Chang, Ha-Joon, ed. 2001. *Joseph Stiglitz and the World Bank: The Rebel Within – Selected Speeches by Joseph Stiglitz*. London: Wimbledon Publishing Company.

Chauvin, Kyle. 2008. "Don't Change Capitalism, Expand it." In Kinsley 2008, 178–82.

Chernomas, Robert, and Ian Hudson. 2007. *Social Murder: And Other Shortcomings of Conservative Economics*. Winnipeg: Arbeiter Ring Publishing.

Chouliaraki, Lilie. 2008. "The Mediation of Suffering and the Vision of a Cosmopolitan Public." *Television & New Media* 9 (5): 371–91. http://dx.doi. org/10.1177/1527476408315496.

Clarke, Nick. 2008. "From Ethical Consumerism to Political Consumption." *Geography Compass* 2 (6): 1870–84. http://dx.doi.org/10.1111/ j.1749-8198.2008.00170.x.

Clarke, Nick, Clive Barnett, Paul Cloke, and Alice Malpass. 2007. "Globalising the Consumer: Doing Politics in an Ethical Register." *Political Geography* 26 (3): 231–49. http://dx.doi.org/10.1016/j.polgeo.2006.10.009.

ClearSky Climate Solutions. 2011. "ClearSky Projects." Small Dog Solutions. Accessed February 18. http://www.clearskyclimatesolutions.com/work/ projects/index.html.

Climate Change Wales. 2011. "The Average Carbon Footprint per Person in the UK." West Wales Eco Centre. Accessed February 18. http://www. climatechangewales.org.uk/public/?id=112.

Clinton, Bill. 2007. *Giving: How Each of Us Can Change the World*. New York: Knopf.

CNBC. 2009. "Oprah Effect." May 30. http://www.cnbc.com/id/29961298/.

Cohen, Jean L. 1982. *Class and Civil Society: The Limits of Marxian Critical Theory*. Amherst: University of Massachusetts Press.

Commission on Social Determinants of Health. 2008. *Final Report*. Geneva: World Health Organization.

Connolly, William E. 2000. "Speed, Concentric Cultures and Cosmopolitanism." *Political Theory* 28 (5): 596–618. http://dx.doi.org/10.1177/009059170 0028005002.

Cooper, Andrew F. 2007. "Celebrity Diplomacy and the G8: Bono and Bob as Legitimate International Actors." *Centre for International Governance Innovation, Working Paper #29*. September. http://www.cigionline.org/

publications/2007/9/celebrity-diplomacy-and-g8-bono-and-bob-legitimate-international-actors.

Cooper, Andrew F. 2008a. "Beyond One Image Fits All: Bono and the Complexity of Celebrity Diplomacy." *Global Governance* 14: 265–72.

Cooper, Andrew F. 2008b. *Celebrity Diplomacy*. Boulder: Paradigm Publishers.

Corbera, Esteve, Katrina Brown, and Neil Adger. 2007. "The Equity and Legitimacy of Markets for Ecosystem Services." *Development and Change* 38 (4): 587–613. http://dx.doi.org/10.1111/j.1467-7660.2007.00425.x.

Corbera, Esteve, Nicolás Kosoy, and Miguel Martínez Tuna. 2007. "Equity Implications of Marketing Ecosystem Services in Protected Areas and Rural Communities: Case Studies from Meso-America." *Global Environmental Change* 17 (3–4): 365–80. http://dx.doi.org/10.1016/j.gloenvcha.2006.12.005.

Cox, Robert. 1986. "Social Forces, States, and World Orders." In *Neorealism and Its Critics*, ed. Robert O. Keohane, 204–54. New York: Columbia University Press.

Creighton, Scott. 2010. "Neoliberal Dream Legislation Submitted by Obama Regime – The Privatization of All Public Housing in America." *American Everyman*, May 23. http://willyloman.wordpress.com/2010/05/23/neoliberal-wet-dream-submitted-by-obama-regime-privatization-of-all-public-housing-in-america/.

Critchell, Samantha. 2010. "Obama Times Square Billboard: Ad Features President 'Modeling' Weatherproof Jacket." *Huffington Post*, June 1. http://www.huffingtonpost.com/2010/01/06/obama-times-square-billbo_n_413658.html.

Cronon, William. 1995. "The Trouble with Wilderness: Or, Getting Back to the Wrong Nature." In *Uncommon Ground: Toward Reinventing Nature*, ed. William Cronon, 69–90. New York: W.W. Norton.

Crook, Clive. 2008. "The Problem with Gates: Do as I Say, Not as I Did." In Kinsley 2008, 110–14.

Culora, Jill. 2007. "A 'Secret' Oprah Craze Hits New Yorkers." *New York Post*, March 4. http://www.nypost.com/p/news/regional/secret_oprah_craze_hits_new_yorkers_E0s4GjNJuc1bAJYVuLLHAO.

Curan, Catherine. 2010. "Jay-Z's 99 Problems." *New York Post*, May 16. http://www.nypost.com/p/news/business/jay_NJOKUMG51yyYswtQo2zrJL/2.

Curtin, Deane. 2005. *Environmental Ethics for a Postcolonial World*. Oxford: Rowman & Littlefield.

Cushman, Phillip. 1995. *Constructing the Self, Constructing America: A Cultural History of Psychotherapy*. Boston: Addison-Wesley.

Daily Mail Reporter. 2010a. "After Aiding the Haiti Relief Effort John Travolta Returns to His Duties for the Premiere of New Movie *From Paris with Love*."

Mail Online, January 29. http://www.dailymail.co.uk/tvshowbiz/
article-1247036/After-aiding-Haiti-relief-effort-John-Travolta-returns-
duties-premiere-new-movie-From-Paris-With-Love.html.

Daily Mail Reporter. 2010b. "'I Was like a Commander': John Travolta on
Leading Scientology Aid Mission to Haiti." *Mail Online*, February 3. http://
www.dailymail.co.uk/tvshowbiz/article-1248223/Haiti-earthquake-
disaster-John-Travolta-leading-Scientology-aid-mission.html.

Daily Mail Reporter. 2010c. "John Travolta Delivers Aid and Scientologists to
Haiti in His Private Boeing 707." *Mail Online*, January 27. http://www.
dailymail.co.uk/news/worldnews/article-1246290/John-Travolta-flies-
tonnes-aid-Haiti-private-jumbo-jet.html.

Daly, Kieran. 2000. *The Business Response to AIDS: Impacts and Lessons Learned*.
Geneva, London: UNAIDS and the Prince of Wales Business Leaders Forum
and The Global Business Council on HIV&AIDS.

Davidson, Adam, and Alex Blumberg. 2009. "Obama Gives Keynes His First
Real World Test." *NPR*, January 9. http://www.npr.org/templates/story/
story.php?storyId=100018973.

Davidson, Paul. 2010. "Unemployment Rate for College Grads is Highest
Since 1970." *USA Today*. http://www.usatoday.com/money/economy/
employment/2010-12-06-collegegrads06_ST_N.htm.

Davidson, Sara. 2007. "Angelina Jolie Interview: Mama!" *Reader's Digest*, June.

Davis, Mike. 1986. *Prisoners of the American Dream*. London: Verso.

Dawson, Michael. 2003. *The Consumer Trap: Big Business Marketing in American
Life*. Urbana: University of Illinois Press.

Dean, Jodi. 2009. *Democracy and Other Neoliberal Fantasies: Communicative Capitalism and Left Politics*. United States: Duke University Press.

Dean, Mitchell. 2009. *Governmentality: Power and Rule in Modern Society*.
London: Sage.

Delpech-Ramey, Joshua. 2007. "The Idol as Icon." *Angelaki* 12 (1): 87–96.
http://dx.doi.org/10.1080/09697250701309635.

Derby, Michael S. 2011. "Bernanke Presents Grim Metrics for Job Growth."
Wall Street Journal, February 9. http://blogs.wsj.com/economics/
2011/02/09/bernanke-presents-grim-metrics-for-job-growth/.

Der Spiegal (magazine). 2008. "The Messiah Factor (Der Messias-Faktor)." (7).
http://www.spiegel.de/spiegel/print/index-2008-7.html.

Deseret News (Salt Lake, UT). 2003. "Oprah for President? She'll Always Say
'Never.'" June 2, A2.

Deutscher, Isaac. 1969. "Roots of Bureaucracy." In *The Socialist Register 1969*,
ed. Ralph Miliband and John Saville, 9–28. London: Merlin Press.

de Waal, Alex. 2008. "The Humanitarian Carnival: A Celebrity Vogue." *World Affairs*, Fall.

De Winter, Rebecca. 2001. "The Anti-Sweatshop Movement: Constructing Corporate Moral Agency in the Global Apparel Industry." *Ethics & International Affairs* 15 (02): 99–115. http://dx.doi.org/10.1111/j.1747-7093.2001.tb00361.x.

DeWitt, Karen. 1995. "Dial 1-800-MY GURU." *New York Times*, February 5. http://proquest.umi.com/pqdweb?did=675323111&sid=3&Fmt=3&clientId=18938&RQT=309&VName=PQD&cfc=1.

Dhillon, Amrit, and Toby Harnden. 2006. "How Coldplay's Green Hopes Died in the Arid Soil of India." *Sunday Telegraph*, April 30. www.telegraph.co.uk/news/worldnews/asia/india/1517031/How-Coldplays-green-hopes-died-in-the-arid-soil-of-India.html.

Dicum, Gregory, and Nina Luttinger. 1999. *The Coffee Book: Anatomy of an Industry from Crop to the Last Drop*. New York: The New Press.

Dienst, Richard. 2011. "Richard Dienst: The Case against 'Saint Bono' (Excerpt from Dienst's *The Bonds of Debt* posted by Andrea D'cruz)." *Verso.com Blogs*, June 24. http://www.versobooks.com/blogs/600-richard-dienst-the-case-against-saint-bono.

Dieter, Heribert, and Rajiv Kumar. 2008. "The Downside of Celebrity Diplomacy: The Neglected Complexity of Development." *Global Governance* 14:250–64.

Diouf, Mamadou. 2000. "The Senegalese Murid Trade Diaspora and the Making of a Vernacular Cosmopolitanism." *Public Culture* 12 (3): 679–702. http://dx.doi.org/10.1215/08992363-12-3-679.

Dixon, Bruce. 2009. "President Obama Declares His DLC Allegiance: Says 'I Am a New Democrat.'" *Black Agenda Report*, March 18. http://www.blackagendareport.com/content/president-obama-declares-his-dlc-allegiance-says-i-am-new-democrat.

Domhoff, William. 2009. "Wealth, Income and Power." *Who Rules America?*, May. http://www2.ucsc.edu/whorulesamerica/power/wealth.html.

Donahue, Phil. 2010. "The 2010 Time 100: Oprah Winfrey." *Time.com*, April 29. http://www.time.com/time/specials/packages/article/0,28804,1984685_1984940_1985540,00.html.

Dovey, Jon. 2000. *Freakshow: First Person Media and Factual Television*. London: Pluto Press.

Drake, Philip. 2008. "From Hero to Celebrity: The Political Economy of Stardom." In *Heroes in a Global World*, ed. Susan J. Drucker and Gary Gumpert, 435–54. Creskill, NJ: Hampton Press.

Dreammagic.com. 2008. "Oprah for President." Accessed October 15.
    http://www.dreamagic.com/oprah/.

Dumenil, Gerard, and Dominique Levy. 2002. "The Nature and Contradictions
    of Neoliberalism." In *Socialist Register 2002*, ed. Leo Panitch and Colin Leys,
    43–71. London: Merlin Press.

Dyer, Richard. 1979. *Stars*. London: British Film Institute.

Easterly, William. 2008. "Let Old-Fashioned Capitalism Help the Poor." In
    Kinsley 2008, 55–7.

Easterly, William. 2010. "John Lennon vs. Bono: The Death of the Celebrity
    Activist." *Washington Post*, December 10. http://www.washingtonpost.
    com/wp-dyn/content/article/2010/12/09/AR2010120904262.html?
    nav=hcmoduletmv.

Eckholm, Erik. 2010. "Recession Raises Poverty Rate to 15-Year High."
    New York Times, September 16. http://www.nytimes.com/2010/09/17/
    us/17poverty.html.

The Economist. 2002. "Bad Faith: Accusing the IMF." June 8, 100.

The Economist. 2010. "The Smoking Greenhouse Gun: An Alluring Trade in
    'Supergreenhouse' Gas Is Coming Under Scrutiny." September 2.
    http://www.economist.com/node/16944921.

The Economist. 2011a. "Do the Maths (Editorial)." January 15–21.

The Economist. 2011b. "They Work for Us: In Democracies the Elites Serve
    the Masses." January 20. http://www.economist.com/node/17929027?
    story_id=17929027.

Edgecliff-Johnson, Andrew. 2010. "Women of the Decade: Oprah Winfrey.
    " *Financial Times*, December 10. http://www.ft.com/management/
    women-at-the-top.

Edwards, Sebastian. 2003. "Review of Joseph E. Stiglitz's *Globalization and Its
    Discontents*." *Journal of Development Economics* 70 (1): 252–7. http://dx.doi.
    org/10.1016/S0304-3878(02)00097-4.

Ehrenreich, Barbara. 2009. *Smile or Die*. London: Granta.

Eichengreen, Barry. 2002. "The Globalization Wars: An Economist Reports
    from the Front Lines." *Foreign Affairs* 81 (4): 157–64. http://dx.doi.org/
    10.2307/20033248.

Eisenstadt, Samuel N. 1973. *Tradition, Change, and Modernity*. New York: Wiley.

Eisenstadt, Samuel N. 1987. *Patterns of Modernity*. London: Frances Pinter.

Eisenstein, Hester. 2005. "A Dangerous Liaison? Feminism and Corporate
    Globalization." *Science and Society* 69 (3): 487–518. http://dx.doi.org/
    10.1521/siso.69.3.487.66520.

Elber, Lynn. 2010. "Oprah Keeps Hand in Media with OWN, Snubs Politics."
    Washington Times, December 31. http://www.washingtontimes.com/
    news/2010/dec/31/oprah-keeps-hand-in-media-with-own-snubs-politics/.

Emerich, Monica. 2006. "The Spirituality of Sustainability: Healing the Self to Heal the World through Healthy Living Media." PhD dissertation, University of Colorado at Boulder.

Emspak, Jesse. 2011. "NASA: 2010 Warmest Year on Record." *International Business Times*, January 13. http://www.ibtimes.com/nasa-2010-warmest-year-record-254433.

Eng, David. 2003. "Transnational Adoption and Queer Diasporas." *Social Text* 21 (3): 1–37. http://dx.doi.org/10.1215/01642472-21-3_76-1.

Engler, Yves, and Anthony Fenton. 2005. *Canada in Haiti: Waging War on the Poor Majority*. Halifax: Fernwood.

Epstein, Debbie, and Deborah L. Steinberg. 1998. "American Dreamin': Discoursing Liberally on the Oprah Winfrey Show." *Women's Studies International Forum* 21 (1): 77–94. http://dx.doi.org/10.1016/S0277-5395(97)00079-4.

Ervine, Kate. 2010. "Participation Denied: The Global Environment Facility, Its Universal Blueprint, and the Mexico-Mesoamerican Biological Corridor in Chiapas." *Third World Quarterly* 31 (5): 773–90. http://dx.doi.org/10.1080/01436597.2010.502694.

Escobar, Arturo. 1995. *Encountering Development: The Making and Unmaking of the Third World*. Princeton: Princeton University Press.

Eurodad (European Network on Debt and Development). 2006. "Devilish Details: Implications of the G7 Debt Deal." Accessed February 17. http://eurodad.org/uploadstore/cms/docs/Overview_G7_debt_deal.pdf.

Fairtrade Foundation. 2011. "Fairtrade Sales Soar to Well Over £1bn Showing the UK Still Cares in Tough Times." February 28. http://www.fairtrade.org.uk/press_office/press_releases_and_statements/archive_2011/february_2011/fairtrade_sales_soar_to_well_over_1bn_showing_the_uk_still_cares_in_tough_times.aspx.

Faludi, Susan. 1991. *Backlash: The Undeclared War against American Women*. New York: Crown.

Fanon, Frantz. 1967. *The Wretched of the Earth*. Trans. Constance Farrington. Harmondsworth: Penguin.

Fanon, Frantz. 1970. *Black Skin, White Masks*. Trans. Charles Lam Markmann. London: Paladin.

Fassin, Didier. 2007. *When Bodies Remember: Experiences and Politics of AIDS in South Africa*. Berkeley: University of California Press. http://dx.doi.org/10.1525/california/9780520244672.001.0001.

Feeney, Mary K. 2000. "New Territory for the Oprah Winfrey Empire." *Los Angeles Times*, April 17, E3.

Ferguson, J. 2009. "The Uses of Neoliberalism." *Antipode* 41 (1): 166–84.

FERN. 2000. *Sinking the Kyoto Protocol: The Links between Forest, Plantations, and Carbon Sinks.* Moreton-in-Marsh, UK: FERN.

Fernandez, Belen. 2011. *The Imperial Messenger: Thomas Friedman at Work.* London: Verso.

Fine, Ben. 2001. *Social Capital versus Social Theory.* London: Routledge.

Fine, Ben, and Elisa Van Waeyenberge. 2005. "Correcting Stiglitz: From Information to Power in the World of Development." In *Telling the Truth: Socialist Register 2006,* ed. Leo Panitch and Colin Leys, 145–68. London: Merlin.

Fine, Robert. 2001. *Political Investigations: Hegel, Marx, Arendt.* London: Routledge.

Fine, Robert. 2007. *Cosmopolitanism.* London: Routledge.

Finn, John. 1999. "Transformation or Transmogrification? Ackerman, Hobbes (as in Calvin and Hobbes), and the Puzzle of Changing Constitutional Identity." *Constitutional Political Economy* 10 (4): 355–65. http://dx.doi.org/10.1023/A:1009023000354.

Fitch, Jessica M. 2000. "Oprah Winfrey, 46." *Chicago Sun-Times,* October 31, 6.

Forbes. 2009. "World's Billionaires: #234 Oprah Winfrey." March 11. http://www.forbes.com/lists/2009/10/billionaires-2009-richest-people_Oprah-Winfrey_O0ZT.html.

Forbes. 2010a. "The World's Billionaires: Special Report." March 10. http://www.forbes.com/2010/03/10/worlds-richest-people-slim-gates-buffett-billionaires-2010_land.html.

Forbes. 2010b. "The World's Billionaires: Special Report (Rankings)." March 10. http://www.forbes.com/lists/2010/10/billionaires-2010_The-Worlds-Billionaires_Rank.html.

Forbes.com. 2010. "Forbes 400 Richest Americans: Oprah Winfrey." http://www.forbes.com/profile/oprah-winfrey.

Ford, Glen. 2011. "Chamber of Commerce Obamanomics." *Black Agenda Report,* February 9. http://blackagendareport.com/content/chamber-commerce-obamanomics.

Foucault, Michel. 1990. *The History of Sexuality, Volume 1: An Introduction.* Vintage Books: New York.

Freund, Bill. 2003. "A Review of *Globalization and Its Discontents.*" *Transformation: Critical Perspectives on Southern Africa* 52: 102–6.

Fridell, Gavin. 2007. *Fair Trade Coffee: The Prospects and Pitfalls of Market-Driven Social Justice.* Toronto: University of Toronto Press.

Friedman, Thomas L. 2000. *The Lexus and the Olive Tree.* New York: Anchor Books.

Friedman, Thomas L. 2007. *The World Is Flat: A Brief History of the Twenty-First Century.* Vancouver: Douglas & McIntyre.

Fromm, Erich. 1941. *Escape from Freedom*. New York: Holt, Rinehart and Winston.

Fromm, Erich. 1955. *The Sane Society*. New York: Henry Holt.

Fuchs, Thomas. 2005. "Corporealized and Disembodied Minds: A Phenomenological View of the Body in Melancholia and Schizophrenia." *Philosophy, Psychiatry & Psychology* 12 (2): 95–107.

Fukuyama, Francis. 1992. *The End of History and the Last Man*. New York: Free Press.

Gabriel, Trip, and Sam Dillon. 2011. "G.O.P. Governors Take Aim at Teacher Tenure." *New York Times*, January 31. http://www.nytimes.com/2011/02/01/us/01tenure.html.

Gailey, Christine. 2000. "Seeking 'Baby Right': Race, Class, and Gender in US International Adoption." In *Yours, Mine, Ours ... and Theirs: International Adoption*, ed. Anne-Louise Rygold, 52–80. Oslo: University of Oslo Press.

Galston, William, and Elaine C. Kamarck. 1989. *The Politics of Evasion*. Washington: Progressive Policy Institute.

Garrett, Laurie. 2007. "The Challenge of Global Health." *Foreign Affairs*, January/February. http://www.foreignaffairs.org/20070101faessay86103/laurie-garrett/the-challenge-of-global-health.htm.

Garthwaite, Craig, and Timothy Moore. 2008. "The Role of Celebrity Endorsements in Politics: Oprah, Obama, and the 2008 Democratic Primary." *Northwestern University Working Paper*, October 27. http://www.kellogg.northwestern.edu/faculty/garthwaite/htm/celebrityendorsements_garthwaitemoore.pdf.

Garvey, Marcus. 1987. "African Fundamentalism." In *Marcus Garvey: Life and Lessons*, ed. Robert A. Hill and Barbara Bair, 1–28. Berkeley: University of California Press.

Gates, Bill. 2008. "A New Approach to Capitalism." In Kinsley 2008, 7–16.

Geldof in Africa. BBC TV Series (6 parts). Directed by Bob Geldof. 2005.

George, Susan. 2004. *Another World Is Possible, If*. London: Verso.

George, Susan. 2008. *Hijacking America: How the Secular and Religious Right Changed What Americans Think*. Cambridge: Polity Press.

George, Susan. 2010. "Converging Crises: Reality, Fear and Hope." *Globalizations* 7 (1–2): 17–22. http://dx.doi.org/10.1080/14747731003593018.

Ghosh, Bishnupriya. 2010. "Looking through Coca-Cola: Global Icons and the Popular." *Public Culture* 22 (2): 333–68. http://dx.doi.org/10.1215/08992363-2009-031.

Gibson-Graham, J.K. 2006. *A Post-Capitalist Politics*. Minneapolis: University of Minnesota Press.

Giddens, Anthony. 1991. *Modernity and Self-Identity: Self and Society in the Late Modern Age*. Cambridge: Polity Press.

Giddens, Anthony. 1999. "Risk and Responsibility." *Modern Law Review* 62 (1): 1–10. http://dx.doi.org/10.1111/1468-2230.00188.

Gien, Pamela. 2007. "Building a Dream." *O, The Oprah Magazine*, January, 154–60, 217.

Giles, Judy, and Timothy Middleton. 2000. *Studying Culture: A Practical Introduction*. London: Blackwell.

Global Footprint Network. 2007. "Ecological Footprint and Biocapacity." Accessed February 7. http://www.footprintnetwork.org/en/index.php/GFN/page/world_footprint/.

Global Footprint Network. 2011. "Ecological Footprint: Overview." Accessed June 5. http://www.footprintnetwork.org/en/index.php/GFN/page/footprint_basics_overview/.

Global Witness. 2009. "Global Witness Uncovers Foreign Companies' Links to Congo Violence." Accessed May 27, 2013. http://www.globalwitness.org/library/global-witness-uncovers-foreign-companies'-links-congo-violence.

Godelier, Maurice. 1986. *The Mental and the Material*. London: Verso.

Goldman, Michael. 2006. *Imperial Nature: The World Bank and Struggles for Social Justice in the Age of Globalization*. New Haven: Yale University Press.

Goldman, Robert, and Stephen Papson. 1998. *Nike Culture: The Sign of the Swoosh*. London: Sage.

Goldman, Robert, and Stephen Papson. 2000. "Advertising in the Age of Accelerated Meaning." In *The Consumer Society Reader*, ed. Juliet B. Schor and Douglas B. Holt, 81–98. New York: The New Press.

Goodman, David, E. Melanie DuPuis, and Michael Goodman. 2012. *Alternative Food Networks: Knowledge, Place and Politics*. London: Routledge.

Goodman, Michael. 2009. "The Mirror of Consumption: Celebritisation, Developmental Consumption and the Shifting Cultural Politics of Fair Trade." *Environment, Politics and Development Working Paper Series, Working Paper #8, Department of Geography, King's College London*. http://www.kcl.ac.uk/sspp/departments/geography/research/epd/workingpapers.aspx.

Goodman, Michael. 2010. "The Mirror of Consumption: Celebritization, Developmental Consumption and the Shifting Cultural Politics of Fair Trade." *Geoforum* 41 (1): 104–16. http://dx.doi.org/10.1016/j.geoforum.2009.08.003.

Goodman, Michael K., and Christine Barnes. 2011. "Star/Poverty Space: The Making of the 'Development Celebrity.'" *Celebrity Studies* 2 (1): 69–85. http://dx.doi.org/10.1080/19392397.2011.544164.

Goodman, Michael, and Emily Boyd. 2011. "A Social Life for Carbon? Commodification, Markets and Care." *Geographical Journal* 177 (2): 102–9. http://dx.doi.org/10.1111/j.1475-4959.2011.00401.x.

Goudreau, Jenna. 2010. "How to Lead like Oprah." *Forbes.com*, October 22. http://blogs.forbes.com/jennagoudreau/2010/10/22/how-to-lead-like-oprah-winfrey-own-rachael-ray-dr-oz-phil/.

Goudreau, Jenna. 2011. "Will the Oprah Winfrey Network Heal America?" *Forbes.com*, January 3. http://blogs.forbes.com/jennagoudreau/2011/01/03/will-the-oprah-winfrey-network-heal-america-own-launch-cable-suze-orman-dr-phil-oz/.

Gowan, Peter. 1999. *The Global Gamble: Washington's Faustian Bid for World Dominance*. London: Verso.

Gramsci, Antonio. 1971. *Selections from the Prison Notebooks*. New York: International Publishers.

Gregory, Derek. 2001. "(Post)Colonialism and the Production of Nature." In *Social Nature: Theory, Practice, and Politics*, ed. Noel Castree and Bruce Braun, 84–111. Oxford: Blackwell Publishing.

Grindstaff, Laura. 2002. *The Money Shot: Trash, Class, and the Making of TV Talk Shows*. Chicago: University of Chicago Press. http://dx.doi.org/10.7208/chicago/9780226309088.001.0001.

The Grio. 2009. "The 'Oprah Effect' Felt across the World" November 24. http://www.thegrio.com/news/the-oprah-effect-felt-across-the-world.php.

Grumley, John E. 1989. *History and Totality: Radical Historicism from Hegel to Foucault*. London: Routledge.

The Guardian. 2005. "Out of Gleneagles." July 11. http://www.guardian.co.uk/news/2005/jul/11/leadersandreply.mainsection.

Gumbel, Peter. 2009. "Rethinking Marx." *Time.com*, January 29. http://www.time.com/time/specials/packages/article/0,28804,1873191_1873190_1873188,00.html.

Guthman, Julie. 2007. "The Polyanyian Way? Voluntary Food Labels and Neoliberal Governance." *Antipode* 39 (3): 456–78. http://dx.doi.org/10.1111/j.1467-8330.2007.00535.x.

Habermas, Jurgen. 1991. *The Structural Transformation of the Public Sphere*. Cambridge, MA: MIT Press.

Hague, Seth, John Street, and Heather Savigny. 2008. "The Voice of the People? Musicians as Political Actors." *Cultural Politics* 4 (1): 5–23. http://dx.doi.org/10.2752/175174308X266370.

Hall, Stuart. 1996. "Introduction." In *Modernity: An Introduction to Modern Societies*, ed. Stuart Hall, David Held, Don Hubert, and Kenneth Thompson, 3–19. Cambridge: Oxford.

Hall, Stuart, and Bram Gieben. 1992. *Formations of Modernity*. Cambridge: Polity Press in Association with the Open University.

Hammad, Suheir. 2011. *Poems of War, Peace, Women, Power*. (TED Video.) February 5. http://www.youtube.com/watch?v=UAj1hsXp18c.

Hart-Landsberg, Martin, and Paul Burkett. 2004. "China's Rise to Model Status." *Monthly Review (New York, NY)* 56 (3): 13–24.

Harvey, David. 2000. "Cosmopolitanism and the Banality of Geographical Evils." *Public Culture* 12 (2): 529–64. http://dx.doi.org/ 10.1215/ 08992363-12-2-529.

Harvey, David. 2003. *The New Imperialism*. Oxford: Oxford University Press.

Harvey, David. 2005. *A Brief History of Neoliberalism*. Oxford: Oxford University Press.

Harvey, David. 2006. *Spaces of Global Capitalism*. London; New York: Verso.

Harvey, David. 2009. "Is This Really the End of Neoliberalism?" *Counterpunch*, March 13–15. http://www.counterpunch.org/harvey03132009. html.

Harvey, Fiona, and Stephen Fidler. 2007. "Industry Caught in Carbon 'Smokescreen' (Carbon Offset Fraud)." *Financial Times Online*, April 25. http://www.ft.com/cms/s/0/48e334ce-f355-11db-9845-000b5df10621. html#axzz1GECNFEIM.

Hastreiter, Kim. 2009. "Rebranding America: PAPER Invited 15 of the Best Visual Communicators to Redefine our Country's Image." *PAPERMAG*, May 1. http://www.papermag.com/arts_and_style/2009/05/rebranding-america.php.

Hawken, Paul, Amory Lovins, and L. Hunter Lovins. 1999. *Natural Capitalism: Creating the Next Industrial Revolution*. Boston: Little Brown.

Held, David. 2006. *Models of Democracy*. Cambridge: Polity Press.

Held, David, and Anthony McGrew, eds. 2000. *The Global Transformations Reader*. Cambridge: Polity Press.

Henwood, Doug. 1996. "Clinton's Liberalism: No Model for the Left." In *Socialist Register 1997: Ruthless Criticism of All That Exists*, ed. Leo Panitch, 159–75. New York: Monthly Review Press.

Henwood, Doug. 1997. "Clinton's Liberalism: No Model for the Left." In *Socialist Register 1997*, ed. Leo Panitch, 159–75. London: Merlin Press.

Hiddleston, Jane. 2008. "The Perplexed Persona of Frantz Fanon's *Peau Noire, Masques Blancs*." *Postcolonial Text* 4 (4): 1–16.

Hiebert, Daniel. 2002. "Cosmopolitanism at the Local Level: The Development of Transnational Neighbourhoods." In *Conceiving Cosmopolitanism*, ed. Steven Vertovec and Robin Cohen, 209–23. Oxford: Oxford University Press.

Hill, Lisa. 2000. "The Two Republicae of the Roman Stoics: Can a Cosmopolite Be a Patriot?" *Citizenship Studies* 4 (1): 65–79. http://dx.doi.org/10.1080/ 136210200110030.

Hinckley, David. 2010. "Rush Limbaugh Haiti Earthquake Comments Are 'Really Stupid,' Says White House Press Secretary Gibbs." *New York*

Daily News, January 15. http://articles.nydailynews.com/2010-01-15/
news/17944705_1_haitian-crisis-white-house-donation.

Hintzen, Percy, C. 2008. "Desire and the Enrapture of Capitalist Consumption:
Product Red, Africa, and the Crisis of Sustainability." *Journal of Pan African
Studies* 2 (6): 77–91.

Hofstadter, Douglas R. 2007. *I Am a Strange Loop*. New York: Basic Books.

Honneth, Axel. 1997. "Is Universalism a Moral Trap? The Presuppositions and
Limits of a Politics of Human Rights." In *Perpetual Peace: Essays on Kant's
Cosmopolitan Ideal*, ed. James Bohman and Matthias Lutz-Bachman. Boston:
MIT Press.

Hornbuckle, David. 2009. "The Oprah Effect." *Inc.com*, August 4. http://
www.inc.com/articles/2009/08/oprah.html.

Horowitz, Jason. 2008. "Barack Obama, D.L.C. Clintonite?" *New York Observer*,
March 3.

Hugman, Richard. 1994. "Consuming Health and Welfare." In *The Authority of
the Consumer*, ed. Russell Keat, Nigel Whiteley, and Nicholas Abercrombie,
207–22. London: Routledge.

Ikas, Karin, and Gerhard Wagner, eds. 2009. *Communicating in the Third Space*.
New York: Routledge.

Illouz, Eva. 2007. *Cold Intimacies: The Making of Emotional Capitalism*. Cambridge: Polity Press.

ILO. 2008. *World of Work Report 2008: Income Inequalities in the Age of Financial
Globalization*. Geneva: International Institute for Labour Studies, International Labour Office.

Irvin, George. 2008. *Super Rich: The Rise of Inequality in Britain and the United
States*. Cambridge: Polity Press.

Isin, Engin. 2004. "The Neurotic Citizen." *Citizenship Studies* 8 (3): 217–35.
http://dx.doi.org/10.1080/1362102042000256970.

Jameson, Fredric. 1992. *Signatures of the Visible*. London: Routledge.

Jicha, Tom. 1993. "Winfrey Is a Standout in Tale of Inner City." *St. Louis
Post-Dispatch*, November 27, 8D.

Jicha, Tom. 2004. "President Oprah, Anyone?" *South Florida Sun-Sentinel*,
June 19. http://www.sun-sentinel.com/features/lifestyle/sfl-tv26tjjun19,
0,1922713.column?soll=sfla-/.

Johnson, Walter. 2004. "Time and Revolution in African America: Temporality
and the History of Atlantic Slavery." In *A New Imperial History*, ed. Kathleen
Wilson, 197–215. Cambridge: Cambridge University Press.

Johnston, Josée. 2008. "The Citizen-Consumer Hybrid: Ideological Tensions
and the Case of Whole Foods Market." *Theory and Society* 37 (3): 229–70.
http://dx.doi.org/10.1007/s11186-007-9058-5.

Jolie, Angelina. 2003. *Notes from My Travels: Visits with Refugees in Africa, Cambodia, Pakistan, and Ecuador*. New York: Pocket Books.

Jones, Juston. 2007. "Beyond Books: Oprah Winfrey's Seal of Approval Goes Presidential." *New York Times*, May 7, C6.

Jones, Mary Lynn F. 2003. "Vote Oprah." *American Prospect Online*, January 21. http://prospect.org/article/vote-oprah.

Jones, Paul. 2004. *Raymond Williams's Sociology of Culture: A Critical Reconstruction*. New York: Palgrave Macmillan.

Jones, Tim. 2000. "The Irony of Oprah Winfrey." *Ottawa Citizen*, April 18, G1.

Jubilee Debt Campaign. 2009. "Hasn't All the Debt Been Cancelled?" Accessed December 11. http://www.jubileedebtcampaign.org.uk/4%20 Hasn%27t%20all%20the%20debt%20been%20cancelled%3F+2651.twl.

Judis, John. 2008. "American Adam: Obama and the Cult of the New." *New Republic*, March 12. http://www.newrepublic.com/article/american-adam.

Kahn, Joseph. 2002. "Are You Better Off Now?" *The New York Times*, June 23.

Kampfner, John. 2010. *Freedom for Sale: Why the World Is Trading Democracy for Security*. New York: Basic Books.

Kant, Immanuel. 1903. *Perpetual Peace*. London: Swan Sonnenschein & Co.

Kapoor, Ilan. 2005. "Participatory Development, Complicity and Desire." *Third World Quarterly* 26 (8): 1203–20. http://dx.doi.org/10.1080/01436590500336849.

Kapoor, Ilan. 2008. *The Postcolonial Politics of Development*. London; New York: Routledge.

Kean, Brian. 2006. "The Psychopharmaceutical Complex." In *Forensic Psychiatry: Influences of Evil*, ed. Tom Mason, 31–66. New Jersey: Humana Press Inc. http://dx.doi.org/10.1007/978-1-59745-006-5_3.

Kellner, Douglas. 2003. *Media Spectacle*. New York: Routledge. http://dx.doi.org/10.4324/9780203166383.

Kellstedt, Paul, Sammy Zahran, and Arnold Vedlitz. 2008. "Personal Efficacy, the Information Environment, and Attitudes towards Global Warming and Climate Change in the United States." *Risk Analysis* 28 (1): 113–26. http://dx.doi.org/10.1111/j.1539-6924.2008.01010.x.

Kennedy, Kevin C. 2003. "A Review of *Globalization and Its Discontents*." *George Washington International Law Review* 35: 251–63.

Killercoke. 2010. "Coke's Crimes." Accessed May 2. http://killercoke.org.

Kinsella, Bridget. 1997. "The Oprah Effect: How TV's Premier Talk Show Host Put Books Over the Top." *Publishers Weekly*, January 20, 276.

Kinsley, Michael, ed. 2008. *Creative Capitalism: A Conversation with Bill Gates, Warren Buffett, and Other Economic Leaders*. New York: Simon & Schuster.

Klein, Naomi. 2007. *The Shock Doctrine: The Rise of Disaster Capitalism*. Canada: Alfred A. Knopf; New York: Metropolitian Books.

Klein, Naomi. 2008. "Obama's Chicago Boys." *The Nation*, June 30. http://www.thenation.com/article/obamas-chicago-boys.

Klein, Naomi. 2010. "Naomi Klein on How Corporate Branding Has Taken Over America." *The Guardian*, January 16. http://www.guardian.co.uk/books/2010/jan/16/naomi-klein-branding-obama-america.

Klinkner, Philip A. 1999. "Bill Clinton and the Politics of the New Liberalism." In *Without Justice for All*, ed. Adolf L. Reed, 11–28. Boulder, CO: Westview Press.

Knight, Franklin W. 1990. *The Caribbean: The Genesis of a Fragmented Nationalism*. 2nd ed. New York: Oxford University Press.

Koch, Wendy. 2010. "How Green Is Al Gore's $9 Million Montecito Ocean Front Villa?" *USA Today*, May 18. http://www.usatoday.com/communities/greenhouse/post/2010/05/how-green-is-al-gores-9-million-montecito-ocean-front-villa/1.

Konings, Martijn. 2010. "The Pragmatic Sources of Modern Power." *European Journal of Sociology* 51 (1): 55–91. http://dx.doi.org/10.1017/S0003975610000032.

Kosova, Weston. 2009. "Live Your Best Life Ever!" *Newsweek*, May 30.

Kotz, David. 2003. "Neoliberalism and the U.S. Economic Expansion of the 1990s." *Monthly Review (New York, NY)* 54 (11): 15–32.

Krestan, Jo-Ann, and Claudia Bepko. 1991. "Codependency: The Social Reconstruction of Female Experience." In *Feminism and Addiction*, ed. Claudia Bepko, 49–66. New York: Haworth Press.

Krugman, Paul. 2009. "All the President's Zombies." *New York Times*, August 24. http://www.nytimes.com/2009/08/24/opinion/24krugman.html?scp=7&sq=zombies&st=cse.

Krugman, Paul. 2010. "When Zombies Win." *New York Times*, December 19. http://www.nytimes.com/2010/12/20/opinion/20krugman.html?_r=1&scp=3&sq=zombies&st=cse.

Kruse, Robert J. 2009. "The Geographical Imagination of Barack Obama: Representing Race and Space in America." *Southeastern Geographer* 49 (3): 221–39. http://dx.doi.org/10.1353/sgo.0.0049.

Laclau, Ernesto. 1995. "Universalism, Particularism and the Question of Identity." In *The Identity in Question*, ed. John Rajchman, 93–110. New York: Routledge.

Landsburg, Steven. 2008. "Why Isn't Regular Capitalism Good Enough?" In Kinsley 2008, 143–5.

Lasch, Christopher. 1979. *The Culture of Narcissism: American Life in an Age of Diminishing Expectations*. New York: W.W. Norton.

Latour, Bruno. 1993. *We Have Never Been Modern*. Cambridge: Harvard University Press.

Latour, Bruno. 2003. "Is Re-Modernization Occurring – And If So, How to Prove it?" *Theory, Culture & Society* 20 (2): 35–48. http://dx.doi.org/10.1177/0263276403020002002.

Latour, Bruno, and Peter Weibel. 2002. "What Is Iconoclash? Or, Is There a World Beyond the Image Wars?" In *Iconoclash: Beyond the Image Wars in Science, Religion, and Art*, 1–41. Cambridge, MA: MIT Press.

Leach, William. 1993. *Land of Desire*. New York: Pantheon.

Lebowitz, Fran. 1996. "Talk Show Host." *Time*, June 17, 65.

Lebowitz, Michael A. 2006. *Build It Now: Socialism for the Twenty-First Century*. New York: Monthly Review Press.

Lee, Don. 2010. "Recession's Over, Economists Say to a Skeptical Public." *Los Angeles Times*, September 21. http://articles.latimes.com/2010/sep/21/business/la-fi-recession-over-20100921.

Lerner, Harriett Goldhor. 1990. "Problems for Profit?" *Women's Review of Books*, April 15–16.

Lertzman, Renée. 2008. "The Myth of Apathy." *The Ecologist*, June 19. http://www.theecologist.org/blogs_and_comments/commentators/other_comments/269433/the_myth_of_apathy.html.

Lewis, Tania, and Emily Potter, eds. 2010. *Ethical Consumption: A Critical Introduction*. London: Routledge.

Leys, Colin. 2001. *Market-Driven Politics: Neoliberal Democracy and the Public Interest*. London: Verso.

Littler, Jo. 2008. "'I Feel Your Pain': Cosmopolitan Charity and the Public Fashioning of the Celebrity Soul." *Social Semiotics* 18 (2): 237–51. http://dx.doi.org/10.1080/10350330802002416.

Littler, Jo. 2009. *Radical Consumption: Shopping for Change in Contemporary Culture*. Maidenhead: Open University Press.

Live8. 2005. "The Story So Far." Accessed March 10, 2010. http://www.live8live.com/whathappened/.

Live Earth. 2011. "Live Earth." Accessed January 14. http://liveearth.org/en/home.

Liverman, Diana. 2004. "Who Governs, at What Scale, and at What Price? Geography, Environmental Governance, and the Commodification of Nature." *Annals of the Association of American Geographers* 94 (4): 734–8.

Lizza, Ryan. 2007. "The Agitator: The Unlikely Political Education of Barack Obama." *The New Republic*, March 19. http://www.newrepublic.com/article/the-agitator .

Lofton, Kathryn. 2006. "Practicing Oprah; Or, the Prescriptive Compulsion of a Spiritual Capitalism." *Journal of Popular Culture* 39 (4): 599–621. http://dx.doi.org/10.1111/j.1540-5931.2006.00281.x.

Lohmann, Larry, ed. 2006. "Special Issue: Carbon Trading: A Critical Conversation on Climate Change, Privatization and Power." *Development Dialogue* 48 (September).

Lohmann, Larry. 2010. "Uncertainty Markets and Carbon Markets: Variations on Polanyian Themes." *New Political Economy* 15 (2): 225–54. http://dx.doi.org/10.1080/13563460903290946.

London Evening Standard. 2007. "With Five Private Jets, Travolta Still Lectures on Global Warming." March 30.

Lovell, Heather, Harriet Bulkeley, and Diana Liverman. 2009. "Carbon Offsetting: Sustaining Consumption?" *Environment and Planning A* 41 (10): 2357–79. http://dx.doi.org/10.1068/a40345.

Lovell, Heather, and Diana Liverman. 2010. "Understanding Carbon Offset Technologies." *New Political Economy* 15 (2): 255–73. http://dx.doi.org/10.1080/13563460903548699.

Lowrey, Annie. 2011. "The Economics of Economists' Ethics." *Slate*, January 5. www.slate.com/id/2279937/.

Lukács, Georg. 1962. *The Historical Novel.* London: Merlin Press.

Lukács, Georg. 1964. *Studies in European Realism.* New York: Grosset & Dunlap.

Ma, Honghong, and Hiroki Takeuchi. 2007. "Depoliticized Politics and the End of the Short Twentieth Century in China: A Talk by Wang Hui." UCLA Asia Institute, University of California–Los Angeles. January 29. http://www.international.ucla.edu/asia/article.asp?parentid=62482.

Ma'anit, Adam. 2006. "If You Go Down to the Woods Today." *New Internationalist*, July 1. http://www.newint.org/features/2006/07/01/keynote/.

MacFaquhar, Larissa. 2007. "The Conciliator: Where is Barack Obama Coming From?" *The New Yorker*, May 7. http://www.newyorker.com/reporting/2007/05/07/070507fa_fact_macfarquhar.

MacIntyre, Alasdair. 1988. *Whose Justice? Which Rationality?* Notre Dame: University of Notre Dame Press.

MacKey, Robert. 2010. "Travolta Flies More Scientologists to Haiti." *The New York Times*, January 26. http://thelede.blogs.nytimes.com/2010/01/26/travolta-flies-more-scientologists-to-haiti/.

MacLean, Nancy. 2002. "Postwar Women's History: The 'Second Wave' Or the End of the Family Wage?" In *A Companion to Post-1945 America*, ed. Jean-Christophe Agnew and Roy Rosenzweig, 235–59. Malden, MA: Blackwell.

Magubane, Zine. 2007a. "Africa and the New Cult of Celebrity." *The Zeleza Post*, April 20. Accessed March 2, 2010. http://www.zeleza.com/blogging/popular-culture/africa-and-new-cult-celebrity.

Magubane, Zine. 2007b. "Oprah in South Africa: The Politics of Coevalness and the Creation of a Black Public Sphere." *Safundi: The Journal of South African and American Studies* 8 (4): 373–93.

Magubane, Zine. 2008. "The (Product) Red Man's Burden: Charity, Celebrity, and the Contradictions of Coevalness." *Journal of Pan African Studies* 2 (6): 2–25.

Mair, George. 1998. *Oprah Winfrey: The Real Story*. Secaucus, NJ: Carol Publishing Group.

Malcolm, Andrew. 2008. "A Surprise: Oprah Pays Real Cost for Supporting Barack Obama." *LA Times Blogs*, May 19. http://latimesblogs.latimes.com/washington/2008/04/oprahobama.html.

Mandel, Michael J. 2002. "Where Global Markets Are Going Wrong." *Bloomberg Businessweek*, June 17. http://www.businessweek.com/stories/2002-06-16/where-global-markets-are-going-wrong.

Maniates, Michael. 2002. "Individualization: Plant a Tree, Buy a Bike, Save the World?" In Princen et al., 43–66.

Manicas, Peter T. 1982. "War, Stasis, and Greek Political Thought." *Comparative Studies in Society and History* 24 (4): 673–88. http://dx.doi.org/10.1017/S0010417500010239.

Manji, Firoze. 1998. "The Depoliticisation of Poverty." In *Development and Rights: A Development and Practice Reader*, ed. Deborah Eade, 12–33. London: Oxfam.

Mansfield, Becky, ed. 2008. *Privatization: Property and the Remaking of Nature*. Oxford: Blackwell. http://dx.doi.org/10.1002/9781444306750.

Marchand, Marianne H., and Anne Sisson Runyan. 2011. "Introduction: Feminist Sightings of Global Restructuring." In *Gender and Global Restructuring: Sightings, Sites and Resistances*, ed. Marianne H. Marchand and Anne Sisson Runyan, 1–23. New York: Routledge.

Marks, Alexandra, and Stacey Vanek Smith. 2007. "Obama and the Oprah Effect: Can She Sway Voters?" *Christian Science Monitor*, December 10. http://proquest.umi.com/pqdweb?did=1395560301&sid=3&Fmt=3&clientId=18938&RQT=309&VName=PQD.

Marsh, David, Paul 't Hart, and Karen Tindall. 2010. "Celebrity Politics: The Politics of Late Modernity." *Political Studies Review* 8 (3): 322–40.

Marshall, P. David. 1997. *Celebrity and Power: Fame in Contemporary Culture*. Minneapolis: University of Minnesota Press.

Marshall, P. David, ed. 2006. *The Celebrity Culture Reader*. New York: Routledge.

Marshall, P. David. 2010. "The Promotion and Presentation of the Self: Celebrity as Marker of Presentational Media." *Celebrity Studies* 1 (1): 35–48. http://dx.doi.org/10.1080/19392390903519057.

Martinelli, Alberto. 2005. *Global Modernization: Rethinking the Project of Modernity*. London: SAGE.

Martinot, Steve, and Jared Sexton. 2003. "The Avant-Garde of White Supremacy." *Social Identities* 9 (2): 169–81. http://dx.doi.org/10.1080/1350463032000101542.

Marx, Karl. 1963. *The 18th Brumaire of Louis Bonaparte*. New York: International Publishers.

Max, D.T. 1999. "The Oprah Effect." *New York Times Magazine*, 37–41.

McAfee, Kathleen. 1999. "Selling Nature to Save It? Biodiversity and the Rise of Green Developmentalism." *Environment and Planning D: Society & Space* 17 (2): 133–54. http://dx.doi.org/10.1068/d170133.

McCarthy, James, and Scott Prudham. 2004. "Neoliberal Nature and the Nature of Neoliberalism." *Geoforum* 35 (3): 275–83. http://dx.doi.org/10.1016/j.geoforum.2003.07.003.

McCarthy, Thomas. 2002. "On Reconciling Cosmopolitan Unity and National Diversity." In *Global Justice and Transnational Politics*, ed. Pablo De Greiff and Ciaran P. Cronin, 235–74. Cambridge: MIT Press.

McChesney, Robert. 2008. *The Political Economy of Media: Enduring Issues, Emerging Dilemmas*. New York: Monthly Review Press.

McGee, Micki. 2005. *Self-Help, Inc*. Oxford, UK: Oxford University Press. http://dx.doi.org/10.1093/acprof:oso/9780195171242.001.0001.

McGee, Micki. 2007. "The Secret's Success." *The Nation*, June 4, 4–6.

McGirt, Ellen. 2008. "The Brand Called Obama." *Fast Company*, April 1. http://www.fastcompany.com/magazine/124/the-brand-called-obama.html.

McKinney, Cynthia. 2008. "A Discussion of Race Worth Having." *All Things Cynthia McKinney*, March 18. http://www.allthingscynthiamckinney.com/ADiscussionOfRaceThatMatters.

McNally, David. 2002. *Another World Is Possible: Globalization and Anti-Capitalism*. Winnipeg: Arbeiter Ring Publishing.

McNally, David. 2010. *Global Slump: The Economics and Politics of Crisis and Resistance*. Oakland, CA: PM Press/Spectre.

Mead, George Herbert. 1934. *Mind, Self, and Society*. Chicago: University of Chicago Press.

Meadows, Donella, Dennis Meadows, Jørgen Randers, and William Behrens. 1972. *The Limits to Growth*. New York: Universe Books.

Meštrovi , Stjepan. 2003. *Thorstein Veblen on Culture and Society*. London: Sage.

Micheletti, Michele, and Dietlind Stolle. 2008. "Fashioning Social Justice through Political Consumerism, Capitalism, and the Internet." *Cultural Studies* 22 (5): 749–69. http://dx.doi.org/10.1080/09502380802246009.

Mignolo, Walter D. 2000. "The Many Faces of Cosmo-Polis: Border Thinking and Critical Cosmopolitanism." *Public Culture* 12 (3): 721–48. http://dx.doi.org/10.1215/08992363-12-3-721.

Miller, Peter, and Nikolas Rose. 2008. *Governing the Present: Administering Economic, Social and Political Life.* Cambridge: Polity Press.

Millman, Joyce. 2000. "The Road to the White House Goes through Oprah." *Salon,* September 25. http://www.salon.com/ent/col/mill/2000/09/25/oprah/print.html/.

Mills, C. Wright. 1959. *The Sociological Imagination.* Oxford: Oxford University Press.

Milonakis, Dimitris, and Ben Fine. 2009. *From Political Economy to Economics: Method, the Social and the Historical in the Evolution of Economic Theory.* London: Routledge.

Mishkin, Budd. 2010. "One on 1: Joseph Stiglitz Stocks Up on Economic Insight." *NY1.com.* Accessed June 6. http://www.ny1.com/content/top_stories/118024/-i-one-on-1---i--joseph-stiglitz-stocks-up-on-economic-insight.

Mitchell, Alison. 2000. "Full of Banter, Bush Takes On 'Oprah' Circuit." *New York Times,* September 20, A1.

Mitchell, W.J.T. 2009. "Obama as Icon." *Journal of Visual Culture* 8 (2): 125–9. http://dx.doi.org/10.1177/14704129090080020201.

Mohandas, Siddharth. 2002. "Market Fundamentalism: A Review of Joseph Stiglitz's Globalization and Its Discontents." *Washington Monthly.* http://www.cfr.org/publication/4663/market_fundamentalism.html.

Monbiot, George. 2005a. "Africa's New Best Friends." *The Guardian,* July 5. http://www.guardian.co.uk/politics/2005/jul/05/internationalaidand development.development.

Monbiot, George. 2005b. "Bards of the Powerful." *The Guardian,* June 21. http://www.guardian.co.uk/politics/2005/jun/21/development.g8.

Mooney, Mark, and Russell Goldman. 2009. "Blagojevich Says He Thought of Oprah for Senate." *ABC News,* January 26. http://abcnews.go.com/Politics/US/story?id=6730220&page=1.

Mooney Nickel, Patricia. 2009. "Text, Portrayal, and Power: A Critique of the Transformation of the State Thesis." *Journal of Power* 2 (3): 383–401.

Moore, Michael. 2004. "Draft Oprah for President." Accessed July 8. http://www.michaelmoore.com/books-films/dudewheresmycountry/draftoprah/index/php/.

Myerson, Allen. 1997. "In Principle, a Case for More 'Sweatshops.'" *New York Times,* June 22. http://www.nytimes.com/1997/06/22/weekinreview/in-principle-a-case-for-more-sweatshops.html.

Nash, Kate. 2008. "Global Citizenship as Show Business: The Cultural Politics of Make Poverty History." *Media, Culture & Society* 30 (2): 167–81. http://dx.doi.org/10.1177/0163443707086859.

Newell, Peter. 2008. "The Political Economy of Global Environmental Governance." *Review of International Studies* 34 (3): 507–29. http://dx.doi.org/10.1017/S0260210508008140.

New Internationalist. 2006. "Bob Geldof." Accessed March 29, 2010. http://www.newint.org/columns/worldbeaters/2006/01/01/bob-geldof/index.php.

New York Times. 2009. "Hardcover Advice & Misc. (*New York Times* Bestseller List)." September 13. http://www.nytimes.com/best-sellers-books/2009-09-13/hardcover-advice/list.html.

Nickel, Patricia, and Angela Eikenberry. 2009. "A Critique of the Discourse of Marketized Philanthropy." *American Behavioral Scientist* 52 (7): 974–89. http://dx.doi.org/10.1177/0002764208327670.

Nixon, Ron. 2008. "Bottom Line for (Red)." *The New York Times*, February 6. http://www.nytimes.com/2008/02/06/business/06red.html.

Norwood, Robin. 1985. *Women Who Love Too Much*. Los Angeles: J.P. Tarcher.

Nunn, Heather, and Anita Biressi. 2010. "'A Trust Betrayed': Celebrity and the Work of Emotion." *Celebrity Studies* 1 (1): 49–64. http://dx.doi.org/10.1080/19392390903519065.

Nussbaum, Martha C. 1996. "Patriotism and Cosmopolitanism." In *For Love of Country*, ed. Joshua Cohen, 3–20. Boston: Beacon Press.

Olatunbosun-Alakija, Ayoade. 2008. "(RED) Spells H.O.P.E." *Journal of Pan African Studies* 2 (6): 68–70.

Olsen, Johan P. 2005. "Maybe It Is Time to Rediscover Bureaucracy." *Journal of Public Administration: Research and Theory* 16 (1): 1–24. http://dx.doi.org/10.1093/jopart/mui027.

O'Manique, Colleen. 2004. *Neoliberalism and AIDS Crisis in Sub-Saharan Africa: Globalization's Pandemic*. Basingstoke: Palgrave-Macmillan. http://dx.doi.org/10.1057/9780230504080.

O'Manique, Colleen, and Ronald Labonte. 2008a. "Re-Thinking Product (RED)." *Lancet* 371 (9624): 1561–3.

O'Manique, Colleen, and Ronald Labonte. 2008b. "Seeing (RED) – Authors' Reply." *Lancet* 371 (9627): 1836. http://dx.doi.org/10.1016/S0140-6736(08)60791-6.

The Oprah Effect. 2009. (TV documentary.) Chicago: Kurtis Productions/CNBC Network.

Oprah Winfrey Show. 1994. "Moral Dilemmas: What Would You Do?" (TV Program.) January 14.

Oprah Winfrey Show. 2007a. (TV Program.) February 7.

Oprah Winfrey Show. 2007b. "One Week Later: The Huge Reaction to the Secret." (TV Program.) February 16.

Oprah Winfrey Show. 2012. *Oprah Winfrey Show* Global Distribution List. Accessed May 14. http://www.oprah.com/pressroom/Global-Distribution-List-of-The-Oprah-Winfrey-Show.

Oprah's Angel Network Fact Sheet. 2009. *Oprah.com*. Available at: http://www.oprah.com/pressroom/About-Oprahs-Angel-Network. Accessed April 28, 2009.

Orman, Suze. 1999. *The Courage to Be Rich: Creating a Life of Material and Spiritual Abundance*. New York: Riverhead Books.

Ortiz, Ana, and Laura Briggs. 2003. "The Culture of Poverty, Crack Babies, and Welfare Cheats: The Making of the 'Healthy White Baby Crisis.'" *Social Text* 21 (3): 39–57. http://dx.doi.org/10.1215/01642472-21-3_76-39.

Ouellette, Laurie, and James Hay. 2008. "Makeover Television, Governmentality and the Good Citizen." *Continuum: Journal of Media & Cultural Studies* 22 (4): 471–84. http://dx.doi.org/10.1080/10304310801982930.

Oxford Dictionaries. 2011. "Carbon Neutral." Oxford University Press. Accessed February 3. http://www.oxforddictionaries.com/view/entry/m_en_gb0978180#m_en_gb0978180.

Panagia, Davide. 2001. "The Predicative Function in Ideology: On the Political Uses of Analogical Reasoning in Contemporary Political Thought." *Journal of Political Ideologies* 6 (1): 55–74. http://dx.doi.org/10.1080/13569310120040159.

Paterson, Matthew, David Humphreys, and Lloyd Pettiford. 2003. "Conceptualizing Global Environmental Governance: From Interstate Regimes to Counter-Hegemonic Struggles." *Global Environmental Politics* 3 (2): 1–10. http://dx.doi.org/10.1162/152638003322068173.

Peck, Janice. 1995. "TV Talk Shows as Therapeutic Discourse: The Ideological Labor of the Televised Talking Cure." *Communication Theory* 5 (1): 58–81. http://dx.doi.org/10.1111/j.1468-2885.1995.tb00098.x.

Peck, Jamie. 2010. *Constructions of Neoliberal Reason*. Oxford: Oxford University Press. http://dx.doi.org/10.1093/acprof:oso/9780199580576.001.0001.

Peck, Janice. 2008. *The Age of Oprah: Cultural Icon for the Neoliberal Era*. Boulder, CO: Paradigm Publishers.

Peluso, Nancy, and Michael Watts. 2001. *Violent Environments*. Ithaca: Cornell University Press.

People's Health Movement, Medact, and Global Equity Gauge Alliance. 2008. *Global Health Watch 2: An Alternative World Health Report*. London: Zed Books.

Perlstein, Rick. 2009. *Before the Storm: Barry Goldwater and the Unmaking of the American Consensus*. New York: Nation Books.

Petridis, Alexis. 2011. "Come Earthquake or Tsunami, There's Always a Celebrity There to Help." *The Guardian (Lost in Showbiz Blog)*, March 17. http://www.guardian.co.uk/lifeandstyle/lostinshowbiz/2011/mar/17/earthquake-tsunami-celebrities-offer-help.

Pieterse, Jan Nederveen. 2004. *Globalization and Culture*. Lanham: Rowman & Littlefield.

Poku, Nana. 2004. "Confronting AIDS with Debt: Africa's Silent Crisis." In *The Political Economy of AIDS in Africa*, ed. Nana Poku and Alan Whiteside, 33–49. Aldershot: Ashgate Press.

Polanyi, Karl. 1944. *The Great Transformation: The Political and Economic Origins of Our Time*. Boston: Beacon Press.

Pollin, Robert. 2003. *Contours of Descent*. London: Verso.

Pollin, Robert. 2009. "Be Utopian: Demand the Realistic." *The Nation*, March 9. http://www.thenation.com/article/be-utopian-demand-realistic.

Ponte, Stefano, Lisa Ann Richey, and Mike Baab. 2009. "Bono's Product (RED) Initiative: Corporate Social Responsibility That Solves the Problem of 'Distant Others.'" *Third World Quarterly* 30 (2): 301–17. http://dx.doi.org/10.1080/01436590802681074.

Porter, Roy. 1993. "Baudrillard: History, Hysteria and Consumption." In *Forget Baudrillard?*, ed. Chris Rojek and Bryan Turner, 1–21. London: Routledge.

Posner, Richard. 2008. "Why Creative Capitalism Would Make Things Worse." In Kinsley 2008, 63–7.

Poster, Mark, ed. 2001. *Jean Baudrillard: Selected Writings*. 2nd ed. Cambridge: Polity Press.

Poulantzas, Nicos. 1975. *Classes in Contemporary Capitalism*. London: New Left Books.

Powell, Michael. 2011. "Obama the Liberal Irks a Liberal Lion." *New York Times*, January 7. http://www.nytimes.com/2011/01/08/business/economy/08reich.html.

"'President Oprah' Hits the Web." 1999. *BBC News Online*, October 6. http://news.bbc.co.uk/2/hi/entertainment/466767.stm.

Press, Eyal. 2002. "Rebel with a Cause: The Re-Education of Joseph Stiglitz." *The Nation*, June 10. http://www.thenation.com/article/rebel-cause.

Princen, Thomas, Michael Maniates, and Ken Conca, eds. 2002. *Confronting Consumption*. Boston: MIT Press.

Pringle, Hamish. 2004. *Celebrity Sells*. Chichester: John Wiley.

Product (RED). 2011. Accessed March 1. www.joinred.com.

Prudham, Scott. 2009. "Pimping Climate Change: Richard Branson, Global Warming, and the Performance of Green Capitalism." *Environment and Planning A* 41 (7): 1594–613. http://dx.doi.org/10.1068/a4071.

Putnam, Robert. 2000. *Bowling Alone: The Collapse and Revival of American Community*. New York: Simon & Schuster. http://dx.doi.org/10.1145/358916.361990.

Quantcast. 2009. "Monthly Traffic Oprah.com." Accessed September 9. http://www.quantcast.com/oprah.com.

Quebedeaux, Richard. 1982. *By What Authority: The Rise of Personality Cults in American Christianity*. San Francisco: Harper and Row.

Rachman, Gideon. 2007. "The Aid Crusade and Bono's Brigade." *Financial Times*, October 30. http://blogs.ft.com/rachmanblog/2007/10/column-the-aid-html/.

Rahman, Momin. 2004. "David Beckham as a Historical Moment in the Representation of Masculinity." *Labour History Review* 69 (2): 219–33.

Rancière, Jacques. 1994. "Post-Democracy, Politics, and Philosophy: An Interview with Jacques Rancière." *Angelaki* 1 (3): 171–8.

Rancière, Jacques. 1998. *Disagreement*. Minneapolis: University of Minnesota Press.

Rancière, Jacques. 2003. "Comment and Response." *Theory & Event* 6 (4). http://muse.jhu.edu/login?uri=/journals/theory_and_event/v006/6.4ranciere.html.

Rancière, Jacques. 2006. *Hatred of Democracy*. Trans. Steve Corcoran. London; New York: Verso.

Rancière, Jacques. 2010. *Dissensus: On Politics and Aesthetics*. Trans. Steve Corcoran. New York: Continuum.

Randers, Jørgen, and Donella Meadows. 1973. "The Carrying Capacity of Our Global Environment: A Look at the Ethical Alternatives." In *Toward a Steady-State Economy*, ed. Herman Daly. San Francisco: W.H. Freeman and Company, 283–306.

Rapping, Elayne. 1996. *The Culture of Recovery*. Boston: Beacon Press.

Reed, Adolph, Jr. 2008. "Where Obamaism Seems to Be Going." *The Progressive*, July 29.

Reed, Adolph L. 1999. "Introduction: The New Liberal Orthodoxy on Race and Inequality." In *Without Justice for All*, ed. Adolph L. Reed, 1–10. Boulder, CO: Westview Press.

Reeves, Jimmie L., and Richard Campbell. 1994. *Cracked Coverage: Television News, the Anti-Cocaine Crusade, and the Reagan Legacy*. Durham, NC: Duke University Press.

Reich, Robert. 2010. *Aftershock: The Next Economy and America's Future*. New York: Alfred A. Knopf.

Richey, Lisa Anne, and Stefano Ponte. 2008. "Better (Red)™ than Dead? Celebrities, Consumption and International Aid." *Third World Quarterly* 29 (4): 711–29. http://dx.doi.org/10.1080/01436590802052649.

Richey, Lisa Ann, and Stefano Ponte. 2011. *Brand Aid: Shopping Well to Save the World*. Minneapolis: University of Minnesota Press.

Riesman, David. 1950. *The Lonely Crowd*. New Haven: Yale University Press.

Roberts, Kevin. 2009. "Rebranding America." *PAPERMAG*, May 6. http://www.papermag.com/arts_and_style/2009/05/rebranding-america-kevin-roberts-satchi-satchi-4.php.

Robinson, William. 2007. "Transformative Possibilities in Latin America." In *Socialist Register 2008: Global Flashpoints: Reactions to Imperialism and Neoliberalism*, ed. Leo Panitch and Colin Leys, 141–59. London: Merlin Press.

Roemer, John. 1995. "An Anti-Hayekian Manifesto." *New Left Review* 211 (May–June): 112–29.

Roeper, Richard. 2000. "O, What an Ego Trip." *Chicago Sun-Times*, April 30, 11.

Rojek, Chris. 2001. *Celebrity*. London: Sage/Reaktion Books.

Roof, Wade Clark. 1993. *A Generation of Seekers*. New York: HarperCollins.

Roof, Wade Clark. 1999. *The Spiritual Marketplace*. Princeton, NJ: Princeton University Press.

Rose, Nikolas. 1998. *Inventing Our Selves*. Cambridge: Cambridge University Press.

Rosin, Hanna. 2010. "The End of Men?" *The Atlantic*, July.

Rothschild, Matthew. 2009. "The Great Recession." *The Progressive* 73 (1) (January): 8. Proquest Central Database.

Rowley, Michelle V. 2011. "Where the Streets Have No Name: Getting Development Out of the (RED)™." In *Gender and Global Restructuring: Sightings, Sites and Resistances*, ed. Marianne H. Marchand and Anne Sisson Runyan, 78–9. New York: Routledge.

Russo, Anthony. 2006. "How to Translate 'Cultural Revolution.'" *Inter-Asia Cultural Studies* 7 (4): 673–82. http://dx.doi.org/10.1080/14649370 600983295.

Rutherford, Stephanie. 2007. "Green Governmentality: Insights and Opportunities in the Study of Nature's Rule." *Progress in Human Geography* 31 (3): 291–307. http://dx.doi.org/10.1177/0309132507077080.

Sachs, Jeffrey. 2005. *The End of Poverty*. London: Penguin.

Said, Edward W. 1978. *Orientalism*. New York: Pantheon.

Samman, Emma, Eilish McAuliffe, and Malcolm MacLachlan. 2009. "The Role of Celebrity in Endorsing Poverty Reduction through International Aid." *International Journal of Nonprofit and Voluntary Sector Marketing* 14 (2): 137–48. http://dx.doi.org/10.1002/nvsm.339.

Sarna-Wojcicki, Margaret. 2008. "Refigu(Red): Talking Africa and Aids in 'Causumer Culture.'" *Journal of Pan African Studies* 2 (6): 14–31.

Satter, Beryl. 1999. *Each Mind a Kingdom: American Women, Sexual Purity, and the New Thought Movement, 1875–1920*. Berkeley: University of California Press.

Saunders, Robert. 2007. "Transnational Reproduction and Its Discontents: The Politics of Intercountry Adoption in a Global Society." *Journal of Global Change and Governance* 1 (1): 1–23.

Saurin, Julian. 2001. "Global Environmental Crisis as the 'Disaster Triumphant': The Private Capture of Public Goods." *Environmental Politics* 10 (4): 63–84. http://dx.doi.org/10.1080/714000578.

Schmitt, John. 2005. *How Good Is the Economy at Creating Good Jobs?*. Washington, DC: Center for Economic and Policy Research. http://www.cepr.net/documents/publications/labor_markets_2005_10.pdf.

Schom, Alan. 1997. *Napoleon Bonaparte*. New York: HarperCollins Publishers.

Schwartz, Daniel. 2010. "Haiti's Unhappy History." *CBC News*, January 14. http://www.cbc.ca/news/world/story/2010/01/13/f-haiti-earthquake-history.html.

Scott, James C. 1999. *Seeing like a State: How Certain Schemes to Improve the Human Condition Have Failed*. New Haven: Yale University Press.

Sellers, Patricia. 2002. "The Business of Being Oprah." *Fortune*, April 1, 50–4, 58, 60, 64.

Sennett, Richard. 1974. *The Fall of Public Man*. New York: Alfred A. Knopf.

Sennett, Richard. 2000. *The Corrosion of Character*. New York: W.W. Norton.

Sexton, Jared. 2010. "People-of-Color-Blindness Notes on the Afterlife of Slavery." *Social Text* 28 (2): 31–56. http://dx.doi.org/10.1215/01642472-2009-066.

Shah, Anup. 2006. "G8 Summit 2005 Outcome." Accessed February 17. http://www.globalissues.org/TradeRelated/Debt/g8summit2005/outcome.asp.

Shah, Anup. 2010. "Poverty Facts and Stats." *Global Issues (Washington, DC)*. September 20. http://www.globalissues.org/article/26/poverty-facts-and-stats.

Shapiro, Michael. 2008. "Is an Icon Iconic?" *Language* 84 (4): 815–19. http://dx.doi.org/10.1353/lan.0.0057.

Shattuc, Jane. 1997. *The Talking Cure*. New York: Routledge.

Skinner, David. 2000a. "Gore's Soft Sell on 'Oprah.'" *Salon*, September 12. http://www.salon.com/2000/09/12/oprah_8/.

Skinner, David. 2000b. "George W. Bush Gets the Oprah Gig Right, All the Way Down to the Tears." *Salon*, September 20. http://www.salon.com/2000/09/20/oprah_9/.

Sklar, Martin. 1988. *The Corporate Reconstruction of American Capitalism, 1890–1916*. Cambridge, UK: Cambridge University Press. http://dx.doi. org/10.1017/CBO9780511528781.

Sloterdijk, Peter. 1987. *Critique of Cynical Reason*. London: Verso.

Smart, Barry. 2005. *The Sport Star: Modern Sport and the Cultural Economy of Sporting Celebrity*. London: Sage.

Smith, Neil. 1984. *Uneven Development: Nature, Capital, and the Production of Space*. Athens: University of Georgia Press.

Smith, Neil. 2007. "Nature as Accumulation Strategy." In *Socialist Register 2007: Coming to Terms with Nature*, ed. Leo Panitch and Colin Leys, 16–36. London: Merlin Press.

Smith, Toby. 1998. *The Myth of Green Marketing: Tending Our Goats at the Edge of Apocalypse*. Toronto: University of Toronto Press.

Soederberg, Susanne. 2007. "Taming Corporations or Buttressing Market-Led Development? A Critical Assessment of the Global Compact." *Globalizations* 4 (4): 500–13. http://dx.doi.org/10.1080/14747730701695760.

Spash, Clive. 2010. "The Brave New World of Carbon Trading." *New Political Economy* 15 (2): 169–95. http://dx.doi.org/10.1080/13563460903556049.

Spivak, Gayatri. 1988. "Can the Subaltern Speak?" In *Marxism and Interpretation of Culture*, ed. Cary Nelson and Lawrence Grossberg, 271–313. Chicago: University of Illinois Press.

Stacey, Judith. 1990. "Sexism by a Subtler Name?" In *Women, Class, and the Feminist Imagination*, ed. Karen V. Hansen and Ilene J. Philipson, 338–55. Philadelphia: Temple University Press.

Starker, Steven. 1988. *Oracle at the Supermarket: The American Preoccupation with Self-Help Books*. New Brunswick, NJ: Transaction Publishers.

Stephens, Michelle. 2003. "Re-Imagining the Shape and Borders of Black Political Space." *Radical History Review* 87 (Fall): 169–82. http://dx.doi. org/10.1215/01636545-2003-87-169.

Stiglitz, Joseph. 1994. *Whither Socialism?* Cambridge, MA: The MIT Press.

Stiglitz, Joseph. 2000. "What I Learned at the World Economic Crisis." *New Republic*, April 17. http://www2.gsb.columbia.edu/faculty/jstiglitz/download/opeds/What_I_Learned_at_the_World_Economic_Crisis.htm.

Stiglitz, Joseph. 2002a. "Autobiography." In *The Nobel Prizes 2001*, ed. Tore Frängsmyr. Stockholm: Nobel Foundation. http://nobelprize.org/nobel_prizes/economics/laureates/2001/stiglitz-autobio.html.

Stiglitz, Joseph. 2002b. *Globalization and Its Discontents*. New York: W.W. Norton.

Stiglitz, Joseph. 2003. *The Roaring Nineties: A New History of the World's Most Prosperous Decade*. New York: W.W. Norton.

Stiglitz, Joseph. 2007a. "The Economic Consequences of Mr. Bush." *Vanity Fair*, December. http://www.vanityfair.com/politics/features/2007/12/bush200712.

Stiglitz, Joseph. 2007b. *Making Globalization Work*. New York: W.W. Norton.

Stiglitz, Joseph E. 2008."The End of Neo-liberalism?" Project Syndicate. July 7. http://www.projectsyndicate.org/commentary/stiglitz101/English.

Stiglitz, Joseph. 2010. *Freefall: America, Free Markets, and the Sinking of the American Economy*. New York: W.W. Norton.

Stiglitz, Joseph, and Linda Bilmes. 2008. *The Three Trillion Dollar War: The True Cost of the War in Iraq*. New York: W.W. Norton.

Stiglitz, Joseph, and Andrew Charlton. 2006. *Fair Trade for All: How Trade Can Promote Development*. New York: Oxford University Press.

Stiglitz, Joseph, Amartya Sen, and Jean-Paul Fitoussi. 2009. *Report by the Commission on the Measurement of Economic Performance and Social Progress*. Commission on the Measurement of Economic Performance and Social Progress. http://www.stiglitz-sen-fitoussi.fr/documents/rapport_anglais.pdf.

Stiglitz, Joseph, and Carl Walsh. 2006. *Economics*. 4th ed. New York: W.W. Norton.

Street, Paul. 2009. *Barack Obama and the Future of American Politics*. Boulder: Paradigm Publishers.

Stockpickr. 2011. "Al Gore – Generation Investment Management." Accessed February 22. http://stockpickr.com/pro/portfolio/al-gore-generation-investment-management/.

Street, J. 2004. "Celebrity Politicians: Popular Culture and Political Representation." *British Journal of Politics and International Relations* 6 (4): 435–52. http://dx.doi.org/10.1111/j.1467-856X.2004.00149.x.

Street, John. 2006. "The Celebrity Politician: Political Style and Popular Culture." In Marshall 2006, 359–70.

Street, Paul. 2008. "Barack Obama: The Empire's New Clothes (Reposted from Black Agenda Report)." *Films for Action*, November 15. http://lawrence.filmsforaction.org/Blog/Barack_Obama_The_Empires_New_Clothes.

Street, Paul. 2009a. *Barack Obama and the Future of American Politics*. Boulder: Paradigm Publishers.

Street, Paul. 2009b. "Reflections on Empire, Inequality, and 'Brand Obama.'" *Z Magazine International*, January 12. http://www.stwr.org/united-states-of-america/no-peace-dividend-reflections-on-empire-inequality-and-brand-obama.html.

Street, Paul. 2010. "Obama Isn't Spineless, He's Conservative." *Znet*, December 11. http://zcommunications.org/obama-isn-t-spineless-he-s-conservative-reflections-on-chutzpah-theirs-and-ours-by-paul-street.

Stuart, Elizabeth. 2008. "To Gates's Critics: You're Making Perfect the Enemy of the Good." In Kinsley 2008, 107–19.

Swibel, Matthew. 2006. "Bad Girl Interrupted." *Forbes* 178 (1): 118–19.

Szerszynski, Bronislaw, and John Urry. 2002. "Cultures of Cosmopolitanism." *Sociological Review* 50 (4): 461–81. http://dx.doi.org/10.1111/1467-954X. 00394.

Tabb, William. 2007. "The Power of the Rich." In *More Unequal*, ed. Michael D. Yates, 34–45. New York: Monthly Review Press.

Taiyab, Nadaa. 2006. *Exploring the Market for Voluntary Carbon Offsets*. London: International Institute for Environment and Development.

Tallen, Betty S. 1990. "Co-Dependency: A Feminist Critique." *Sojourner: The Women's Forum* (January): 20–1.

Tapper, Jake. 2007. "Al Gore's 'Inconvenient Truth'? – A $30,000 Utility Bill." *ABC News*, February 26. http://abcnews.go.com/Politics/GlobalWarming/story?id=2906888&page=1.

Tauber, Michelle, and Jennifer Wulff. 2006. "Brad Pitt and Angelina Jolie's Baby Girl." *People Magazine*, June 12. http://www.people.com/people/archive/article/0,20061158,00.html.

Taylor, Marcus. 2005. "Opening the World Bank: International Organisations and the Contradictions of Global Capitalism." *Historical Materialism* 13 (1): 153–70. http://dx.doi.org/10.1163/1569206053620870.

Tennessee Center for Policy Research. 2007. "Al Gore's Personal Energy Use Is His Own 'Inconvenient Truth. '" February 25. http://www.tennesseepolicy.org/2007/02/al-gore%e2%80%99s-personal-energy-use-is-his-own-%e2%80%9 cinconvenient-truth/.

Tennessee Valley Authority. 2011. "Green Power Switch." Accessed January 27. www.tva.com/greenpowerswitch/green_mainfaq.htm.

Terranova, Tiziana. 2004. "Communication Beyond Meaning: On the Cultural Politics of Information." *Social Text* 22 (3): 51–73. http://dx.doi.org/10.1215/01642472-22-3_80-51.

Tie, Warwick. 2004. "The Psychic Life of Governmentality." *Culture, Theory & Critique* 45 (2): 161–76. http://dx.doi.org/10.1080/1473578042000283844.

Tillich, Paul. 2000 [1952]. *The Courage to Be*. New Haven: Yale University Press.

The Times of India. 2012. "Jaipur Literature Festival: Oprah Winfrey Charms 'Chaotic' India," January 22. http://timesofindia.indiatimes.com/india/Jaipur-Literature-Festival-Oprah-Winfrey-charms-chaotic-India/articleshow/11592200.cms.

Time.com. 1999. "TIME 100 Persons of the Century." June 14. http://www.time.com/time/magazine/article/0,9171,991227,00.html.

Tolstoy, Leo. 1993 [1869]. *War and Peace*. Hertfordshire, UK: Wordsworth Editions Limited.

Torgerson, Douglas. 2010. "Policy Discourse and Public Spheres: The Habermas Paradox." *Critical Policy Studies* 4 (1): 1–17. http://dx.doi.org/ 10.1080/19460171003714914.

Travis, Trysh. 2009. *The Language of the Heart: A Cultural History of the Recovery Movement from Alcoholics Anonymous to Oprah Winfrey*. Durham: University of North Carolina Press.

Trimble, Carrie S., and Nora J. Rifon. 2006. "Consumer Perceptions of Compatibility in Cause-Related Marketing Messages." *International Journal of Nonprofit and Voluntary Sector Marketing* 11 (1): 29–47. http://dx.doi. org/10.1002/nvsm.42.

Turner, Graeme. 2004. *Understanding Celebrity*. London: SAGE Publications.

Turner, Graeme. 2010. "Approaching Celebrity Studies." *Celebrity Studies* 1 (1): 11–20. http://dx.doi.org/10.1080/19392390903519024.

Turque, Bill. 2000. *Inventing Al Gore*. New York: Mariner Books.

Uchitelle, Louis. 2006. *The Disposable American: Layoffs and Their Consequences*. New York: Alfred A. Knopf.

Uchitelle, Louis. 2007. "The Richest of the Rich, Proud of a New Gilded Age." *New York Times*, July 15, 1, 18–19.

Ulrich, Carmen W. 2006. "The Oprah Effect: The $1.4 Billion Woman Influences Pop Culture, Creates Stars, and Drives Entire Industries." *Essence* (October): 190.

UNDP. 1990. *Human Development Report 1990*. New York: United Nations Development Programme.

UNDP. 2009. *Human Development Report 2009*. New York: United Nations Development Programme.

United Nations. 1998. *Human Development Report 1998 [Online]*. New York.

United Nations. 2009. *Report of the Commission of Experts of the President of the United Nations General Assembly on Reforms of the International Monetary and Financial System*. New York: United Nations.

Valelly, Paul. 2007. "Editorial." *The Independent*, March 9.

Van Der Pijl, Kees. 2006. "A Lockean Europe?" *New Left Review* 37 (January– February): 9–37.

Veblen, Thorstein. 1953 [1899]. *The Theory of the Leisure Class*. New York, Oxford: Mentor Books and Oxford University Press.

Vedantam, Shankar. 2008. "The Oprah Effect." *Washington Post*, September 1. http://www.washingtonpost.com/wp-dyn/content/story/2008/08/31/ ST2008083101952.html.

Vertovec, Steven, and Joshua Cohen. 2002. "Introduction: Conceiving Cosmopolitanism." In *Conceiving Cosmopolitanism*, ed. Steven Vertovec and Joshua
Cohen, 1–24. New York: Oxford University Press.

Vidal, Gore. 2004. "State of the Union, 2004." *The Nation*, September 13.
http://www.thenation.com/doc/20040913/vidal/.

Wade, Robert. 2001. "Showdown at the World Bank." *New Left Review* 7
(January–February): 124–37.

Waldinger, Roger, and Michael Lichter. 2009. *How the Other Half Works:
Immigration and the Social Organization of Labour*. Berkeley: University of
California Press.

Wallerstein, Immanuel. 1974. *The Modern World-System, Vol. I: Capitalist Agri-
culture and the Origins of the European World-Economy in the Sixteenth Century*.
New York: Academic Press.

Wallerstein, Immanuel. 1980. *The Modern World-System, Vol. II: Mercantilism
and the Consolidation of the European World-Economy, 1600–1750*. New York:
Academic Press.

Wallerstein, Immanuel. 1989. *The Modern World-System, Vol. III: The Second
Great Expansion of the Capitalist World-Economy, 1730–1840s*. San Diego:
Academic Press.

Wallerstein, Immanuel. 2004. *World-Systems Analysis: An Introduction*. Durham:
Duke University Press.

Wallerstein, Immanuel. 2010. "Reading Fanon in the 21st Century." *New Left
Review* 57 (April–May): 117–25.

Walsh, Kieron. 1994. "Citizens, Charters and Contracts." In *The Authority of
the Consumer*, ed. Russell Keat, Nigel Whiteley, and Nicholas Abercrombie,
189–206. London: Routledge.

Walzer, Michael. 1996. "Spheres of Affection." In *For Love of Country*, ed.
Joshua Cohen, 125–30. Boston: Beacon Press.

Wang, Hui. 2006a. "Depoliticized Politics from East to West." *New Left Review*
41 (September–October): 29–45.

Wang, Hui. 2006b. "Depoliticized Politics, Multiple Components of Hegemony,
and the Eclipse of the Sixties." *Inter-Asia Cultural Studies* 7 (4): 682–700.

Wang, Hui. 2007. "Depoliticized Politics and the End of the Short Twentieth
Century in China." (Talk given to UCLA Asia Institute, University of
California-Los Angeles.) http://www.international.ucla.edu/asia/article.
asp?parentid=62482.

Watson, Sean. 1999. "Policing the Affective Society: Beyond Governmentality
in the Theory of Social Control." *Social & Legal Studies* 8 (2): 227–51. http://
dx.doi.org/10.1177/096466399900800204.

Weart, Spencer. 2010. "The Discovery of Global Warming." American Institute of Physics. Accessed January 3. http://www.aip.org/history/climate/summary.htm.

Weber, Max. 1970. *From Max Weber: Essays in Sociology*. Ed. H.H. Gerth and C. Wright Mills. London: Routledge.

Weber, Max. 2002. *Sociological Writings*. Trans. Wolf Heydebrand. New York: Continuum Press.

Weisbrot, Mark, Dean Baker, and David Rosnick. 2005. *The Scorecard on Development: 25 Years of Diminished Progress*. Washington, DC: Center for Economic and Policy Research.

Weiss, Piper. 2011. "Critics Mixed on Oprah's New Network. What Do You Think?" *Allthingsnow.com*, January 3. http://shine.yahoo.com/channel/life/critics-mixed-on-oprahs-new-network-what-do-you-think-2435870.

Whitaker, Robert. 2010. *Anatomy of an Epidemic: Magic Bullets, Psychiatric Drugs, and the Astonishing Rise of Mental Illness*. New York: Crown Publishing Group.

Wilderson, Frank. 2005. "Gramsci's Black Marx: Whither the Slave in Civil Society?" *We Write* 2 (1): 1–17.

Wilderson, Frank. 2010. *Red, White, and Black: Cinema and the Structure of US Antagonisms*. Durham, NC: Duke University Press.

Williams, Alex. 2006. "Into Africa." *New York Times*, August 13. http://www.nytimes.com/2006/08/13/fashion/13AFRICA.html.

Williams, Patricia. 2007. "The Audacity of Oprah." *The Nation*, December 6. http://www.thenation.com/doc/20071224/williams.

Williams, Raymond. 1977. *Marxism and Literature*. Oxford: Oxford University Press.

Wirgau, Jessica S., Kathryn Webb Farley, and Courtney Jensen. 2010. "Is Business Discourse Colonizing Philanthropy? A Critical Discourse Analysis of (PRODUCT) RED." *Voluntas* 21 (4): 611–30. http://dx.doi.org/10.1007/s11266-010-9122-z.

Wolf, Richard. 2010. "Number of Uninsured Americans Rises to 50.7 Percent." *USA Today*, September 17. http://www.usatoday.com/news/nation/2010-09-17-uninsured17_ST_N.htm?loc=interstitialskip.

Wood, Ellen Meiksins. 1995. *Democracy against Capitalism: Renewing Historical Materialism*. Cambridge: Cambridge University Press. http://dx.doi.org/10.1017/CBO9780511558344.

Wood, Ellen Meiksins. 1999. *The Origin of Capitalism*. New York: Monthly Review Press.

World Bank. 2007. *State and Trends of the Carbon Market 2007*. Washington, DC: World Bank.

World Bank. 2011. "Open Data Online: The World Bank Group." Accessed March 1. http://data.worldbank.org.

World Development Movement. 2006. "Small Change." Accessed March 12, 2010. http://www.wdm.org.uk/sites/default/files/smallchange01062006. pdf.

Wuthnow, Robert, and Robert C. Liebman. 1983. *The New Christian Right*. Hawthorne, NY: Aldine Publishing.

Wyatt, Edward. 2008. "A Few Tremors in Oprahland." *New York Times*, May 26. http://www.nytimes.com/2008/05/26/business/media/26oprah.html.

Wymer, Walter. 2006. "Editorial: Special Issue on Corporate Philanthropy." *International Journal of Nonprofit and Voluntary Sector Marketing* 11 (1): 1–2. http://dx.doi.org/10.1002/nvsm.43.

Yen, Hope. 2009. "Census: Number without Health Insurance at 46.3 Million." *The Oklahoman Online*, September 10. http://newsok.com/census-number-of-uninsured-americans-rises-to-46.3-million/article/3399828?custom_click=pod_headline_health.

Youde, Jeremy. 2009. "Ethical Consumerism or Reified Neoliberalism? Product (RED) and Private Funding for Public Goods." *New Political Science* 31 (2): 201–20. http://dx.doi.org/10.1080/07393140902872369.

Young, Robert J.C. 2001. *Postcolonialism: An Historical Introduction*. Oxford: Blackwell Publishers.

Zdravkovic, Srdan, Peter Magnusson, and Sarah M. Stanley. 2010. "Dimensions of Fit between a Brand and a Social Cause and Their Influence on Attitudes." *International Journal of Research in Marketing* 27 (2): 151–60. http://dx.doi.org/10.1016/j.ijresmar.2010.01.005.

Zeleza, Paul Tiyambe. 2009. *Pan Africanism in the Age of Obama* (International African Institute's Lugard Lecture). International African Institute. http://www.internationalafricaninstitute.org/downloads/Lugard%20lecture%20 2009%20Pan-Africanism%20in%20the%20Age%20of%20Obama.pdf.

Zepf, Siegfried. 2010. "Consumerism and Identity: Some Psychoanalytical Considerations." *International Forum of Psychoanalysis* 19 (3): 144–54. http://dx.doi.org/10.1080/08037060903143992.

Žižek, Slavoj. 1989. *The Sublime Object of Ideology*. London: Verso.

Žižek, Slavoj. 1993. *Tarrying with the Negative: Kant, Hegel, and the Critique of Ideology*. Durham: Duke University Press.

Žižek, Slavoj. 1999. *The Ticklish Subject: The Absent Centre of Political Ontology*. London; New York: Verso.

Žižek, Slavoj. 2006a. *The Parallax View*. Cambridge, MA: MIT Press.

Žižek, Slavoj. 2006b. *The Universal Exception*. New York: Continuum.

Žižek, Slavoj. 2008. *Violence: Six Sideways Reflections*. New York: Picador.

Žižek, Slavoj. 2009. *First as Tragedy, Then as Farce*. London: Verso.
Žižek, Slavoj. 2011. *Living in the End Times*. London: Verso.
Zubaida, Sami. 2002. "Middle Eastern Experiences of Cosmopolitanism." In
    Conceiving Cosmopolitanism, ed. Steven Vertovec and Joshua Cohen, 32–41.
    New York: Oxford University Press.

Contributors

Feyzi Baban is an associate professor of International Development Studies at Trent University.

Kate Ervine is an assistant professor in the International Development Studies Program at Saint Mary's University.

Gavin Fridell is an associate professor and Canada Research Chair in International Development Studies at Saint Mary's University.

Michael K. Goodman is a professor of Environment and Development at University of Reading in the Department of Geography and Environmental Science.

Ilan Kapoor is a professor in the Faculty of Environmental Studies at York University.

Martijn Konings is senior lecturer and Australian Research Council DECRA Fellow in the Department of Political Economy at the University of Sydney.

Colleen O'Manique is an associate professor of Women's Studies at Trent University.

Janice Peck is an associate professor in the School of Journalism at the University of Colorado, Boulder.

Momin Rahman is an associate professor in the Department of Sociology at Trent University.